PHILLIS WHEATLEY CHOOSES FREEDOM

ALSO BY G. J. BARKER-BENFIELD

The Horrors of the Half-Known Life: Male Attitudes Toward Women and Sexuality in Nineteenth-Century America, 1976 and 2000

The Culture of Sensibility: Sex and Society in Eighteenth-Century Britain, 1992

Abigail and John Adams: The Americanization of Sensibility, 2010

Portraits of American Women: From European Settlement to the Present, edited with Catherine Clinton, 1991 and 1998

Phillis Wheatley Chooses Freedom

History, Poetry, and the Ideals
of the American Revolution

G. J. Barker-Benfield

NEW YORK UNIVERSITY PRESS
New York

NEW YORK UNIVERSITY PRESS
New York
www.nyupress.org

References to Internet websites (URLs) were accurate at the time of writing. Neither the author nor New York University Press is responsible for URLs that may have expired or changed since the manuscript was prepared.

Library of Congress Cataloging-in-Publication Data
Names: Barker-Benfield, G. J., author.
Title: Phillis Wheatley chooses freedom : history, poetry, and the ideals of the American Revolution / G.J. Barker-Benfield.
Description: New York : New York University Press, 2019. |
Includes bibliographical references and index.
Identifiers: LCCN 2017054988 | ISBN 9781479879250 (cl : alk. paper)
Subjects: LCSH: Wheatley, Phillis, 1753–1784. | African American women poets—Biography. | Poets, American—Colonial period, ca. 1600–1775—Biography. | Women slaves—United States—Biography.
Classification: LCC PS866.W5 Z56 2019 | DDC 811/.1 [B] —dc23
LC record available at https://lccn.loc.gov/2017054988

New York University Press books are printed on acid-free paper, and their binding materials are chosen for strength and durability. We strive to use environmentally responsible suppliers and materials to the greatest extent possible in publishing our books.

Manufactured in the United States of America
10 9 8 7 6 5 4 3 2 1

Also available as an ebook

To Linda

You have my heart always

Should you, my lord, while you peruse my song,
Wonder from whence my love of *Freedom* sprung,
Whence flow these wishes for the common good,
By feeling hearts alone best understood,
I, young in life, by seeming cruel fate
Was snatch'd from *Afric's* fancied happy seat;
What pangs excruciating must molest,
What sorrows labour in my parent's breast?
Steel'd was that soul and by no misery mov'd
That from a father seiz'd his babe belov'd.
—Wheatley, "To the Right Honourable
   WILLIAM, Earl of DARTMOUTH ..." 1772

in every human Breast, God has implanted a Principle,
which we call Love of Freedom; it is impatient of
Oppression, and pants for Deliverance, and by the
Leave of our Modern Egyptians I will assert, that the
same Principle lives in us.
—Wheatley to Samson Occom, February 11, 1774

CONTENTS

Introduction

In 1774, at the age of nineteen or twenty, the recently emancipated Phillis Wheatley chose not to go to West Africa as the wife of a Christianized African man she had never met; instead, she continued in the life of a poet she had made for herself in revolutionary America. This decision is the subject of this book.

Under another name we do not know, Wheatley probably spent the first six or seven years of her life in a village in "Africa," a term used very loosely by Europeans. She was enslaved as a child, in all probability by African traders from another place, perhaps when she was close to the age at which she was shipped across the Atlantic to Massachusetts.[1] If she had been enslaved literally as the "babe" she writes she was in a poem, the intervening years are a mystery.[2] She was roughly seven when she was unloaded in Boston, where she spent the rest of her life, apart from a voyage to London and back in 1773, to publish her book of poems written in formal English, in which she incorporated direct and indirect references to her enslavement and her Africanness. This is a major subject because of its bearing on her 1774 choice. Each chapter is intended to explain Wheatley's choice, and the last one, its outcome.

Wheatley understood what would likely happen to her in Africa because she had read some of the correspondence of the Rev. Philip Quaque, the subject of chapter 1. Born "Cuaco" in 1741, either a Feta or Fante, in present-day Ghana, he was sent to England as a child, there educated and made an Anglican Christian, and returned to the British slave fort Cape Coast Castle and the adjoining town as chaplain and missionary. He wrote regularly to his London employer, the Society for the Propagation of the Gospel in Foreign Parts.[3]

Quaque was also in correspondence with the Rev. Samuel Hopkins of Rhode Island about the proposed mission of two of Hopkins's African congregants, John Quamine and Bristol Yamma. Hopkins's proposal included that Phillis Wheatley, by 1773 famous in America and England as an African poet, but famous, too, as a Christianized African, marry either Quamine or Yamma. This correspondence is the chief subject of chapter 2, which concludes with an account of the relation, under revolutionary circumstances, between the proposed emancipation of African Americans and the Christianization of Africans in Africa, of which the return of Wheatley and her husband was to be a beginning.

A British evangelical who urged Wheatley to subordinate herself to Hopkins's plan was John Thornton, a powerful supporter of Selina, Lady Huntingdon, head of the Huntingdon Connexion, an early Methodist group, at first within the Anglican church. She promoted the Christianization of peoples in places subject to British political and economic imperialism. Because Phillis Wheatley became her protégée, the Countess of Huntingdon is the first subject of chapter 3. One of her agents in America was Susanna Wheatley, wife of the Boston merchant who bought the seven- or eight-year-old African child on the Boston wharf in 1761. Susanna Wheatley taught Phillis English and the Christianity preached by the Rev. George Whitefield in Boston, who visited her in her house. Phillis Wheatley gained Lady Huntingdon's personal interest by sending her the elegy "On the Death of the Rev. Mr. GEORGE WHITEFIELD," published in a pamphlet in 1770, which, addressing the "Great Countess, we Americans revere thy name," noted Whitefield had been Lady Huntingdon's chaplain.[4]

Chapter 3 suggests that Wheatley's many poems on the deaths of children and bereavement of parents were the expression of her African and transatlantic trauma. She came to see Susanna Wheatley as her virtual mother, in whose family she had been reborn.

Chapter 4 describes Wheatley's public emergence as an African genius, under the aegis of the Huntingdon Connexion, which saw her as a useful prospect, like the Christianized Mohegan Samson Occom. The Huntingdon Connexion helped sponsor Occom's mission to Native Americans, its sponsorship implemented by John Thornton. Wheatley was required to prove herself a Christian poet by Lady Huntingdon's agents, who visited her at the Wheatleys' house to do so. Wheatley, in turn, contacted Lady Huntingdon's most powerful and aristocratic acolyte, the Earl of Dartmouth, sending him her poem "To the Right Honourable WILLIAM, EARL of DARTMOUTH, His Majesty's Principal Secretary of State for North America, &c." While this, too, was a bid for patronage, Wheatley took the opportunity to tell Dartmouth that her love of freedom and of republicanism stemmed from having been enslaved as a child; she made enslavement and, implicitly, being brought to America into resources for the writing of poetry.[5]

While Wheatley published individual poems in New England, she and Susanna were unable to find enough subscribers for the collection of poems Wheatley proposed. But her successfully demonstrated and widely publicized writing of Christian poems could be of considerable use to Lady Huntingdon's evangelical purposes: hence Wheatley's voyage to London in 1773 and the publication there of her *Poems on Various Subjects: Religious and Moral*, the subject of chapter 5. It was a lucky moment, a pause in the deterioration of relations between Britain and her American colonies, the occasion for her poem to Dartmouth, one registered by the combined list of loyalist and revolutionary Americans endorsing the book. Wheatley selected its poems accordingly.

Wheatley's opening poem "To Maecenas," Virgil's patron, was a self-assertive tribute to her own patron. She proclaimed, moreover, her lineage from the African playwright Terence, and other poems incorporated her confidence in being African, even as she wrote in the long tradition of classical English literature.[6] This is a major subject of chapter 5. I suggest that Wheatley's "Niobe in Distress for her Children slain by Apollo, from *Ovid's* Metamorphoses, Book VI, and from a View of the Painting by *Richard Wilson*," written in London, referred to her African mother's bereavement, as that poem to Dartmouth had referred to her being seized by a slave-trader from her African father.[7] The chapter concludes with some consideration of Wheatley's reception, including being deemed a republican and a feminist, as well as her poems' subsequent appearance in antislavery writings, apart from her inevitable racist stereotyping.

Analysis and assessment by literary scholars have brought out the brilliant facets of Wheatley's poetry for modern readers: her mastery of English poetry from Milton to Pope; her absorption and transmutation of Biblical and classical knowledge, of contemporary political thought, and of the language of sensibility.[8] She drew on all this to come to terms with her traumatic past and racist surroundings: she insisted on the value of being African, to imagine a multiracial, more cosmopolitan world, inclusive of all human hearts.[9]

Chapter 6 opens with the subject of Wheatley's preoccupation with selling her *Poems*, in consequence of her manumission on her return to Boston. She resisted pressures brought on her by Thornton to control her now that she was free and potentially independent, despite the likelihood he had been instrumental in having her freed. Wheatley was in touch with Occom at the time Hopkins made his proposal to her; she replied to Occom's criticism of the hypocrisy of ministers who supported slavery, her letter embracing the freedom for everyone potentiated by the American Revolution. It was widely published. Then she refused the Hopkins proposal, endorsed by Thornton, representing the Connexion that had played such a valuable part in Wheatley's life. Her letter of refusal is extraordinary in its combination of play and seriousness. She then wrote a series of witty poems portraying white stand-ins for the aborted Quamine-Yamma mission to an Africa she could celebrate positively, now that she no longer faced a return there. The pain she had endured and mastered was very liable to have been reawakened had she chosen to return, permanently and intimately subordinated to an African man she had never met. Wheatley wished to continue to write and to publish her poetry, to extend the selfhood she had made since 1761.

Chapter 7 describes the transformation of Wheatley's poetry's subject under revolutionary circumstances. Now she attempted to gain the patronage of George Washington and Benjamin Franklin. Her own breaking of ties to Britain (notably to the Huntingdon Connexion—Susanna died in March 1774) coincided with the breach made by the new nation's revolutionary leaders. She chose to marry an African American man and probably gave birth to three children. The hardships of wartime and postwar economic dislocation were compounded by racism, but Wheatley wrote until the end. She died in 1784 aged about thirty-four.

The Rev. Hopkins's rhetoric linking the emancipation of African Americans to their living in colonies in Africa became orthodoxy among white abolitionists for decades. One proponent of such a link was Jefferson. Wheatley had opposed his and other revolutionaries' "monstrous inconsistency" in demanding freedom for themselves and denying it to black people. [10] Wheatley took the ideals of the revolution seriously, not as mere rhetoric, and called for freedom for all, women and men, black and white.

1

Britain Sends an African Missionary to Africa

An African Pledge

On February 6, 1753, twenty-five Fante leaders agreed to a treaty with British leaders at the slave fort of Cape Coast Castle, on the African Gold Coast. The treaty recognized "the Right of the British Nation" to occupy that fort, and excluded the demands of the French.[1] Africans, there and elsewhere, played off imperial powers for their own purposes, particularly the British and the French in the eighteenth century, as did their contemporary indigenies in North America, and later, on the subcontinent of India.[2] The African signatories gave pledges, in the language of the treaty, "of our mutual observance of the above Law," five boys, who were sent to London in 1753 and 1754. The Rev. Thomas Thompson, chaplain of the fort and missionary to local Africans, contacted the headquarters of the Society for the Propagation of the Gospel in Foreign Parts, in London, asking the Society to approve designating some of them for education. In return, the Society, he recorded, "sent me an Order for four, or to the Number of six Negro Boys, none of them exceeding ten Years of Age, to be maintained and educated at their sole Charge." Thompson wrote that Cudjo, aka Cudjoe Caboceer and Kwadwo Egyir, "expressed Satisfaction, and spoke handsomely and worthily of the Society's intended Bounty." He had been paid as a "company 'translator'" since 1729, and exercising "effective political power at Cape Coast . . . , played an essential role in the local slave trade."[3]

Thompson had hoped to send three boys from "Annamaboe," but another local leader, John Corrente, did not agree in time (he preferred negotiating separately with European powers).[4] So Thompson settled on the three supplied by the Cape Coast town. They arrived in London in 1752, each aged about ten as the SPG had wished, and were put under the charge of a Mr. Hickman, schoolmaster, in Islington. The SPG paid him 25 pounds a year for each one. We can only imagine the shock and bewilderment of these children, having traveled weeks across the seas from their families, to be immersed amidst very differently looking and behaving people (inclined to look askance and down on them in virtue of their age as well as Africanness), and daily facing an authority paid to discipline them according to strict and alien standards.[5]

After graduating from Christ's College, Cambridge, Thompson had become a missionary for the SPG, licensed, therefore, by the Bishop of London. He landed in New York, August 29, 1745, and served six years as a minister in New Jersey. The SPG had been founded in 1701, shortly after the founding of the Society for the Propagation of Christian Knowledge, corollaries of the founding of the Society for the Reformation of Manners, all in the aftermath of the "Glorious Revolution" and in reaction to the perceived immorality of Charles II's court and the Catholicism of his heir, James II. The SPG and the SPCK were intended to spread to British colonies the reforms attempted in Britain, "to improve the lax Christian presence in America." Thompson was one of the Anglican ministers who "were flocking to Maryland, Virginia and the Carolinas" in the early eighteenth century. By the time of the American Revolution, the "SPG had sent over 600 ministers" and SPCK "thousands of books," disseminating the Anglican message in a variety of accessible literary forms.[6] These efforts were inspired not only by the colonists' irreligion but also by the "Sectaries," as Thompson called them, first Baptists and then Methodists, but many others too, all competing for the same potential congregants.[7]

Thompson recollected, "I was not unconcerned for the poor Negroes, who wanted enlightenment more than any." The missionary efforts of the SPG coincided with the rapid increase in slavery, especially in the southern colonies, but in the middle colonies, too, along with the formulation of legal codes governing imported Africans and their now perpetually enslaved descendants.[8] The SPG itself was bequeathed two sugar plantations and three hundred slaves in Barbados, Britain's richest colony in virtue of its production of sugar. This was in 1710, the donor Colonel Christopher Codrington. In the 1711 Annual Sermon to the SPG (a high point of its calendar), Bishop William Fleetwood (a founder of the SPG, who had published a book in 1706 addressing the "potential difficulties," that is, for Anglican Christians, "in American slaveholding") "enunciated principles regarding slaveholding and planter ethics that the SPG followed for the next half century in America." While Fleetwood accepted "the Africans' full humanity" and said, in theory, that on being baptized, they could be emancipated, he also declared that the "Liberty of Christianity is entirely Spiritual," so Baptism "left Men under all the obligations that it found them." "'To the slaves and Captives [Paul] would say, 'Obey your Master in all things as becomes your sad Condition, and make your Chains as easier as you can by your Compliance and Submission.'" This Anglican position "fitted with un-canny precision the elaboration of slave codes . . . that increasingly spec-ified the degraded condition of captive Africans."[9]

Inspired by "Prophecies," Thompson requested the SPG "to grant me a Mission to the Coast of Guiney that I might make a trial with the Natives, and see what Hopes there would be of introducing them to the Christian religion." He "requested that his salary [L70] be taken out of the Fund for Negroes Conversion." The SPG agreed. Its founder, the Rev. Thomas Bray, had bruted a scheme to send missionaries to Africa in 1721, but it was not implemented.[10]

Thompson sailed from New York in November 1751 on the *Prince George*. "Captain Williams had a Negro Youth, whom he had brought from *Africa* for Education, a Grandson of *Peter*, King of *Cape Monte*. He had him baptized and was now carrying him *Home*." Touching other slave forts, the *Prince George* reached Cape Coast Castle, "the princi-pal *English* settlement on the Coast of Guiney," on May 13, 1752; "the Governor thereof was Thomas Melvil." A month later, Melvil wrote the African Committee (of the CMTA, Company of Merchants Trading to Africa—British slave traders), telling them of his answer to Thompson's pressing him for his opinion of his undertaking "to convert the Negroes." Melvil based what he said on "the Circumstances of the Country, and the Character of the People." It was Melvil who reported Thompson had been brought to Africa "by Prophecies." If the supernatural helped, he might hope, said Melvil, but "if it was left to himself he could do no good and . . . ought not to throw away his time and Constitution to no Purpose." He added that Thompson had gone to Anomabu "where if he can put old John's morals to rights he will perform a miracle." This was John Corrente.[11]

Cudjo spoke some English, but it was his son, Frederick Adoy, sent to England to learn English, who was Thompson's (and then Quaque's) principal interpreter in the attempt to convert Africans to Christianity: "Some Years ago [Adoy] was brought to London with another young Man, Son of *John Courantee*, Cabosheer of Anamabu, and both had their Education under the Reverend Mr. Tirnt of the Temple." Thompson wanted to spend his time at Anomabu, a town not far from Cape Coast Castle. William Ansah, another son of John Corrente, invited him there, where the reverend met Corrente, "then about eighty," still formidable.[12]

We should note that William Ansah had been treacherously enslaved by an archetypally crooked captain, sold in America, but then "redeemed" when it was discovered he was a prince, the son of an important partner in Britain's slave trade, and he was sent back to his father under the auspices of the Earl of Halifax, Lord Commissioner of the Board of Trade and Plantations. This was one among quite a number of comparable episodes of the enslavement of high-ranking African sons, deemed wrongful because of their rank, becoming a theme in English literature, "Guinea's Captive Kings." During a second visit there, when he witnessed the post-treaty rebuilding of the fort, Thompson gave William Ansah a copy of "a short Instructions for the Blacks," that is, in Christianity, and Thompson said "he made a conscientious point of it . . . to bring those when he could to the Knowledge of Christianity."[13]

Cuaco Becomes the Rev. Philip Quaque

Thompson tried to improve the Christianity of "Mulattoes," of whom the town next to the fort (called Cape Coast by the English and Oquaa by the Africans) had "a good number." They were, he wrote, "betwixt a *Negro* and a *White*, this same as in *England* we commonly called *Tawnies*." Most of the adults had been christened "by Chaplains of Men of War," or by preceding chaplains of the garrison. He tried to use their sense of being privileged in having a Christian name by preaching to them separately but, "I may truly say, they are more *heathenish* than the *Negroes*." But those Africans, he wrote, "had no Principles to graft anything upon. . . . As to their Sense of Vice and of Virtue, they have only cold, and unaffecting Notions of both." This was equivalent to stating that Africans lacked sensibility, including the moral sense, according to his psychological model, and one frequently asserted by proslavery writers.[14]

Thompson continued: "The Christian Religion they call white Men's Fashion, and white Men, they say, *know best*, but *black Man* follow *Black Man's Fashion.*" This, too, must have been translated for Thompson. His "not being acquainted with the Language" he considered "as a Disadvantage." Even when he had an interpreter, "it were impossible to know how to express, the Doctrines and Articles of the Christian Religion by suitable words." He devoted half a dozen pages to describing "the very various Language of the Coast." According to Rebecca Shumway's history of the eighteenth-century evolution of Fante identity, "the Akan language became more widely used across Fanteland. A new language, Fante, which blended Akan, Guan, and Etsi dialects and . . . incorporated words and phrases from Portuguese, English, and Dutch, became commonly used across Fanteland."[15] Thompson tried to learn "the Fante" by writing down what he could from those he asked, giving a description of "sounds expressed" in a kind of "melted voice," spoken quickly because of "that Impetuosity in the Temper." Thompson's ignorance made him miserable. In bad health, he resigned his mission, sailing from West Africa to London via a transatlantic leg to St. Christopher. Thompson concluded his retrospective account by declaring that the "Propagation of the Gospel," particularly "in the Conversion of the Negroes in . . . Guiney," was probable. Missionaries should appeal "to the material Creation," the Book of Nature, but God's "word . . . should be published by every Nation," to rescue "these poor *Pagans* out of their Subjection in this tyranny of Satan." Thompson could envision the three African lads he had sent to England preaching to Africans in their own tongue.[16]

In December 1754, those three boys were examined in London and "one of them could repeat the Lords Prayer and the Apostles Creed, and the other two answered well to the questions put to them." They were examined again in 1756 and the SPG Committee found them proficient in reading, writing, and repeating the Catechism. Caboro died of consumption in 1758, but in January 1759, Cuaco and Cudjo were baptized as Philip and William; their education was taken over by the Rev. John Moore, "a member of both the SPCK and the SPG . . . [who] had previously cooperated" with the CMTA "in training Atlantic creoles." In January 1766, Moore wrote the SPG: "It is now 7 years since I undertook the Care of the two Negroes at the Request of the Society. . . . One of them has rewarded my Labours by improving in every branch of Knowledge in this Station for which he was designed, and it is hoped will approve a worthy Miss[ionary]." He had largely lost his Fante language and culture, replacing them with English and Anglicanism. This was Cuaco, henceforth transliterated as Quaque, who became deeply attached to Moore.[17]

But the design for the remaining African boy had failed dramatically. On January 15, 1764, Moore wrote to the Board of the SPG about him: "The other (Wm. Cudjo) who never discovered any great Talent for Learning tho' otherwise well behaved, was put out of the Reach of Instruction by a Lunacy which seized him in December 1764. He has been confined near twelve Months in St. Luke's, &, by the Rules of the Hospital, must be returned upon my Hands in a few Days, which will expose me to fresh Trouble & Expence till I can provide him in St. Luke's, Bedlam, or Guy's Hospital." Moore said he was "willing to undertake the Trouble" but could not afford "the Expence, which may attend this unhappy Affair," and asked the SPG to reimburse him for it, and the "Securities" for the young man's perhaps permanent confinement. Very soon after his return to Africa, Quaque would write to the SPG on behalf of William Cudjo's parents, thanking the Society for its "Care & Pains in the Education of their unfortunate Son," and, if he was somewhat better, that the SPG "would free themselves of that Burthen," begging "that he may be sent over by the next Committee Ship . . . for they are very uneasy about him, and are impatient of his return, especially his Father, who laments daily after him, being himself also in a bad State, and wants greatly to see his deplorable Son before his Departure." A few months later, Quaque reported that "Mr. Cudjo's Father died soon after this letter." Since he was dead, "it will be much better . . . to let him remain in [the London asylum] rather than send him. His Relations are almost [all] dead, & even those who are left will, I am certain, do Nothing for him." He did not mention Cudjo's mother.[18]

Quaque had been ordained on May 4, 1765, by the Bishop of London (in charge of Anglicanism in Britain's colonies) and sent back to Cape Coast Castle. Before he left, the twenty-four-year-old Quaque wrote to the Rev. Daniel Burton, Secretary of the SPG, expressing, as he often would, his profound gratitude to the "Venerable Society the Fruit of whose Benevolence I have enjoyed ever since their Compassion snatched me from the Bondage of Sin & Satan, and that Miserable Condition I was then involved in." This view of Christianization was widely expressed; as metaphor, "it could bolster the acceptability of slavery in the real world," diminishing the significance of its literal form, even rationalizing slavery of the body as unimportant, in contrast to the salvation of the soul. Fleetwood preached as much to the SPG in 1711. Whitefield interpreted the enslavement of Africans according to this vision, bringing them from the bonds of Satan in pagan Africa, to Christian lands, where slavery to whites offered the chance of freedom in Christ. Wheatley wrote a poem on this theme in 1768, published in 1773.[19]

As in the case of Thompson, Quaque's mission for the SPG was combined with his chaplaincy for the African Committee, the first intended to convert local Africans, the second to serve white officials in the fort, as well as those Quaque called "Mulatoes." He prayed for "the success of the Society in this Work of the Ministry, that the Kingdom of our God may soon be made known in the remotest Regions of the Universe, that those wretched Creatures who are now languishing under & despair & in the shadow of Death may soon be brought to the Truth of the Glorious light of the Gospel of our Lord & Saviour." Quaque's repeated "our" identified him with the other members of this Anglican society, remote from the particular region where "those" to whom he intended to bring light were still under the "bondage" from which the SPG had rescued Quaque.[20]

The Rev. Quaque in Africa

Throughout his life, Quaque was contemptuous of those he wished to convert. His first letter from Africa characterized "the great work [he has] undertak[en] of Propagating the Gospel of our Saviour to them who now groan under a gross Superstition and Idolatry in the Land of Darkness and Ignorance." In his first "conference with Cabosheer Cudjo, explaining the Utility & Legality of the Ordinance of Baptism, . . . I stated also . . . the Excellency of our Religion above that of any other in the World." Quaque repeatedly ridiculed African religion in terms far harsher than those he reported Africans expressed for his.[21]

Consistent with seeing himself as a "New comer," albeit among those he slipped into calling "my countrymen," Quaque was virtually as incompetent in the Fantee language as Thompson had been. He tried to explain "the sacrament of Baptism in my own Lingo as well as I was able to," tried to interpret "the Liturgy in my own language," and got his African listeners to ask that central Christian question, "What must I do to be saved?"—incomprehensible to non-Christians. In 1769, the SPG "urged Quaque 'to recover his own language,'" to fulfill Thompson's and the SPG's hopes for him, "but he was unwilling to do so." He had lost most of his first language during all those years in London, and had to depend on Thompson's translator, Frederick Adoy, Cudjo's son.[22]

Quaque's first visit to Anomabu was in January 1767, when he baptized slave-trader Richard Brew's granddaughter by way of his "wench," Effina Ansah. Her descendants "belonged to the matrilineal family of the Rev. Philip Quaque. Effina Ansah, John Corrente's daughter, had been married to Brew when he was Governor of the fort at Anomabu." That was part of the negotiations in the treaty between Corrente and the British in 1753, supplementing the one that had sent "Cuaco" to England.[23]

In explanation of his promised audience's failure to turn up for his service, Quaque wrote to the SPG about another part of the culture of his infancy he had replaced with that under the aegis of the SPG: "They were going to offer Sacrifice to their chief God, the Goddess Aminsor. A superstitious & Infamous Offering indeed." They sacrificed sheep to "Taberah, . . . a prodigious high rock whereon the better part of [Cape Coast] Castle stands," to procure fish. Quaque asked Cudjo whether his people expected results "of their deceitful Dum lying Fetishes." Cudjo—who played along with Quaque to some extent—"answered No. Why then, said I, You all so silly & so very deluded as to place yr Confidence in Dum Stones and Bushes." This was precisely the approach Thompson had taken, arguing that before infidels could receive Christian truth their minds had to be purged of false belief.[24]

One of the "Panims" (elders) told Quaque they had heard the same from the Rev. Thompson. Quaque's report suggests why Thompson had tried to have Africans minister "to Negroes." He notes, "The same Person remarked that as to Us Christians"—by "us," Quaque means himself, with his interlocutors saying, "you Christians," then continues speaking in their voices—"the Almighty has super abundantly blessed Us, and that We are peculiarly his Children because said he, . . . God has not distained to give to Us his own Book, by w[hich] means We comprehend everything. . . . And tho' We whose religion it is (pointing to the Gentl[emen] in the Fort) do not so much regard it." As Cudjo had told Thompson, "as for Me [i.e. Quaque] to press it upon them. Moreover, [he] said that, as for them, they were but Black Men, and the only Means or Books afforded by Him [your god] to them is their Fetishes." But, he added, if Quaque would tell them the things they should avoid, they would try to follow his instructions. Despite his interpreting that statement as "Nothing but deceit in Him," Quaque said he would keep trying, but he accompanied that effort with a stream of denigration of the Africans' "Fetishes & False Gods," the "Means of our Spiritual Enemy the Devil," who had thereby "brought Evil into the World." Quaque was forced to compromise, bribing Africans with liquor and presenting Caboocer Cudjo with "a piece or Two of Silken Garment," remarking, "For it is not so much the terrours of the Lord we serenade Men, but oft wrought by gentle and Captivate Admonitions."[25]

Quaque had hoped to be able to give a more pleasing account to the SPG of the white "Inhabitants of the Garrison than what I could relate concerning these illiterate People." It was impossible, "as they have grown even more degenerate" since "the reign of John Hippisley," the Governor at the time Quaque arrived, when they regularly attended Sunday service. If they came, he believed, it was "out of Curiosity" to see a black chaplain. They have cast "a stain upon the Professions where with they were called, by the Corruption of Morals and the Inhuman Practice and the love of Mammon which they hold in great Esteem." Though imprecise, this is Quaque's earliest reference in this correspondence to the fort's chief purposes, a collection point and market for the transatlantic slave trade. To him, however, more pressing evidence of white men's degeneracy and corruption of morals was the practice of consorting.[26]

The "Curiosity" Quaque remarked was one expression of the racism he continually faced. On his arrival, and under Hippisley's direction, the fort's chief accountant had ordered his subordinates to attend service. One of them (named Cahune) rebelled: "I don't chose to attend to hear any . . . black man whatsoever." Hippisley observed, "As to the Colour of the preacher's Complexion none but the most illiberal could make any objection . . . as under any colour, piety & good sense might inhabit, and we ought to suppose this was the case with the person in Question, as a most disinterested Society . . . very attentive . . . to their missionaries, had recommended him." Hippisley added that the good example—that is, of a black man—was necessary, as he had been informed by the African Committee, according to the design "to make Converts among the Natives." Quaque recorded another white man's remark as directly racist as Cahune's, exclaimed by Richard Brew. To his face Brew showed civility and friendship, and Quaque "baptized his two Mullattoe Daughters by his own earnest desires." Then, after "a few trifling words," Brew declared "he would never come to Cape Coast to be Subservient to, & to sit under the Nose of a Black Boy, to hear Him pointing or laying out their faults before them."[27]

Most of the other governors of Cape Coast Castle Quaque served during his very long tenure were similarly irreligious and contemptuous of him. John Grossle excluded Quaque from his table (being invited there would have been a mark of public acceptance), and turned "the bare mention of Religious Subjects into Ridicule and Prophaneness." Quaque wrote to SPG that he was a "hideous Libertine or Freethinker." On being shown notes that Quaque had sent a "gentleman" under his command, expressing Quaque's dispute with him, Grossle said one of them was "a very dirty & indecent Note, & for . . . it [he] deserves to be kickt, were it not for a disgrace for a Gentleman to enter into a list with a Negro Priest."[28]

Another governor, David Mill, like Hippisley, had "a true benevolent Disposition, and one whose tender feelings extended to the Distresses of his fellow Creatures," but, unlike Hippisley, he did not attend to his religious duties. His successor, Richard Miles, was suspended, as Hippisley had been, charged by the African Committee with buying slaves privately from the Dutch, "obstructing the free market . . . selling skilled CMTA slaves for high prices to the West Indies." Quaque wrote the SPG that this was defamation by some self-serving competitor, and he thought Miles and his accomplices would be exonerated. He asserted that he wrote impartially on these matters, which were outside his "cognizance," despite his gratitude to those gentlemen for acting to get "a new supply of Canonicals" from the African Committee. The SPG neglected his request. Quaque always fulfilled his duty to send semiannual reports (*Notitae Scholasticae*) to the successive SPG secretaries in London. Their neglect caused Quaque great distress, as he continued to express his love for the SPG. Years went by before he heard from headquarters, but he continued to pile on expressions of gratitude. Eventually they were tinged with irony.[29]

Quaque's Marriages and Family

The day after Quaque was ordained he married Catherine Blunt, in all probability one of Moore's parishioners. His first letter from Cape Coast Castle, dated February 29, 1766, reported their safe arrival, and gave a detailed account of the voyage. He thanked God for preserving "my Family & life, particularly Cudjo. He was very glad to see me and his New Daughter," that is, Mrs. Quaque, thus formally accepted into Cudjo's family. Quaque knew how much he would need Cudjo's help in his mission to Africans.[30]

During their first year at Cape Coast Castle, the rains made the Quaques' room uninhabitable, foreseeably for every rainy season. "My poor Spouse & Bosom Companion had been but very indifferent since we came upon the Coast, who now lies at the point of Death . . . I would willingly send her . . . Home again," or come with her, but, "if leave cannot be obtained & no known Captn. to convey her . . . she must inevitably perish, as here is no proper Remedy for the female Sex." Catherine Quaque was pregnant. Quaque himself was suffering from "a severe fit of the flux and fever." She soon died, along with her newborn baby. He described his feelings the following spring in his report to the SPG secretary, the Rev. Doctor Daniel Burton: "The heaviness w[hic]h surrounds me . . . for the los of so dear and worthy a Spouse," Providence "for wiser Ends," depriving him of "the sweet Consolation I rece[ived] from her tender Breast on Nov last." As a "Young unskillful fellow in these incidental Scenes of Nature & a doting Husb[an]d withal, am not able as yet to Eradicate." The deaths of her and "a Child, too," had in some ways incapacitated him. Quaque conveyed "her dying Words & Circumstances" to the SPG, his paraphrase expressing the religious belief she shared with her husband. "God called her away from the world's vanities, and put an end to her grievous & heavy Sufferings," and she thanked him for the "safe Delivery" of her child, and the opportunity of embracing this last legacy. Immediately after, she "dropt a tender tear & then departed in peace like a Lamb." So she died before her baby.[31]

Quaque was two years a widower. Then, in 1769, he reported to the SPG that he had "once more entered into the Holy State of Matrimony, with my Spouse's waiting Maid." The editors of his letters assumed she was a "slave given to Philip and Catherine by Cudjoe Caboceer," although William St. Clair writes she was "probably also white," assuming she had come to Cape Coast Castle with Catherine Quaque.[32]

Quaque explained he had remarried after having "suffered the jealous lashes of so many Scandalous Tongues, in order to silence those Reproaches & deadly Aspersions thrown against Me." This was in the context of his attempt to persuade men at the fort to get properly married, giving up consorting or the fig-leaf of celibacy. The then-governor, John Grossle, a "hideous libertine," was one source of the aspersions. Along with "some other Chiefs," he said "publickly at Dinner before Strangers, that since I was disappointed in my Amour of a Mustee Young Lady, if I did not get One to marry, I should meet with no Countenance from them (particularly the Gov.) then what they always treated Me with, i.e. with Defidence & Coldness." Grossle wanted Quaque to marry as Quaque importuned white officers to do. Quaque did get married, hoping "as a true Christian" to see "mutual Harmony" established between himself and the governor.[33]

But within a year, Quaque wrote to the SPG "of loosing my Second [wife], also in Child-Bed, thro' the bitter hatred & enemy held against me by my own Relations. . . . She has left Me, however, a Female Child to provide for." He interpreted the loss and its cause, compounded by "the same Affliction & Troubles from Slanderous, Suspicious, & Censorious People," as a "Trial of my Faith & Patience" by God, unfathomable to "we frail Beings."[34]

In 1772, Quaque reported baptizing two people, "one an Infant Mulattoe Boy, and the other an adult Black Girl whom I afterwards Married." He explained to the SPG that the "chief motive of my embracing this Opportunity was owing to a previous advice of Mr. Thompson, who judging it the most prudent step I could pursue as a means whereby to quench the flames of jealous Dispositions and the deadly Suspicions & Censors of Many." Quaque suggested that this expressed white officials' projection, intensified by racism. It seems likely Thompson believed Quaque's marrying an African woman would contribute to a more successful mission to the "Negroes." Similarly, the Rev. Dr. Johnson had urged Quaque to marry an African "daughter." All this is suggestive context for Thornton's and Hopkins's wanting Quamine/Yamma to marry Wheatley.

Quaque added to his account of this third marriage that the "Woman whom it has pleased God to give me, I hope thro' his gracious Assitance to bring her up in the Nurture & fear of the Lord, and to the praise of his Holy Name." Presumably she had been converted from her African beliefs and baptized to marry Quaque. "She is very tractable, and seems willing & mindful for the little Time she has been with me, which [is] now two Months & better."[35] By 1781 he had three children, "a son and two Daughters," and the following year, "another very lately brought forth." One of the daughters seems to have been the survivor of his second wife."[36]

Quaque's third wife continued to represent the African culture he had lost and continuously scorned: he had "pitched upon this method," taking his children to England to be educated, "to secure Minds from receiving bad Impressions of the Country [Africa], the vile, Customs and Practices, & above all the loosing of their Mother's vile Jargon, the only obstacles of Learning in these Parts."[37] This raises the question of how much English Quaque had been able to teach his wife as he tried to nourish her faith in Christianity and in him. Evidently she had taught her children her own language. Sending these children to be educated by whites in England would "be an Everlasting Provision for 'em after I am . . . intered in the Sepulchre of my Ancestors." That provision would be "a superior Knowledge of Things over their Countrymen," his pronoun representing Quaque's children's absorption of the ambiguities that had bedeviled him.

Nearly a year after his proposal to the SPG, the secretary told him that those Quaque called "my most Munificent and Venerable Patrons" permitted him "the Indulgence of a Tour to England whenever . . . Convenient," but "that the Care of my Children is quite out of their Province" and "must rest entirely on [his] own Disposal." The Society granted him a leave to return to England, Quaque noted, just as peace in the Revolutionary War had been proclaimed. Seven weeks later, he wrote the secretary that "the Commissary of His Majesty's Troops on the Coat of Africa," son of a dear friend, the Rev. John Fountaine of St. Mary's Church, Islington, would bring Quaque's son Samuel to London, "to be consigned under the Care of the Rev. Mr. Moore." Quaque himself came to London with his daughter (never named) between 1784 and 1785, joining Samuel at the Rev. Moore's, thereafter often reminding the SPG to recompense Moore for his expenses.[38]

For a while at least, Samuel began to fulfill Quaque's hopes. In 1789, Quaque reported that a "Society of Gentlemen," patronized by the governor and calling themselves "Torridzonian, a Name analogous to the climate," joined together to clothe, feed, and educate "twelve colour'd Children of this Country, principally the Offspring of distressed and deceased Parents." Quaque said the Torridzonians' plan was "calculated to produce Virtue and Religion," viewing "profligacy in a very severe exemplary manner." The twelve children whose education they sponsored were to exemplify the reformation of manners and Christianity to "other of the Natives." Quaque was put in charge and, he wrote to the SPG, made "my little Boy, Samuel, lately under the Tuition of the Rev[eren]d Fountaine of Marybone, my Assistant. The Boy has proved himself diligent and careful and has acquired the countenance of these Gentleman." Quaque hoped he would further merit their esteem and therefore that of the SPG.[39]

In 1795, he sent the SPG specimens of his scholars' writing, apparently done under the auspices of the Torridzonians, hoping this promised well for the future. Quaque did not mention Samuel. Probably Samuel was the son for whom Quaque asked the African Committee the position of "writer," the job to which William Ansah had applied his English education.[40] This may have been a come-down from Quaque's hopes for his son: he had been sharply disappointed when his other protegees had left off their education, boys to become "Soldiers and Fifers" for the CMTA, and "females" to get married as soon as they could.[41]

Quaque's relations with his children only worsened, a subject of his last extant letter, written sixteen years later. The state of the country paralleled the wretched state of his health (he was in his seventies), grown worse and worse, "nothing but confusion and rumours of War." The American Revolutionary War had been followed by Britain's war with revolutionary France. Quaque's familial "disadvantage . . . was too shocking to relate. My own family, whom I have brought up, one would naturally imagine would be the most near and dear tye to me, but instead of which they are plotting my ruin, more particularly raising up a malicious dispute with Mrs. Quaque merely thro' jealousy and hatred and envy, and opposing every measure I take for the further benefit of my Wife, as if a Man has not power and authority to do and dispute of his own Property as he pleaseth, without the controlling and interfering of any one." Presumably, this would have been the orientation either Quamine or Yamma would have had toward Wheatley.[42]

Quaque presented his children's psychology and values as typical of Africans, writing as if he was not black. "Thus You see the avaricious dispassions of the Blacks, who are all for themselves, and wish not that the inferior People should ever rise, in equality with themselves." Elsewhere he had said his difficulties were compounded because Africans "foolishly look upon" him "as in no other light than as one of themselves."[43] Here he continued, "That a man's foes shall be of his own Household," his amplification of Christ's declaration, "a Prophet has no honour in his own Country.' This is the case now with me." Yet he had spent his life ridiculing his family's African religion and culture. Even here, he went on, he had been "casting so many purls before Swens [swine]." But he had not given up, telling the SPG he hoped "that the Almighty God, who has all along supported Her innocent cause will no doubt finish the same, . . . to the utter shame and confusion of all her cruel enemies." "Her" refers to Mrs. Quaque. He also noted in the report that Parliament had refused the African Committee more money for the upkeep of its forts, although this was not the reason for its eventual banning of the slave trade. Quaque's last paragraph opened: "The State of this unsuccessful Mission, I formerly had some hopes of its growth, but at present. . . . I have my doubts of its increase." On October 4, 1816, Governor Dawson wrote the African Committee that "from age and indisposition" Mr. Quaque had long been "unable to perform divine service for many years." Quaque died two weeks later.[44]

Matrimony and Inter-Racial Sex

In that first letter from Cape Coast Castle Quaque had reported to the SPG that "the greatest Task that I shall have to encounter will be the Europeans at the Factory. The prevailing Vice that reigns among them is that of Consorting, which they seem to glory in, in abundance." In St. Clair's view, one of the attractions for men to join the African service was "the prospect of plentiful sex." "Consorting" was the form of their relations with local African women they called "wenches." According to St. Clair, wenches' contracts with such white men "were unequal and exploitative," although some wenches "lived with them, day by day, year after year, in some cases as least in sexual, caring, and affectionate unions, brought up their children, grieved at their funerals."[45]

Quaque saw "consorting" as emblematic of the irreligion and immorality of whites at the fort in particular, but also of the Africans who lived there and in the adjoining town. Quaque reported that he had "expounded in a[s] familiar style as possible, showing them the utility of one Wife." He preached this to native Africans and to Europeans, but "all in vain, and their Custom they will follow, yet at the same time do modestly allow the reasonableness of our way of Marriage." He continued: "But for the Europeans to defile themselves with such sort of Notions, may even partaking with them, and dis[d]aining not to turn them away at Pleasure for the least trifle of Misdemeanors and soon after, taking another at Will, I cannot away with it. [A]nd to their shame be it spoken, it is not so rigorous with the poor Natives themselves." Quaque's calling whites' consorting with blacks defilement referred to a Mosaic text that Rev. Thompson, retired from his missions and living in Reculver in Kent, made the title of a sermon published in 1757, when Quaque was a young student in London. "Defile not yourselves, says he in any of these Things, as it is in the verse before my Text [*Leviticus* xviii, 25] *for in all these* (the unlawful Marriages and Lusts here specified in this Chapter) *the Nations are defiled which I cast before you.* And then it follows, *And the Land is defiled, therefore do I visit the Iniquity thereof upon it.*"[46]

Quaque addressed the subject at length in letters to Dr. Samuel Johnson, an American minister who, from 1754, was president of King's College in New York. Evidently he had told Johnson of Mrs. Quaque's death because Johnson advised Quaque to marry "the Daughter of some Eminent Person for the Sake of the good Design in View." That "design," as Quaque's letter to him implied, was his mission to "Negroes," and, in Johnson's view, Quaque's bride should be African. Quaque answered, calling himself "a young lad," as he did at other times to his authoritative, white, male correspondents: "But permit me, as a young Lad, to suggest to You that the Marriages here are vulgarly termed Consor[t] ing, and Celebecy too being much in Demand with the better most Sort, as may nominally be called, to our Shame be it spoken, as well as those whose established Custom it is." "Our Shame" referred to Christian officials, with whom he thus identified himself; "those," to the Africans living nearby. Neither group, he implied, actually practiced celibacy. He explained to Johnson that were he to follow proper Anglican ritual and marry an African woman, "a person, in my Character, and the only One here," that is, an African but adhering to Anglican orthodoxy, "would look black in the Eyes of them, very insignificant and worthless, and which would in all likelihood render his Public Orations to be of no weight and influence with them." This was either conscious or unconscious irony, given his "complection," and the connotation of blackness in English, which Quaque had internalized. Africans would scorn him as an African for following British ritual, and the British for not following their custom, their chaplain showing his true colors, betraying his Britishness. Quaque believed it fundamental to the success of his mission that he maintain the status he had earned in London as a lad, somehow able to seem white to his audience.[47]

Quaque's next paragraph concentrates on the predictable response of those Africans about whose conversion the Anglican American minister had questioned him. "But as to those ignorant and unpolished People, whose Minds are not for Confinement, the proposal of such schemes," including Quaque's marriage to an African woman, "in every Respect foreign to their unaltered and bigoted Principles, wou'd appear to them . . . as one who wants to wheedle them of their Independency, by a false Notion of better prospects which they know Nothing of." Those better prospects included eternal life in heaven.

Their answer to him when he talked to them "upon the Principles of Religion touching upon Matrimony" resembled, he wrote, that made by "the Pagans in the East, when they hear that such and such Plan," presented to them by the East India Company, "as laying out to enrich their Nation," evidence of Quaque's awareness of the operation of empire, seeing an analogy between economic and sexual exploitation and resistance. "Ah!" those Indian pagans exclaim, "let them come and cultivate our Country, build Houses and teach Us Husbandry and all Sciences necessary for Us to know, but still the Possession of the Ground shall remain ours. Likewise here," at Cape Coast Castle in Africa, "who says that the Europeans may Consor[t] them if they think proper, but as to the little kept in reserve against the Rainy Day, shall not be mixed with theirs, so as to give them an Opportunity of Laying claims to it, some time or other, and then at last leave them Destitute by shameful Dismission." He tells Johnson this is what Africans apprehend would be the case were he to marry an African daughter according to his definition of matrimony, understanding what that meant for a wife's property. "And God forbid! That this ever shou'd be my case."

2

Prospects of an American Mission to Anomabu

Quaque Comes to View Slavery Critically

Much of what Quaque wrote about slavery was in summaries of his replies to American ministers who asked him about it, expressing great interest in his success in converting Africans to Christianity, in the new context of the "monstrous inconsistency" dramatized by the American Revolution.

The first of these was this reply to that 1767 letter from Dr. Johnson. Quaque thought he was from Rhode Island, probably because the captain who put them in touch sailed from Newport, a major slaving port with a congregation of Christianized Africans. Quaque told Johnson that while he had hoped "as a Native," and therefore to be more successful than Thompson had been in "bringing over these People to their Duty and Religion," "they seem to be a very Stubborn & stiff-necked People, extremely bigoted to their own Principals & Customs . . . the hardest Thing in Nature for the most sagacious Man . . . [that] ever lived to root out." He was "young and unskillful . . . amongst so many Ravenous Wolfs." Acknowledging that Johnson was better educated than he was, Quaque asked his advice. Johnson sent him "two Grammars for the Use of Schools."[1]

Quaque was profusely grateful in the letter he then sent to Johnson and, as he often did, contrasted the success Anglicans enjoyed in America with his failure in Africa. He added that "the stir of Religion & its Everlasting Recompense is not so much in vogue as the vicious Practice of purchasing Flesh & Blood like Oxens in the Market Places." These African nations, living "under the confines of Usurping and Arbitrary Government . . . are kept in Ignorance for Interest and lucre's sake. " This refers to the African side of the slave trade, Quaque's account resembling Anthony Benezet's: "while Xtian Humanity and fellow feeling," here referring to the whites' side of the trade, "are blinded with Profit and Loss." This was "the only Hindrance that the name of Christ is not known to these unhappy Nations." He had written earlier that whites did not come to communion because of a sense of guilt, then specified consorting, although his words could have subsumed slavery, too. Here he went on to describe consorting, in responding to Johnson's suggestion that he marry "the Daughter of some Eminent Person for the sake of the good Design in View."[2]

A second letter to Johnson, conveying Quaque's "Proposals for the Government of Wenches," also addressed the slave trade. We can note the contiguity of subjects, "their Dependence so entirely upon these Men." Quaque asked Johnson, "May I have the Liberty to suggest that just remark of yours with respect to that cursed Slave Trade is the only Obstruction to the Ministering in these desolate Parts." Quaque's writing the same in his previous letter was his conscious echo of what Johnson had written him—"& as Necessity has driven many Youths to get their Fortunes by way of Trafick," including St. Clair's black sheep and ne'er do wells, operators of empire. Quaque makes clear they grouped him with enslaved Africans: "I am afraid . . . it will be impossible for Me, whom they look upon not better than those unhappy creatures they come to purchase, so that as it is their aim & Interest to oppose the means I try to make Religion flourish & abound, it will methinks be kicking against the Pricks or Goads as to make my poor Countrymen fully sensible what a horrid thing it is." This spelled out how the slave trade was an obstruction to conversion. White slave traders would not be able to enslave Christianized Africans, in Quaque's view, consistent with the belief that others held, which had to be officially refuted by the SPG, itself owning slaves in Barbados. Some runaway slaves in the England of Quaque's youth had had themselves baptized with that belief in mind. Quaque held that Africans did not see enslavement as morally repugnant, not distinguishing here between usurping, arbitrary governments, and "nations." "Could this Mallady"—the slave trade—"be easily removed, there might then I believe be some hopes of doing little Good amongst my deluded Countrymen."[3]

Johnson had written him of the conversion of Africans in America, so Quaque continued, "But on the other hand, I am truly joyful to hear of your Admission of two of my Countrymen into that sacred Function as well as the hopes of those whom You are shortly to invite to the awful Table of our Lord"—communion, refused by Cape Coast Castle officers. "I am lead to wish You & all the Brethren that are in America better prospect of Success in the Name of God, than what I here heavily labour under." SPG missionaries circulated their news among each other, and apparently to other Anglican ministers, and sometimes other Anglophone denominations' ministers, too, all "Brethren" laboring in God's vineyard. Quaque asked Johnson to intervene with the SPG in London on behalf of an increase in his salary.[4]

Quaque wrote the SPG ten days after that letter to Johnson, reflecting on "how desperately degenerated Mankind are from the Touch stone of Faith. . . . while the God of Mammon carries the greater sway." Two years later (still not having heard from the SPG since he left England four years earlier), he wrote of his failure in both of his roles, chaplain and missionary. The garrison disapproved of his "shewing Christianity to the Indigents belonging to the Town," and neither did it "approve of Service [attending communion], on Account of the Branch of Business which they are obliged to follow." That was trading in slaves.[5]

Quaque then reported a letter he had received from "the Rev. Mr. [Edward] Bass of Newbury Port, New England," an Anglican minister like Johnson, who, like Johnson, wanted to know "what success I meet with in this Quarter[,] whether there is any seeming prospect of establishing Christianity, or whether that cursed Slave Trade was not the chief Obstruction?" This was precisely how Johnson had framed the question.[6] Quaque described his reply in his next report to the SPG. Bass, he said, "earnestly and zealously requested to know the religious State of this Part of the World." Quaque answered, "First, Of the many Obstacles & Difficulties attending the Labours of those who are unfortunately situated here, principally the horrid Slave Trade, of which [Bass] himself makes a Mention. . . . Secondly the want of a good President" who would exemplify Christianity. But "instead . . . Interest or the love of gain and Ambition on the one hand," meaning the whites, and "Superstition and Bigotry on the other," the Africans, "is the chief Hindrance. So that it is Impossibility, one thinks, to bring them over to our Faith, unless the Professors of Christianity join strenuously in this glorious & laudable Undertaking."[7]

In 1772, the year after Quaque's reply to Bass, the retired Rev. Thompson, provoked by the Mansfield decision (he refers sarcastically to "learned lawyers and casuists" who argued that slavery is "contrary to the law of nature"), published *The African Trade for Negro Slaves Shown to be Consistent with the Principles of Humanity and the Laws of Revealed Religion*.[8] The pamphlet opened by declaring that alongside the "the happy free constitution of this kingdom," Great Britain has "an excellent religion," so that the slave trade, necessarily arising to supply "our West India and American colonies with the fittest hands for plantations," is "generally considered with feelings of tenderness, and but seldom spoken of without great humanity." The implicit debate had been very much sharpened by the Mansfield case decided that year, its terms fraught with the language of humanity, of sensibility.[9] (Mansfield freed Virginian James Somerset, arguing that the laws of England did not recognize slavery.) Similarly, Thompson acknowledged something "very affecting and disagreeable in the notion of human creatures, even the lowest of such, being treated like mere beasts or cattle." This was a common comparison—Quaque said the same—referring to bringing people to market to be sold, whipped, and forced by violence to work, their offspring enduring the same fate forever.[10]

Thompson contrasts such British humanity with "the negroes[']" own imperviousness to the trade. "For the negroes so to misuse each other,—this passes in detail without any special remark upon it"—a tad exaggerated he admits—"but considering them as pagans and of as dark a mind as complexion, one does not much admire of monstrous things as are reported of them. But that Christians maintain a commerce with those people" (he means African enslavers, pagans with dark minds and skins) "for the numberless poor wretches, which they enslave, and drive down from the country." The last phrase stands for the vast geographical networks within which Africans were gathered. (Governor Hippisley wrote that slaves were "natives of the utmost extremities of Africa." Slaves "purchased at *Angola* are brought from the interior parts of *Ethiopia*, and the borders of the *Indian Ocean*.") Africans were driven to "the factories and lending places on the coast, to be sold like bullocks at a fair;—this is a fact that seems hardly capable of a defense, notwithstanding that our plantations cannot be cultivated without them." We do not know where the small child, shipped to Boston, sold there, and named Phillis, came from.[11]

But Thompson defends the slave trade further by declaring that the cost of purchasing enslaved "negroes" and then freeing them "would exhaust the Treasury," so should not be attempted, even though it would express "the spirit of our benevolent religion." With similar, apparent ambivalence, he says the slave trade is as "vindicable as any species of trade," open and public, and "encouraged and promoted by acts of parliament" (as the other critics of the 1772 Mansfield decision pointed out), even though "being contrary to religion, it must be deemed a national sin," with "a consequence that would always be dreaded." This echoed Anthony Benezet's antislavery pamphlet, *A Caution and Warning to Great Britain and Her Colonies in a Short Representation of the Calamitous State of Enslaved Negroes in the British Dominions. Collected from various authors, and submitted to the serious consideration of all, more especially of those in Power.* Such defensive assertion and qualifications all manifested growing opposition to the slave trade in moral terms, intertwining Christianity and sensibility.[12]

Thompson pressed on, citing biblical justification from the Old and New Testaments, and arguing that slavery originated in Europe "as a principle of humanity," an alternative to putting prisoners to death. Furthermore, "hard usage" in transatlantic slavery arises from "the injustice and cruelty of masters" and is not intrinsic to slavery. He returns to his particular knowledge of African enslavement, arguing that it was not the result of mere force or subterfuge, "for every negro nation has its form of government," upholding custom and policy. People are enslaved partly "by the fortune of war, and partly from the national custom of equal authority with laws: as the selling of criminals and insolvent debtors." Thompson adds that the "seizing and carrying off of negroes from the coast, which is called *panyarring* is what the masters of ships in the African trade are sometimes obliged to, done by reprisal for theft or damage committed by the natives." It was "practice . . . established by the natives themselves," the rationale given by William Ansah's captor to his father.[13]

Thompson applies to traders in slaves what we can see as the Protestant rationale for any calling, and challenged explicitly in the case of the slave trade a hundred years earlier by the Rev. Richard Baxter, an authority for Benezet. "Anything being made a subject of trade, which to sell is not contrary to godliness, to moral virtue, to humanity, to legal right and justice, nor to the laws in being, is lawful trade." He declares that the slave trade is not contrary to these standards, all construed from the point of view of the traders, rather than the traded, whom Thompson relegated to commodities: "The property in such individuals is transferable like all other property," and therefore is "no violation of humanity."[14]

Thompson wrote "several Letters" to him, Quaque reported to the SPG in 1771. Perhaps he continued to do so for a while. But Quaque had lost trace of him when, in 1778, he asked the SPG Secretary "whether the Reverend Thomas Thompson, my predecessor is still in Being or Translated into the Bliss above, there to receive the Recompense of his Labor." The following year he said he heard of Thompson's death "some years ago." Quaque was coming to differ sharply from Thompson in his view of slavery.[15]

Before he received a reply from the Rev. Bass in Massachusetts, Quaque reported a letter from the Rev. Samuel Fayerweather of Rhode Island, another SPG missionary "and a slave owner," who quizzed Quaque on the success of his mission, as well as that of Thompson. He had written, he said, because of Johnson's favorable opinion of Quaque.[16]

The African Quaque and the American Hopkins

On May 12, 1773, Quaque wrote to the Rev. Richard Hind, the new Secretary of the SPG, telling him that two months earlier he had received a letter from the Rev. Samuel Hopkins, also of Rhode Island, who "earnestly Petitions to be informed of the Manner and Customs of the People of Africa, the way of Life, and method of the Slave Trade, and whether the Introduction of two Natives belonging to Annamaboe could be happily effected without losing their lives, either from their Tribe or Town's People or from the more Unchristian the more Savage Traders." Hopkins apprehended there could be deadly threats to his protégés, from both African and European slavetraders. Quaque's report of Hopkin's letter continued, "And if these two Black Persons, whom he vouches to be men of more than common Understanding in Things of Religion, can be introduced, what Assistance could I give to such a Design? And what would be necessary to support them in such a Situation? Because they are willing to come and live among their Brethren to attempt to convert them to Christianity." Quaque told Hind that this "Mr. Hopkins, I believe, *followeth not after US*," (referring to the Book of Matthew), meaning he was not an Anglican, as other American correspondents had been, "but he is the Pastor of the First Congregational Church in Newport."[17]

Hopkins (1721–1803), called "the most controversial and the most influential theologian of the American Revolutionary period," "almost single handedly set in motion the . . . abolition of slavery in New England," meaning whites' abolitionism. He was at the same time the "father" of "colonization," the efforts to plant a colony of manumitted American black people in Africa. The proposal he sent to Quaque, inherited from the British SPG, was the seed of this effort, which lasted until the American Civil War, and much longer if one includes Martin Delaney and Alabama Senator John Tyler Morgan as Hopkin's heirs.[18]

Hopkins, a remarkably sober student at Yale, "lived and studied with [Jonathan] Edwards after his graduation," absorbing the Calvinism that emphasized entire obedience to God's will. Notably he elaborated that obedience to "universal benevolence," the love of all his fellow creatures, overlapped with the terms of the culture of sensibility, which Hopkins believed should be translated into social action. Hopkins had been a minister in Great Barrington, Massachusetts, for a quarter of a century but in January 1769, his congregation dismissed him, refusing "to abide theological controversy." Invited to preach at the First Congregational Church in Newport, Rhode Island, later that summer, he was appointed its pastor on April 11, 1770.[19]

In Newport, Hopkins, under Sarah Osborne's influence, joined her efforts to evangelize African and native-born black people.[20] In 1773, together with Ezra Stiles, pastor of the Second Congregational Church in Newport, Hopkins published "To the Public. There has been a design formed . . . to send the Gospel to Guinea," by way of "two Negroe men," members of Hopkin's church. Their circular gave the names of these proposed African missionaries, Bristol Yamma and John Quamine, who they said were "hopefully converted some years ago." Their account of Quamine was a familiar one, recalling those stories, true and false, of "Guinea's Captive Kings."

The latter is son of a rich man at Annamaboe, and was sent by his father to this place for an education among the English and then to return home: Which person to whom he was committed engaged to perform for a good reward. Instead of being faithful to his trust, he sold him a slave for life. But God in his providence has put it in the power of both of them to obtain his freedom.

That freedom was from physical slavery, but also the freedom to serve God that Quaque so relished.[21]

In a longer, private version of this story, Hopkins wrote Quaque (in Quaque's paraphrase), "This man, about Nineteen Years ago [i.e. about 1753] was taken off the Coast with one Captain Linsey of Newport, Rhode Island, not as a Captive, but free, to be educated in the Principles of Christianity, and when fit to return him back to his Father. [B]ut instead of which the unchristian Captain took no manner of care of Him but sold him as a Slave for Life. However, in process of Time the Captain died, and Since his Death it has pleased the Overruling Providence that this Man should purchase that Liberty wherewith the Son of God. Christ Jesus our Saviour has made Us all free." Ex-slave captain John Newton "redeemed" a free boy who had been taken illegally to Rhode Island and returned him home.[22]

The Hopkins-Stiles circular described Bristol Yamma and John Quamine as "apparently devoted to the service of Christ." The qualifying adverb strengthened the suggestion in the phrase "hopefully converted"—the reverends had some doubt about the completeness of their Africans' conversion. But they assured the public that their candidates for this American mission to Guinea "have good natural abilities; are apt, steady, and judicious, and speak their native language; the language of a numerous potent nation in Guinea to which they both belong." In Quamine's case that would be the language spoken in "Anamabue." Later they would learn that Yamma was Asante, speaking a variant of Fante. Language was evidently an issue of basic importance for would-be missionaries, an insuperable impediment to Quaque, let alone Thompson, one recognized by Wheatley. The circular continued, "They are not only willing but *very desirous* to quit all worldly prospects and risqué their lives, in attempting to open a door for the propagation of Christianity among their poor, ignorant, perishing, heathen brethren."[23]

The purpose for which Hopkins and Stiles solicited funds, in addition to paying the rest of Yamma's purchase price, was to send the Africans to Princeton, "to be taught to read and write better than they now can; and he instructed more fully in divinity, &c." They were not yet ready to attempt to convert the heathen. It was only "if, upon trial, they appear to make good proficiency; and shall be thought by competent judges, to be fit for such a mission, it is not doubted that money may be procured, to execute" this design. "God in his providence" opened the way to this, a unique opportunity, they wrote, for an American contribution of "patronage and assistance" to show themselves "pious and benevolent."[24]

Hopkins and Stiles also made the case that to contribute to the promotion of this mission was an expression of opposition to "the iniquity of the *slave trade*." This was in contrast to the exceptional cases of enslaved African princes, and in keeping with the argument being made by Benezet, and the following year, by John Wesley. (Hopkins was in touch with Granville Sharp, the British antislavery campaigner who had been inspired by Benezet.) They appealed to those who "are sensible of the great inhumanity and cruelty of enslaving so many thousands of our fellow men every year." The contributors would "bear testimony against it in all proper ways and do their utmost to put a stop to it . . . by contributing . . . to the mission proposed." The authors suggested that by thus contributing "we are able to make the best [compensation] to the poor Africans, for the injuries they are receiving by this unrighteous practice and all its attendants." The pamphlet's conclusion summarizes that compensation by declaring the mission will bring about the wish of the Lord's Prayer, "*Thy kingdom come*" by sending "the glorious gospel of the blessed God to the nations who now worship false gods, and dwell in the habitation of cruelty, and the land of the shadow of death." In a later pamphlet Hopkins spelled out more fully the compensatory relationship between the slave trade and Christianizing Africa.[25]

Quaque's report to the SPG of this Hopkins proposal had continued, "And if these two Black Person, whom [Hopkins] vouches to be men of more than common Understanding in Things of Religion, can be introduced, what is the best way of doing it?" Hopkins had asked Quaque what assistance he could give and how much would it cost, because "these two Black Persons . . . are willing to come and live among their Brethren, to attempt to convert them to Christianity."[26]

Five days later, Quaque replied to Hopkins, referring to the fact that Hopkins had been "excited to open a path for frequent Correspondence" because he had seen "a Scrawl of mine" in that letter to Fayerweather." He was hungry for such a correspondence. He said he would attempt, "as far as my weak judgement in Matters that are quite foreign to me will permit, of affording you a secret Satisfaction." That inner feeling was one of the religious motives that Quaque learned to articulate during his education in England and his preparation for the ministry, in the Anglicanism modified by Latitudinarianism and cognate with the moral sense. The same can be said of the opening of his next sentence: "And I rejoice with Joy unspeakable" (1 Peter 1:8), a quotation he used elsewhere, the figure of incapacity becoming a mark of sensibility, related to the "self-approving Joy" with which Latitudinarians encouraged themselves and their congregations to feel in performing unselfish actions. In this case, Quaque's "Joy unspeakable" was stimulated by his finding "there are still Numbers of Africans, the supposed race of Ham, able to embrace Christianity, were they in a Country that yields that Light and Knowledge." He implied that this was not the case among the Africans he was attempting to convert.[27]

Quaque took the opportunity though, in answer to a presumably sympathetic American minister, to challenge the "mark" of Cain, the black skin conferred on him and other black people according to an interpretation of Genesis, in shaming retaliation for Ham's looking on his father Noah's nakedness as Noah lay in a drunken stupor. The marking was accompanied by the curse that Ham and his descendants should be "the servant of servants," in Quaque's phrase, "entailed upon him and his numerous offspring forever." Quaque does not mention blackness explicitly, as he asserted that the mark "is likely to be effaced because it appears there are no Disparagement[s] to their increase or growth in Grace, since all by Exception are invited, and the Gates of Religion opened to the Reception of the Gentiles as well as the Christians." This was an African's direct refutation of the assertion that people are permanently subordinated and inferior because of color. Wheatley made the same point in regard to "*Christians*, Negros, black as Cain." Quaque goes on: many "piercing scenes might be ruminated upon this subject." Perhaps he recalled the discrimination he had faced as a child and young man in London, as well as what he had told Johnson and reported to the SPG about white men's treatment of him at Cape Coast Castle. But he restrains himself, "for fear I should loose my self in the attempt and come of in utter Disgrace. And not only that but to avoid the horrid and uncharitable Opinions of Individuals about Us unhappy Africans."[28]

Quaque cannot restrain himself entirely. "However, to be candid, that Justice may take it's rights, I cannot help confessing the Certainty of the wretched condition in which they [Africans] are deeply involved, which speaks but very little for them. A Misery! That ought to be much [more] pitied, then be held in Scorn and Contempt." The immediate reason was their "savagery," implicitly their apparent impermeability to Christianity, with direct bearing on what Hopkin's prospective missionaries would face. "As to those Men of more than common Understanding in Things of Religion"—Hopkin's description of Yamma and Quamine—"believe me, could not spring from a Race more *Savage, Villainous, Revengeful, Malicious,* and none more *Blood-thirsty* then those of Annamaboe, the adjacent Places and the interior Parts of that Country, who make it their daily Practice of distressing their Brethren by frequent Palavors, id. est. Disputes, Causes, or Trials incessantly held by Men of fashion and worth, merely or politically to ruin others who are in a fare way of advancing forward in Life." This was an earlier statement of that bitter characterization of "Blacks" quoted above, making it clear that Quaque saw Christianization as a means whereby "the inferior People should rise in equality with themselves," presumably believing that is what it had done for him.[29]

Quaque's passionate outburst conveyed one of the obstacles he had faced in his missionary efforts. Evidently he felt it would give ammunition to racists, although it bore directly on Hopkins's protégés' prospects, if they tried to do what Quaque had. "I give this as not only my own Opinion, but the Judgement of many that were they to put their feet again on Africa's shore without the Support of the African Committee and my Great Benefactors, the Venerable Society they bitterly would rue the Day on which they with Reluctance parted with their happy Place of abode." That mission would fail without the support of the two metropolitan British organizations that sponsored him. This was a challenge to an effort by America, then on the verge of rebellion against Britain.

Quaque adds a prophecy: "Besides, were they to accomplish their End, and be Stationed anywhere on the Coast, unless the place of their Nativity, . . . in very little Time they would soon be enticed into all manner of Debaucheries the Enducement of which would lead them to commit such Actions as will entangle them in such Difficulties that they will not easily Eradicate." One method that had helped Quaque avoid illicit, sexual debaucheries was to be married to a Christian woman before he returned to Africa as a missionary.

Yet Quaque backs off in his next sentence, denying that he means "to frighten, hinder or discourage them from pursuing the laudable Plan they have undertaken, nor even"—and he turns to their reverend white sponsors—"the godlike Intensions of those Worthy Gentlemen be slackened, or put them out of Conceit of executing [their] Design." But Quaque then repeats that the difficulties Quamine and Yamma must face are daunting, specifying the financial costs. "The repeated welcomes of many, for Instance, would make them distracted, and the Annual Income which might be gathered for their Support, in less then three Weeks be spent . . . without the least Prospect of any Success."

Quaque criticizes Hopkins for not having had "the presence of Mind . . . to have mentioned their [the two African men's] Original Names, and of what Family." He expected Hopkins's next letter to tell him. While he intimated Hopkins's scheme was likely to fail, Quaque wanted him to keep writing, and to try it, a hope for a frustrated and isolated missionary "to the Negroes."

Quaque then answers Hopkins's inquiry about the slave trade, making Africans decisively the creators and perpetuators of it, just as Thompson had in that 1772 pamphlet. Quaque declares that Europeans had only entered the slave trade because they witnessed "the Natives . . . continually depopulate themselves by frequent Wars." According to Quaque's explanation of the origins of the slave trade, some warring Africans once brought "the head of a Captive Slave to an European Chief who in return gave them . . . a small Present." So the natives wanted to keep bringing him heads, but he refused and "desired that they for the future might not be killed, but brought him a live . . . in Barter." Therefore, Europeans entered the slave trade out of humanity. The "Natives," Quaque continues, "have now gone to such a pitch that they not only dispose of their Brethren as captive slaves taken in war, but make the Practice of stealing and kidnapping their Neighbors, and secretly making away, with them, especially in case of Adultery, which the Fantees, id.est the Quarter from which they were." The Fantees then, "encourage and force their Wenches to that vile and brutal action by way of gain." In short, the Fantees invented "consorting," too, a preoccupation from which Quaque cannot stay away when laying out the immoral horrors of Africans.[30]

Hopkins received his reply from Quaque in September, and dated his own 10th December 1773. He does not doubt Quaque's judgement in laying out "the difficulties and discouragements" that his proposed missionaries "among ye blacks" would face and cannot see that the African Committee or the SPG would be able to remove them. Hopkins tells Quaque that since his first letter, he had sent him "A particular account of . . . John Quamine, that you might inquire after his relatives, and inform me . . . ye result of your inquiry. To this I have not received . . . any answer yet." He does add that the name of the other "is Yamma (now called Bristol Yamma). He is a Shantee [Asante]. Was born far up in ye country . . . taken captive when he was quite young by some neighboring nation, and passed thro' several hands & was sold several times before he got ye sea at Annamaboe. He cannot give any particular account of his parents and ye family from which he sprang." We can assume he was traumatized. If Quamine was sent on the mission to Anomabu in part because that was where his family was, Yamma had no such connection. Along with this letter to Quaque, Hopkins sent him a copy of the 1773 circular he had written with Stiles, telling him that it had "met with as much encouragement as could be expected."[31]

In 1776, Hopkins and Stiles published an updated version of their 1773 circular. The American Revolution was now well under way. They reported that the SPG in Scotland had made a donation, as had a "gentleman in London," evidently John Thornton, with whom they must have been in touch about Phillis Wheatley. The directors of the Scots SPG rejoiced "at the fair prospect now extended to those nations who dwell at present, in the habitation of cruelty, and in the land of the shadow of death." They gave the plan their "warmest approbation."[32]

Then Hopkins and Stiles quoted an extract of a letter "from an African, *Phillis Wheatley*, dated February 9, 1774." The previous year, Wheatley had published *Poems on Various Subjects, Religious and Moral*, under the patronage of the Countess of Huntingdon. The countess was a founder of Methodism, which was headquartered in Britain, and also had a significant following in America, including Wheatley's owners.[33]

Thornton, a merchant, was probably her wealthiest follower. In the extract Hopkins sent Quaque, Wheatley had written, "I have received a paper, by which I understand there are two Negro men, who are desirous of returning to their native country, to preach the gospel. What I can do in influencing my Christian friends and acquaintances to promote this laudable design shall not be wanting." The extract continued, Wheatley's prose resembling Quaque's in its sentimental religiosity, a combination typical of both Wheatley's evangelicalism and the Anglicanism to which Quaque subscribed. Clearly Hopkins and Stiles believed it would affect their audiences positively: "My heart expanded with sympathetic joy to see at distant time the thick cloud of ignorance dispersing from the face of my benighted country."[34]

Wheatley had been sold to an American slaving captain in 1761 when she was between seven and eight years old, probably at Fort Lewis in Senegal, a slaving entrepot which the British had recently captured from the French, and distant from Cape Coast Castle.[35] So she was between twenty and twenty-one when she had written this reply to Hopkins. The circular's extract continued, "Europe and America have long been fed with the heavenly provision, and I fear they loath it, while Africa is perishing with a Spiritual Famine." Wheatley's praise of her god for nourishing Christians with his words—the Bible—and not Africans, recalls one of Quaque's interlocutor's making the same point. But she implies that the Africans in their innocence of God's words are morally superior to those Americans and Europeans who have passionately repudiated it. She prays for Africans: "O but they could partake of the crumbs, the precious crumbs, which fall from the table of these distinguished children of the kingdom!" This refers to the "two negro men" whom Hopkins proposed to send to Africa. In her next sentence, Wheatley asserts that the imagined African recipients of Christian crumbs "are unprejudiced against the truth, therefore it is hoped they would receive it with their whole heart." Hopkins chose not to publish this. It ran counter to what Quaque had told him, but it was consistent with her earlier suggestion of Africans' hunger for Christianity. Hopkins ended his extract with Wheatley's next sentence. "I hope that which the divine royal Psalmist [David, with whom Wheatley identified in her poetry] says by inspiration is now on the point of being accomplished, viz 'Ethiopia shall stretch forth her hands unto God' [Psalm 68:31]."[36]

Hopkins also sent Quaque "the *proposals* &c., supposing it will give you pleasure to see what a remarkable African appears in N. England." Wheatley's "Proposals" for a book of poems were published as an advertisement in the *Boston Censor* in February 1772, describing "a Negro girl . . . an uncultivated Barbarian from Africa." Hopkins continued, "She has lately been to Europe," where she stayed with Thornton, "and was much taken notice of there. She will I hope be a means of promoting ye best interest of Africans." She had published *Poems on Various Subjects,* dedicated to the Countess of Huntingdon. Hopkins hoped she would accompany Quamine and Yamma on their mission, not that he mentioned this to Quaque.[37]

In this 1776 version of the circular, Hopkins and Stiles could report that "the two men . . . have spent one winter under the care of Dr. Witherspon" at Princeton, and were now qualified for the mission to Anomabu. Hopkins and Stiles were also able to publish endorsements of Quamine's authenticity. They told their American audience they had written "to Philip Quaque, a black, and native of Guinea, who is missionary from the society in London for propagating the gospel in foreign parts, and resided at Cape Coast Castle." In this letter to him, they had "related the manner of [John Quamine's] being brought from Guinea; and sending his description of his father's family, and informing that he was now free, and has thoughts of returning to his native country, &c." The writers ignored Quaque's devastating criticism of the inhabitants of Anomabu, instead quoting a second extremely positive response of Quaque's to Hopkin's information about Quamine's family. "It is with inexpressible pleasure and satisfaction I acquaint you that my enquiries after the friends and relations of that gentleman have not been fruitless, but have met with the desired success." Hopkins could infer this was on one of Quaque's visits to Anomabu; presumably he depended on an interpreter. "His minute account he entertains you with, of his family and kindred is just." This must refer to another letter we do not have. "I have found the father's name to be the same as you mention, who has been dead many years. His mother's name is as you wrote it, who is still alive, and whom I had the pleasure of seeing." He described her response. The "bowels of maternal affection, in truth do I declare it, seem ready to burst; and break forth in tears of joy, like Jacob when he heard his son Joseph was still alive. The joy it kindled . . . throws her into extacies. . . . And in raptures she breaks forth and says, 'It is enough My son is yet alive I hope by God's blessing to see him before I die.'" The reader must assume either she spoke this kind of English or that Quaque rendered it from what his translator told him. Quaque sent this to Hopkins, knowing Hopkins had an antislavery audience in mind in appealing for funds, although it is very similar to the representation of other sentimental scenes, the redeemed slave's purported reunification with his family, for example.[38]

Quaque's account includes his encounter with "a great personage of Quamine's family, whose name is Oforee, who now enjoys his [Quamine's] father's estate, desires with great importunity, that I would earnestly petition you that he may be returned to them as soon as may be," promising to make Quamine "comfortable and happy among his own kindred." They thanked Hopkins, begging Quaque to tell him "that as it not in their power to requite you for all your trouble, they therefore hope that the good God of Heaven will recompense you hereafter for your labor of love bestowed on him." While in Akan religion, there was "a Supreme Being and a belief" in lesser deities inhabiting . . . sea, rocks and rivers," Quaque presents them as "the children of Jehovah."[39]

In a second, undated letter to Hopkins, also quoted in the 1776 circular, Quaque again takes up the subject of Quamine's family's anticipation of his return to them. Quamine's "mother is still looking with impatience for the return of her son, once dead and lost." She and that "cousin," presumably Oforee, "joined earnestly in entreating you would, in your Christian love and charity to them, send the lad again, that he may receive their cordial embraces, looking upon themselves sufficient to support him." This bore on one of the circular's purposes in trying to raise money for the mission. It seems clear, when one thinks of the audiences Quaque had in mind—Hopkins first, then his circular's public, together with Quaque's desperate loneliness and sense of abandonment—why he couched his account in the terms he did. Willy nilly, his sentimental extracts fed into antislavery's appeal to Anglophone, domestic ideology, its emphasis on the slave trade's tearing apart of families, and from a Christian, African source.[40]

Quaque thanks Hopkins for these "charitable proposals," referring to Wheatley's poetry, repeating he is "joyful to hear there are Africans with you who partake of the blessings of the Gospel, and in time may be the means of promoting the greatest and best interest of Africans here. I wish to God for its speedy accomplishment, when the nation, who are now called the children of Jehovah, shall become the prophets of the LORD, and the children, of the living God." Hopkins and Stiles omitted Quaque's letter's accounts of the formidable difficulties their missionaries must face.[41]

Instead, their 1776 update added the news that a "native of Annamaboe has lately arrived at Newport, who is a free man, and appears to be a sensible, inquisitive person, and is recommended by the captain he came with as a man of integrity and good behavior." Perhaps he was a sailor; Africans were notably part of ships' complements. "He is a relation of John Quamine's, well acquainted with his family, and confirms the above account." This "Annamaboe" relative, purportedly cognizant of the prospects advanced by the authors of this document, "expresses a desire to learn to read, &c., and be instructed on the Christian religion; sensible that he and his countrymen are ignorant of the way in which men may find favor with God; and that they stand in need of revelation from him, in order to know what he requires of them. He says he has heard we have such a revelation among us, and he desires to know what it contains." Here was an African ripe for conversion. His account of the similar potential in the place where Hopkins proposes to send Quamine and Yamma contradicted Quaque's. "He informs, that he knows of a number of youths at Annamaboe, who have a great desire to learn to read and write &'s and would come into these parts for that end, were they not afraid of being cheated and sold." It could be deduced that the best place to Christianize Africans was in Africa, the conviction of which motivated Hopkins's future career.[42]

Just by chance this African supplied an invaluable, first-hand endorsement of the proposal at hand. "He appears pleased with the proposal to send blacks to teach his people and thinks they will be kindly received, and attended to." And there was yet another African voice the authors could paraphrase, "another black, named *Salmas Nuba*, a member of the second congregational church, in Newport [this was Stiles's], who is promising as a person of good genius, and giving evidence of real piety. He is about twenty years old, and has lately had his freedom given to him." The circular suggests he would be a good investment. "He is greatly desirous and engaged, in some way, to promote the spread of the gospel among the Africans. We think there is good encouragement to be at the expense of fitting him for a missionary, or a school master among them."[43]

The Monstrous Inconsistency

Hopkins and Stiles assumed their vision of Christianizing Africa was God's, and though this particular mission was "small in its beginning, [it] may hopefully issue in something very great, and open the way to the happiness and salvation of many nations who are now in the most deplorable state, ready to perish in the darkness of heathenism." These terms were identical to Quaque's, but significantly, Hopkins and Stiles link them to the outbreak of the American Revolution: "The present state of our publick affairs," in 1776, "is so far from being a reason for neglecting this proposal, that it seems rather to afford strong motives to encourage it. For which we are struggling for our civil and religious liberties, it will be peculiarly becoming and laudable to exert ourselves to procure the same blessings for others, so far as it is in our power." James A. Levernier notes that "throughout the sermons and tracts of the preachers whom Wheatley knew, slavery becomes the major metaphor through which the conflict between England and the colonies is dramatized." Hopkins and Stiles conclude by referring to the opening of the war for independence, which brought that inconsistency to a head. "And when God is so remarkably interposing and ordering . . . events in our favor, in this time of general distress, is there not a special call to pay this tribute to him, according as he has prospered us. . . . to obtain the countenance of his love and protection?" If not, they would incur God's punishment.[44]

That same year, Hopkins called for the emancipation of American slaves in his *A Dialogue Concerning the Slavery of the Africans, Showing it to be the Duty and Interest of the American States to Emancipate All their African Slaves*,[45] expressing his outrage at the "inconsistence" of the liberty white Americans claimed while they kept other human beings in slavery. Enslaved Africans, he tells the members of the Continental Congress, to whom his pamphlet was addressed, "see the *slavery* the *Americans* dread as worse than death, as lighter than a feather, compared to their heavy doom." Mansfield's 1772 decision, freeing a Virginian's slave in Britain, had injected a dramatic moral issue into the growing dispute between pro-revolutionary and pro-monarchist writers on both sides of the Atlantic. In 1774, wishing to neutralize Britain's moral superiority, Congress had passed a resolution prohibiting slave imports and American participation in the slave trade. Hopkins tells the members (to whom Alexander Hamilton distributed his pamphlet), "We have the satisfaction of best assurance that you have done this not merely from political reasons; but from a conviction of the unrighteousness and cruelty of that trade, and a regard to justice and benevolence, deeply sensible of the inconsistence of promoting the slavery of the Africans, at the same time we are asserting our own civil liberty, at the risqué of our fortunes and lives." So Hopkins deliberately links his call for emancipation of "Africans" to the Declaration of Independence.[46]

Being "sensible"—conscious with feeling—is coupled with "a hope and confidence that the cries and tears of these oppressed will be regarded by you." He asserts the process that the members of the Continental Congress will irresistibly experience when they "attentively considered the slave trade in its real nature." It "will lead us to think of it with a detestation and horror, ... this scene of inhumanity, oppression and cruelty, exceeding everything of its kind . . . ever perpetrated by the sons of man," including, he makes explicit, the claim Britain is enslaving white Americans. The "scene of inhumanity . . . is suited to excite and awaken us to a proper indignation against the authors of this violence and outrage done to their fellow men, and to feelings of humanity and pity to their brethren." Antislavery writers, applying their Christian assumption of common ancestry in Adam, and their customary mode of address, one assumes, too, by Enlightenment philosophers in asserting the kinship of all humanity, had insisted Africans were their brothers. The Declaration of Independence had, with ostentatious reluctance, announced the necessity of "separation" from "our British brethren." Hopkins rhetorically assumes his audience's acceptance of such kinship with their enslaved Africans and African Americans.[47]

Hopkins describes in some detail the horror of the slave trade, whereby many "millions have been torn from their native country, their relations, and friends," enslaved forever, "worse than death," marketed, "burned with a hot iron . . . crowded together in a close hold" on board a ship, "put in irons, except some of the women perhaps, and the small children"—

little Phillis or Bristol Yamma may have come to his mind—and if they survive, thousands are, in effect, "murdered" *en route*, the survivors then again "separated . . . without any regard to their friendships or relations, of husbands and wives, parents and children, brothers and sisters . . . being torn from each other." We see all this, writes Hopkins, having placed it in the context of white Americans' opposition to their own enslavement, "and yet we have not the least pity." His pronoun implies whites generally are complicitous in not sympathizing with enslaved blacks. "They have a thousand times more discernment and sensibility . . . than their masters, or most others." He repeats this contrast: "We behold vast numbers of blacks among us, torn from their native country, and all their relatives . . . and yet have not the least feelings for them, or their desire for freedom!" By contrast, the "poor Negroes have sense enough to see and feel it, but have no friend to speak a word for them."[48]

And Hopkins returns to this contrast: many masters fondly believe they are good to their slaves, who they believe prefer slavery to freedom. "They have not so much as put themselves in the place of their slaves, so as properly and with one sensibility to consult what would be their own feelings on such a supposition." This invokes the operation of sensibility, of the moral sense, formulated at length by Adam Smith at the opening of *The Theory of Moral Sentiments*, that we conceive "what we ourselves should feel in a like situation," that is, of "our brother upon the rack." Hopkins asks, "Why are we not so much affected with the many thousands of blacks among ourselves whose miserable state is before our eyes?" One of his two epigraphs from the Bible on the title page is "And as ye would that men should do to you, ye do also to them like wise, Luke VI, 31" which must be seen to refer to the monstrous inconsistency.[49]

Affect should lead to action: "And why should we not be as . . . engaged to relieve them? The reason is obvious. 'Tis because they are Negroes, and fit for nothing but slaves; and we have been used to look on them in a mean contemptible light; and our education, has filled us with strong prejudices against them, and led us to consider them not as our brethren, or in any degree on a level with us; but as quite another species of animals, made only to serve us and our children."[50]

Hopkins's assertion of brotherhood is thus contradicted. Antislavery campaigners on both sides of the Atlantic faced the challenge of increasing popular support to decisively influence legislators, by appealing to white feelings of sympathy, even identification, across the apparent divide of color. Hopkins says that required a change in white Americans' psychology: "If we could only divest ourselves of these strong prejudices which have insensibly fixed themselves in our minds, and consider them as, by nature, and by right on a level with one brethren and children, and those our neighbors," act as Christ's injunction to keep the commandments (referring to Leviticus 19:18): "Thou shalt love thy neighbors as thy self" (Matthew 19:19). Like Benezet, Hopkins warns that Britain "admonishes us to reform . . . and [we are] amazingly guilty if we refuse." Historian Davis writes of Hopkins and his fellow "heirs of the Great Awakening," that "however free and virtuous individuals might be the sins of the nation would be repaid in kind." His use of the word "guilt" carries psychological as well as existential, religious meaning: "And just as the punishment, of taxes and commercial restraints pointed to the sins of greed and luxury, so the threat of political bondage pointed to the source of the colonists' deepest guilt." Hopkins had sold his female slave before he came to Newport. Here he concludes that "if we obstinately refuse to refer what we have implicitly declared to be wrong" and abolish slavery, God will withdraw his kind protection." Implicitly, Britain will win.[51]

In contrast to Quaque and Thompson, Hopkins writes that it was Europeans who "have taken advantage of African ignorance and barbarity to persuade them to enter into the inhuman practice of selling one another . . . for the commodities of which they have no real need . . . particularly spirituous liquors, which are carried to them in great quantities by the *Americans*." African inhabitants of towns near the sea enslave one another "and sell them to us for rum, by which they intoxicate them selves, and become more brutish and savage . . . so there are but few instances of sobriety, honesty, or even humanity." But those who live furthest from these slaving sea ports are "much more civil and humane." This is promising. Hopkins shows how slavery projects this sin of alcohol into "my part of the world": Africans enslaved in return for alcohol were transported to the West Indies, where they produced incredible quantities of molasses to ruin mainland America. Stanley K. Schultz points out, "There were more than thirty rum distilleries in Rhode Island."[52]

The *Dialogue* incorporates the missionary vision Hopkins and Stiles outlined in their circular. If slave traders create a horrid scene of barbarity in Africa, most "of the Africans are in a state of heathenism; and sunk down into that ignorance and barbarity, into which mankind naturally fall, when destitute of divine revelation." The 1776 version of their circular reported that a "native of Annamaboe" stood in "need of a revelation" from God, which he had heard "we have among us." Hopkins's later pamphlet is constructed as a series of "dialogues" between himself and an imaginary proponent of slavery and opponent of emancipation who asserts that in spite of the "evils" of the slave trade, "we bring the slaves from a heathen land, to places of gospel light, and to put them under special advantages to be saved." Hopkins retorts that the masters of slaves in the West Indies "guard against their having any instruction . . . if any one would attempt any such thing, it would be at the risk of his life." Those "who call themselves Christians . . . prejudice Africans . . . against the Christian religion." In the southern mainland colonies, and even in New England, "it is a very great wonder and owing to an extraordinary divine interposition . . . that any of them should think favorably of Christianity and cordially embrace it." He had described Wheatley to Quaque as "a remarkable African [who] appears in New England." But, his *Dialogues* had continued, "most have imbibed the deepest prejudices against it."[53]

Even if Africans were enslaved with their successful Christianization as the result, it "would not justify the slave trade or continuing them in a state of slavery: For to take this method to Christianize them would be direct and gross violation of the laws of Christ." In fact, Christ wished Christianization to be borne in the opposite direction. Christ "commands us to go and preach the gospel to all nations; to carry the gospel to them, and not . . . with violence bring them from their native country." Had Europeans and Americans been as "engaged" in Christianizing Africans as enslaving them in Africa, "that extensive country, containing a vast multitude of inhabitants, would have been full of gospel light; and the many nations there, civilized and made happy; . . . and the happy instruments . . . rewarded ten thousand fold for all their labour and expence."[54]

Enslaved Africans and their descendants in America "never forfeited their liberty" and have "as much a right to it as ever they had" when free in Africa. His interlocutor responds that were they to be freed, "they would be in a much worse state than that in which they now are." Many do not know "how to contrive for themselves" and would have to be maintained by their old masters. Others "would make themselves wretched, and become a great trouble to their neighbors, and an injury to the public, by their unrestrained vices." Hopkins concedes something to this but also says whites are given to vices, too, and cannot maintain themselves: should *they* be enslaved? And anyway the character his opponent gives blacks is the effect of slavery. It sinks and contracts the minds of men, "down in darkness and despair," without "encouragements to activity," and "naturally tends to lead the enslaved to . . . stupid carelessness, and to vices of all kinds." The wonder is "there are so many instances of virtue, prudence, knowledge and industry among them." We have reduced them to this miserable state and now "make this an argument" for perpetuating their enslavement.[55]

A Colony in Africa?

Once freed, however, according to Hopkins's forecast, black people would be unable to take care of themselves, needing legislation to protect them but also "restrain them from vicious courses." Such laws would reassure the white public "against any imagined evil consequences of a general manumissions of our slaves." Revolutionary leaders capitalized on widespread fears of what African Americans would do to whites, out of justifiable revenge.[56]

All this sets up Hopkins's argument for colonization—masters would be less reluctant to free their slaves. "And if no public provision be made for them—they may be transported to *Africa*, where they might probably live better than in any other country." He suggests, too, that freed slaves could be "removed" by whites, "to those places in this land, where they might have profitable places, and are wanted," for example, where white men have left their farms to join the revolutionary armies.[57]

Hopkins's attack on slavery; his representative opponent's defense of it, including his expression of fear of freed black people; then Hopkins's accompanying proposal to transport them in light of those "evil consequences" on white minds, were contexts for some black men's proposal to transport themselves to somewhere on the African coast.

Following several "liberty suits" black women as well as men had filed from 1766, black men took another approach, petitioning the Massachusetts government in January 1773, significantly still nominally under loyalist control, although the revolution was under way. It was signed by "Felix." Conceding there were some "vicious" "Negroes," he assured his addressees—Governor Thomas Hutchinson, along with "His Majesty's Council, and the House of Representatives in General Court assembled"—there were "many other of quite a different Character, who if made free, would soon be able as well as willing to bear a Part in the Public Charges." That was to say, on the side of the governmental, antirevolutionary men they addressed. That would be the *quid pro quo* for emancipation.[58]

Felix describes the state of mind of his fellow "Negroes": "discreet, sober, honest and industrious" and "may it not be said of many, that they are virtuous and religious." But in this petition for freedom, Felix downplays the willingness of "negroes" to subordinate themselves, continuing, "although their Condition is in itself so unfriendly to Religion, and every moral virtue except Patience." Implicitly, African Americans had been simmering, "having had every Day of their Lives embittered with this most intolerable Reflection," that whatever their "Behaviour . . . neither they nor their Children to all Generations shall ever be able to do, or to possess and enjoy any Thing, no, not even *Life itself*, but in a Manner as the *Beasts that perish*."

He makes clear in specifying the things they cannot enjoy, that his subjects to enjoy being freed are men. "We have no Property! We have no Wives! No Children! No Country!"—He answers Hutchinson *et al* that granting his fellow blacks such "relief" would not "be productive of the least wrong or Injury to our Masters; but to us will be as Life from the dead." It was published in the pro-revolutionary *Massachusetts Spy*, on January 28, 1773.[59]

The second petition, dated April 20, 1773, written on "behalf of our fellow slaves in this province and by order of their Committee," was signed by Peter Bestes, Sambo Freeman, Felix Holbrook (presumably the author of the first petition), and Chester Joie. This one, however, was addressed to those ascendant, white revolutionary members of the Assembly who had been petitioning for their "freedom." So it opened by referring to their inconsistency in relation to the enslavement of blacks.

"The efforts made by the legislature of this province in their last session to free themselves from slavery, gave us, who are in that deplorable state, a high degree of satisfaction." Not so implicitly, their "state" of slavery was the more deplorable because it was literal. "We expect great things from men who have made such a noble stand against the designs of their *fellow men* to enslave them." The petitioners are their fellow men, too, whom they enslave. They share humanity. "The divine spirit of *freedom*, seems to fire every human breast on this continent, except such as are bribed to assist in executing the execrable plan." (He means loyalists' attempts to put down the revolution.) While the subjects of the paragraph are men, and the breasts male ones, Wheatley, for one, will put this phrase "human breast," literally gender neutral to her own use to make the same point, notably in a letter published early in 1774.[60]

These petitioners conclude, "We are willing to submit to such regulations and laws as may be made relative to us until we leave this province, which we determine to do as soon as we can, from our joynt labours, procure money to transport ourselves to some part of the Coast of *Africa*, where we propose a settlement." That was to say, in response to being freed, they would leave the country, evidently a recognition of the racist apprehensions their being free would arouse, the wrongs and injuries to masters which the other petition guaranteed would not happen and the "imagined consequences of a general manumission of our slaves," to which Hopkins refers.[61]

The vast majority of black people, however, regarded America as their home, and were not interested in going to Africa. The entrenched racism Winthrop Jordan describes in *White Over Black* had been made a unifying force by white revolutionaries, sharpened by emancipation and its prospects in the North, set in motion by the revolution and its rhetoric. Robert G. Parkinson has shown in persuasive detail that white revolutionaries, from disparate and rivalrous colonies, made "common cause" on the basis of subordinating black people—indigenous people, and "Hessians"—laying the basis for a racist national identity. It was an outcome Wheatley challenged.[62]

3

From Africa to America

Selina, Countess of Huntingdon as Evangelical Leader,
Wheatley's Patron

Phillis Wheatley's *Poems on Various Subjects, Religious and Moral* was published in 1773 in London because of the patronage of Selina Hastings (born Shirley), Countess of Huntingdon (1707–91). With Wesley and Whitefield, she was a founder of British Methodism, the head of her own sect, the Huntingdon Connexion, and a congeries of chapels and preaching places. In 1767, Lady Huntingdon established a college at Trefeca, in South Wales, "an alternative to Oxford and Cambridge for training Methodist evangelicals," and modelled on the formers' colleges but with herself as mistress, frequently residing in her house there. Her attention to it and to all of her establishments was ceaseless and intense.[1] One young man reported (in 1773) what a Trefeca student said to him: her "Ladyship . . . is such a woman that no Body can refuse anything she asks them, she is a mother to us all, and indeed calls us her Children."[2]

From early in her life, Lady Huntingdon consciously imitated her half-sister, Lady Betty Hastings, twenty-five years her senior, who, as well as beginning her family's association with what would become Methodism, contributed to the national and international projects of the spck and the spg, Quaque's sponsor. She preceded Lady Huntingdon in sponsoring education, and paid for young men to attend university— one of them was Whitefield. She shared such interests with her close friends, Mary Astell and Elizabeth Elstob, who exemplified the long association between the assertion of women's intellectual equality and the reformation of manners, perpetuated subsequently by "Bluestocking" feminists. Because they published books and thereby entered public life, Astell and Elstob and their successor women writers were attacked as Amazons, a characterization escaped by Lady Betty.[3] Some elite female kin worked on their menfolks' electoral campaigns, but they did so behind the scenes: if they were too public, as the Duchess of Devon-shire was, campaigning for Fox in 1784, they were pilloried mercilessly in sexually explicit ways.[4]

Nonetheless, women occasionally braved such inevitable ridicule. At thirty, Lady Huntingdon joined a group of "noble Ladies" to force their way into the gallery of the House of Lords to witness the debate on the Convention of Pardo, a controversial treaty between Britain and Spain, addressing issues soon brought to armed conflict in the War of Jenkins' Ear. One issue was the extension of "the assiento," the clause of the Treaty of Utrecht formally allowing British traders to enter the transatlantic slave trade, shipping Africans into Spanish possessions. Describing this episode, when the ladies defied their male peers' efforts "to starve them out," Lady Mary Wortley Montagu wrote, "These Ama-zons . . . shewed themselves qualified for the duty even of foot-soldiers." It was, writes one of Huntingdon's biographers, her last "escapade" of this kind, but she was to enter public life far more formidably as a reli-gious leader, scrupulously avoiding publicity.[5]

She took up this ambition full-time when she was widowed in 1746, although she had been converted to Methodism in 1739, developing ties with Charles and John Wesley, as well as with Whitefield. For some years she agreed with Wesley's Arminianism, but in 1747 or 1748, she decided on the unmitigated Calvinist predestinarianism preached by Whitefield, and appointed him one of her chaplains. He proudly added "Chaplain to the Countess of Huntingdon" to his "AB" and wrote her weekly Let-ters "that for frequency and passion exceeded any to his wife," whom he left in America. Historian Harry Stout describes this correspondence as "exaggerated deference and groveling," accompanying Whitefield's sense of accomplishment in being able to hobnob and preach "among great company," with particular effect on aristocratic ladies. But with "all this new found respectability and interest in the English aristocracy," it was the American colonies that "engaged his deepest loyalties."[6]

Lady Huntingdon was long "fascinated by overseas missions," al-though she had begun with coalminers in her English domains. Cus-tomarily she sent Trefeca students to evangelize as part of their course, "Indian nations" in North America among their targets. "She planned to send them to the Pacific and, seeing an opportunity opened by the French Revolution at the end of her life, to continental Europe." At

Whitefield's behest, the countess established the "Orphan House in Georgia and made Whitefield its keeper." She called it "Bethesda" after a pool in Jerusalem, according to the Bible (John 5:2–4), where "lay a great multitude of impotent folk, blind, half, withered, waiting for the movement of the water. For an angel went down at a certain season into the pool and troubled the water: who so ever then first . . . stepped in was made whole."[7]

In his 1766 *Caution*, Benezet quoted Whitefield's publicly expressed sympathy for enslaved Africans, written in 1739, immediately prior to his establishment of the Orphan House. "As I lately passed through your provinces [his audience were correspondents in the southern colonies], I was sensibly touched with a fellow-feeling for the miseries of poor Negroes," a sentimental expression in keeping with Benezet's book. But by 1751, Whitefield had concluded that "hot countries cannot be cultivated without Negroes." This was the year that Oglethorpe's vision of a slave-free Georgia was overthrown, in part through Whitefield's efforts. Whitefield had continued by exclaiming, "What a flourishing country might Georgia have been, had slavery been permitted years ago? How many white people have been destroyed for want of them, and how many thousands of pounds spent to no purpose at all?" He admitted that "negroes . . . are brought in a wrong way from their own country, and it is a trade not to be approved of, yet, it will be carried on whether we will or not."[8]

Whitefield's priority, apart from their forced labor, was Africans' conversion to Christianity. Writing "A Prayer for a poor Negroe" in the voice of an enslaved African, Whitefield began, "Blessed be thy name [Lord], for bringing me over into a Christian country." He looked to the conversion of Africans: "Have mercy in my poor countrymen: Lord, suffer them no longer to sit in darkness, and in the shadow of death. Lighten our darkness, we beseech thee. O Lord, and let us know the truth as it is in Jesus." This was identical to the contemporary Rev. Quaque's hope in Anomabu. Whitefield's "Negroe" prayed to accept enslavement. "Make me contented with my condition, knowing, O Lord, that thou has placed me in it. Let me never be tempted to rebel against my master and mistress."[9]

Whitefield looked forward to purchasing "a large number of them, in order to make their lives comfortable, and to lay a foundation for

breeding up their posterity in the nature and admonition of the Lord."
He told the same correspondent, "It rejoiced my soul, to hear that one
of my poor negroes in Carolina was made a brother in Christ." In short,
Whitefield was a proponent of enslavement, albeit an ameliorator in his
treatment of his slaves. Dying in 1770, he willed them to Lady Huntingdon. She kept them, agreeing with his views, and attempted to imple-
ment his double purpose through her ordained agents. Her precedent
included the SPG's inheritance of that huge sugar plantation in Barbados from Col. Codrington in 1710. He had intended its profits "for
the construction and maintenance of a college for training missionaries,"
also a precedent for Lady Huntingdon's Trefeca.[10]

Benezet wrote her, hoping to persuade her of the inhumanity of
slaveholding: while his "esteemed friend George Whitefield . . . first
clearly saw the iniquity of the horrible abuse of the human race," he
changed that view; "after residing in Georgia & being habituated to
the sight & use of Slaves, his judgement became so much influenced
as to paleate & in some measure defend the use of slaves." Benezet enclosed a page from John Wesley's *Thoughts on Slavery* (1774) and a copy
of fellow antislavery Quaker John Woolman's *Journal*, and he "urge[d]
the Countess to release her slaves" before justifying his outspokenness
"where lives & natural as well as religions welfare of so vast a number
of our Fellow Creatures concerned, to be Silent, where we apprehend
it a duty to speak our sense of that which causes us to go mourning
on our way, would be criminal." But Lady Huntingdon continued to
hold slaves.[11]

She promoted Wheatley's poetry, "religious and moral," as a demonstration of the capacity of Africans for conversion, an aim which
Wheatley recognized. She had been preceded in this demonstration
by a Christianized African man, John Albert Ukawsaw Gronniosaw:
Wheatley wrote Lady Huntingdon while in England in 1773 to tell her
of the "very great satisfaction" it gave her "to hear of an African so worthy to be honored with your Ladiship's approbation & Friendship as
him whom you call your Brother."[12] Gronniosaw knew Whitefield "very
well—I had heard him preach often at NEW YORK," and when Gronniosaw came to England, Whitefield played a decisive part in his life.
It was the Rev. Walter Shirley, Lady Huntingdon's cousin and Whitefield's successor as her chaplain, whose name was on the title page of *A*

Narrative of the Most Remarkable Particulars of the Life of James Albert Gronniosaw, and African Prince, as Related by Himself, published in 1770 and dedicated "to the HONOURABLE the Countess of HUNTINGDON, THIS NARRATIVE OF my LIFE. And of GOD'S wonderful Dealings with me is, (Through Her LADYSHIP's Permission) Most Humbly Declared By her LADYSHIP's Most obliged And obedient Servant, JAMES ALBERT." His African name is omitted for his address to the God he now shared with his patron, and to whom he attributed the course of his life that had brought him to this point.[13]

Shirley, too, gives Gronniosaw only his Christian names, as he vouches for the genuineness of this story, (amidst that of other, putative princes and the racist suspicions of British readers), "taken from his own Mouth and committed to Paper by the elegant Pen of a young Lady of the Town of Leominster," not far from Kidderminster, where Gronniosaw and his family lived. Both towns were in a region of England where the ministers of the Huntingdon Connexion were active, and we can assume that Gronniosaw's amanuensis was a member. Shirley points out to readers that the young lady had written down the African's words "for her own private satisfaction and without any intention at first that it should be made public." Wheatley would make the same conventional disclaimer in the preface to her *Poems,* published three years later, influenced by a sense of the response to women entering public life this way. Shirley emphasizes the young woman's reluctance in the process: "But she has now been prevailed on to commit it to the Press, both with a view to serve ALBERT and his distressed Family, who have the sole Profits arising from the Sale of it." Wheatley had that hope, too, and the British African Ignatius Sancho's *Letters* were published posthumously in part to benefit his widow and children.[14]

Wheatley and Sancho had managed to attain literacy in English, but Gronniosaw had not. Like "the vast majority of laboring peoples in the early modern era, most black men and women living in Britain, he could neither read nor write." So, historian Christopher Leslie Brown continues, Gronniosaw "provides one of the few opportunities to know in detail what [illiterate] blacks were thinking and saying in . . . crucial years." We have his mediated voice only because of Lady Huntingdon's wish to publicize the susceptibility of Africans to Christian conversion.[15]

Shirley continued, "It is apprehended that this little History contains Matter well worthy the Notice and Attention of every Christian Reader. We have here in some Degree a solution of a Question that was perplex'd the Minds of so many serious Persons, viz. In what Manner will God deal with those benighted Parts of the World where the Gospel of Jesus Christ hath never reach'd?" Of course, God does not "save without Knowledge of the Truth," that is, without people learning his word in the Bible. But referring to predestination, "with Respect to those whom he hath fore-known, though born under every outward Disadvantage, and in Regions of the Grossest Darkness and ignorance, he most amazingly acts upon and influences their Minds." Shirley thus lays out how English-speaking Christians are to read this narrative and anticipates how Gronniosaw was presented as recreating his life, emerging from darkest Africa to the brightly lit, Christian West: "In the Course of wisely and most wonderfully appointed Providences, he brings them to the means of spiritual Reformation, gradually opens to their View the Light of his Truth."[16]

Shirley asks rhetorically, "Who can doubt but that the Suggestion so forcibly press'd upon the Mind of ALBERT (when a Boy) that there was a Being superior to the Sun, Moon, and Stars (the object of African idolatry) came from the Father of Lights . . . the first-fruit of the Display of Gospel Glory," God's action assimilable to the operation of Lockean psychology, automatically assumed by eighteenth-century writers. In this African's journey, his enslavement and transportation across the Atlantic, the Rev. Shirley nudges his readers to "discern an All-wise and Omnipotent Direction." His enslavement is transformed into redemption: all along Gronniosaw "belong'd to the Redeemer of lost Sinners; he was the Purchase of the Cross; and therefore the Lord undertook to bring him by a Way that he knew not, out of the Darkness into his marvelous Light." Shirley here acknowledges the gospels, where both Paul and Jude referred to "themselves as the slaves of Jesus Christ." I have mentioned earlier the metaphor's capacity to bolster "the acceptability of slavery in the real world," and Shirley's use of it is consistent with Whitefield's justification of enslavement.[17]

Phillis Wheatley wrote to Lady Huntingdon the same year that Gronniosaw's *Narrative* was published in metropolitan Britain. Wheatley's dedication of her *Poems*, published in London three years later, was virtually identical to the dedication of Gronniosaw's: "DEDICATION to the Right Honourable the COUNTESS OF HUNTINGDON, Inscribed, By her much obliged, Very humble, And devoted Servant, Phillis Wheatley." Susanna Wheatley, Phillis's mistress, had been "originally converted by Whitefield" and maintained strong relationships with the Huntingdon Connexion.[18]

Wheatley's *Poems* began with three items in explanation of "Negro Servant" and testifying to the authenticity of her authoring the poems. The first after the dedication was a preface, written by Wheatley herself. The second, a "Letter," ostensibly "sent by the Author's Master to the Publisher," was also written by Wheatley. It began, "Phillis was brought from *Africa to America* in the Year 1761, between Seven and Eight Years of Age." I will return to these documents, but her enslavement as a child and her relationship with Lady Huntingdon should be the starting points.

Childhood Trauma

"Was brought" stands for the child enduring the Middle Passage. While Wheatley's most recent biographer, Vincent Carretta, writes of the impossibility of knowing where, let along how, her journey began, the verb's passive voice also stands for the adult Africans who captured her (like those with whom John Corrente traded). Wheatley was likely captured quite a way inland and brought on a well-used path from a habitation in the area loosely called "Sinigall," back of "the Windward Coast," where the slave ship picked up the cargo, including Wheatley. John C. Shields makes the case that she came from Gambia.[19] Most likely she had been kidnapped/captured in a violent raid, then marched with others, perhaps family members and other adults, who may have carried her when they could, to the fort, to be traded and held for shipment. We do not know how she was spoken to, or handled. Europeans would have replaced her name with a number, spoken in words she did not understand. She was one of the thirty thousand Africans sold into the northern mainland colonies by 1775.[20]

William H. Robinson and Vincent Carretta have uncovered the history of the transatlantic voyage of the slave ship which brought her, the

Phillis (also called "the *Charming Phyllis*," "The *Phyllis*," and "Schooner *Phyllis*"), after which the child was eventually renamed, although to name an enslaved African after a figure in Greek or Roman mythology or history was a racist convention, intending irony. After a four-month voyage, the ship landed seventy-five Africans in Boston, out of the ninety-six who had been loaded on the African coast. This was an unusually high mortality rate, perhaps because a disproportionate number were young children. Whether any of them were accompanied by kin, we do not know.[21]

The owner of the *Phillis* was Timothy Fitch, a "wealthy merchant living in Medford," north of Boston. He had instructed his captain, Peter Gwinn, "to be sure to bring as Fiew women and Girls as possible" when he gathered slaves along the West African coast. He reminded Gwinn again "to get as few Girl Slaves as possible & as many Prime Boys as you can." So displeased was he with the cargo that arrived in Boston in 1761 that, for the next voyage, Fitch ordered Gwinn "not to take any Children & Especially Girls," but "as many Prime Young Men and Boys as you can get from 14 Years of Age."[22]

Antislavery campaigners and recent historians, notably Marcus Rediker and James Walvin, allow us to imagine the African child's shock of capture, forced march to the coast, and her experience of the Middle Passage in her phrase "from Africa to America." We have intimations of what Africans, enslaved by raiders and purchasers and sold to Europeans since the late fifteenth century at least, may have apprehended and feared previously and *en route*. Despite linguistic differences, there were degrees of intelligibility among Africans from different areas, at least within a radius of 250 miles from the coast where "Phillis Wheatley" was brought.[23]

Large numbers were incarcerated in dungeons like those Quaque knew at Cape Coast Castle, before being sold, branded, and loaded on slavers right away, singly or in small groups, as captains like Gwinn cruised up and down the coast, dependent on what African slavers had available. On board, alien figures ordered their captives about with peremptory signs and blows, Africans calling out in pain, anger, and fear. Evidently there were possibilities for all aboard to learn some words, even develop a "pidgin" language. A child took in these strange sounds and those of the ship as it got under way, sometimes generating prolonged seasickness in its cargo, hatches and portholes battened down in heavy seas; more horrible stenches from all those packed and cramped bodies, mired in excreta, and the effluvia of amoebic dysentery—the "bloody flux"—a prime killer of between 10% and 50% of Africans on board, dead bodies chained to live, before being unchained, hauled out, and thrown into the shark-thrashed sea.[24]

Wheatley mentions being seized from her father's arms and suggests her mother was bereaved by the same event.[25] Because a "primary method used by African enslavers was a 'grand pillage' of entire villages set afire in the middle of the night," families were "swept up by marauding forces" and sold on the coast as "prisoners of war. Husbands and wives, parents and children, siblings . . . found themselves on the same ships." This was by no means always the case; moreover, the genders were separated, men chained below, women and children allowed on deck more often. Little girls might sleep together in a separate place.[26] Females were subject to rape; James Field Stanfield, aboard a slave ship from 1774 to 1776, recorded "something practiced by the captain on an unfortunate female slave of eight or nine," which, in Rediker's words, "must have been the rape of a small girl." Both women and children were suspected of plotting resistance with the men.[27]

Slave ships were designed and operated deliberately as engines of terror, as whites faced the continual threat and reality of blacks rising up against them. Violence "of one kind or another, had brought almost everyone on board" and "most everything that happened . . . had the threat or actuality of violence behind it."[28] Walvin writes that "every single one of the over 11 million Africans who stepped ashore in the Americas had endured . . . a hellish voyage of undreamt of terror," with demonstrably long-term damage to health. Wheatley was sickly, and she died at thirty-four, her body fundamentally weakened before she underwent childbirth possibly three times.[29]

Having seen assaults, whippings, and perhaps forced-feedings during the voyage, a child watched sailors rub grease into the skin of the enslaved before unloading them for sale, stuffing oakum into rectums to stop the flow of diarrhea. "Phillis" was parted from other Africans (perhaps from another child to be named Obour Tanner), even her mother, other kin, or an adult or adults who had sympathized with her. The African child was sold, probably on Avery's Wharf in Boston, to an utter stranger, white like the crew. She would find his name was John Wheatley. From his point of view, in buying the child and leading her to his house, he was fulfilling his wife's wish for a maid, doubling perhaps, as consolation for the girl they had lost.[30]

Particular Experience and Poetic Convention

This child's capture, march to the coast, and voyage were her traumas, amidst the traumas suffered by all the enslaved and shipped. One historian who characterizes extant slave narratives generally finds it "striking that so little is said about the transatlantic crossing."[31] Wheatley mastered English prodigiously; this is how she interpreted her Middle Passage, seven years later, in "On being brought from AFRICA to AMERICA." The title was of profound importance to the author:

> 'TWAS mercy brought me from my *Pagan* land,
> Taught my benighted soul to understand
> That there's a God, that there's a *Saviour* too:
> Once I redemption neither sought nor knew.
> Some view our sable race with scornful eye,
> "Their colour is a diabolic die."
> Remember, *Christians*, *Negros*, black as Cain,
> May be refin'd, and join th' angelic strain.

This was an interpretation Wheatley would repeat in subsequent poems and letters. It was consistent with Whitefield's and Lady Huntingdon's hopes for the enslavement of Africans, as well as rationalization by some planters. Indeed, Wheatley's poem referred to Whitefield's "Prayer for a poor Negroe." ("Blessed be thy name, for bringing me over into a Christian country.") Her poem told the countess—and many subsequent evangelical, antislavery writers—what they wanted to hear. But it meant something very different to Wheatley herself, giving sense and transcendent value to horror.[32]

One can read this particular meaning in Wheatley's poems, consoling parents for the death of children and other family members, transforming sentimental convention's dominating "theme of loss." Of the forty poems published in her book, fourteen are on such losses, and of the other eighteen, five are.[33] For example, Wheatley writes "To a LADY and her Children, on the Death of her Son and their Brother,"

> No more in briny show'rs, ye friends around,
> Or bathe his clay, or waste them on the grounds:
>
> . . .
>
> No more for him the streams of sorrow pour,
> But haste to join him on the heav'nly shore[.]

Or she tells "a GENTLEMAN and a LADY on the Death of the Lady's Brother and Sister, and a Child of the Name, Avis, age one Year,"

> Thine *Avis* give without a murm'ring heart,
> Though half thy soul be fated to depart.
> To shining guards consign thy infant care
> To waft triumphant through the seas of air:

and in "On the Death of J. C. an Infant," the verb repeats how she presented being shipped from Africa to Boston; she urges the weeping parent:

> Enough—forever cease your murm'ring breath;
> Not as a foe, but friend converse with *Death*,
> Since to the port of happiness unknown
> He brought that treasure which you call your own.

One could read this as a consolation offered to her African parents, to see the virtual death of their daughter as she had come to interpret it.[34]

And by the same token, one can read the interpretation Wheatley offered "to a LADY on her remarkable Preservation in a Hurricane in *North Carolina*" as parallel to her own interpretation of her survival of her enslavement and Middle Passage, to become a Protestant, Calvinist Christian:

> But thee, *Maria*, a kind *Nereid's* shield
> Preserv'd from sinking, and thy form upheld:
> And sure some heav'nly oracle design'd

At that dread crisis to instruct thy mind
Things of eternal consequence to weigh,
And to thine heart just feelings to convey
Of things above, and of the future doom,
And what the births of the dread world to come.

"Maria," then, leaves pagan gods, and through an oceanic crisis, reaches a proper knowledge of her Christian fate by way of "God's command," the next stanza tells us. Her parents'

> . . . fears are all reliev'd:
> Thy daughter blooming with superior grace[.]

The last line's exclamation, "And what the blessings of maternal care!," suggests that the child's parents can rejoice not only in her survival in Christianity, but in being taken in by another mother.[35]

Wheatley learned English and evangelical Christian values under the aegis of Susanna. On her death in 1774, Wheatley wrote to Obour Tanner, her enslaved, African "sister" and co-religionist, "I have lately met with a great trial in the death of my mistress; let us imagine the loss of a parent, sister, or brother, the tenderness of all was united in her. I was a poor little outcast &c stranger when she took me in: not only into her house, but I presently became a sharer in her most tender affections. I was treated by her more like her child than her servant; no opportunity was left unimproved of giving me the best advice, but in terms how tender, how engaging!"[36]

She also described her relationship with her mistress to John Thornton (1720–90), that evangelized London merchant and co-worker in the countess's missionary project. It would be at his house that "the Clapham sect was first to gather," evolving from "the Teston Circle," "the heart of the white component of English abolitionism."[37] Wheatley had recently stayed with Thornton in London. She told him of the effects of "the great loss . . . of my best friend. I feel like One forsaken by her parent in a desolate wilderness . . . without my friendly guide. I fear lest every step should lead me into error and confusion." Susanna, she wrote, had bestowed "uncommon tenderness for thirteen years from my earliest youth." She had mothered Phillis for longer than her birth mother.[38]

Obour had been brought from Africa and then presumably sold to the Tanners, but kept her African name, too. She may have been a little older than Wheatley. That Wheatley called her "sister" was with the same Christian significance as when she referred to Gronniosaw as Lady Huntingdon's "brother" (Obour was "baptized and admitted" to Newport's First Congregational Church in 1768—Hopkins became her pastor two years later), but if they had been transported across the Atlantic together, then the term also could have reflected "the strong and tender affection . . . almost equivalent to that of brother or sister" that an eighteenth-century voyager observed among Africans on slave ships.[39] Wheatley's letters to Obour were the most affectionate she wrote, expressing the kinship of both enslavement and conversion. Her first to her "Dear Sister" tells her she "rejoices in that . . . experience of the Saving change which you so emphatically describe." Evidently Obour ("Abour" she calls her in this letter) had initiated the correspondence by describing these experiences. Wheatley continues, "Let us rejoice in and adore the wonders of God's infinite Love in bringing us from land Semblant of darkness itself, and where the divine light of revelation (being obscur'd) is as darkness." This was her prose version of "On being brought from AFRICA to AMERICA," the passage Obour shared. "Here, the knowledge of the true God and eternal life has made manifest: But there, profound ignorance overshadows the land." Able to envision salvation, longing for it was a major subject of their correspondence, which Wheatley in this first letter hoped "may have the happy effect of improving our mutual friendship." Poet Robert Hayden, expanding what Wheatley would tell Obour of her experience in London the following year, imagines the uniqueness of their relationship:

> Sister forgive th' intrusion of
> My Sombreness—Noctural Mood
> I would not share with any save
> your trusted Self.[40]

In all likelihood, Obour was converted by Sarah Osborn, a friend of Whitefield's, through him an acquaintance of Susanna Wheatley's, as well as a colleague of Hopkins. Osborn publicly led the revival in Newport by way of a female prayer society there. These efforts were combined with a school she ran to support herself, founding it, she said, "in the name of God and in deeds of charity to the poor."[41]

By 1767, hundreds of people of all kinds came to Osborn's home "for religious discussion, reading, catechizing, singing and sometimes praying." The largest group, comprised of black people, was the "Ethiopian Society," averaging about seventy attendees, most of them slaves, and at one point one in every six blacks in town. Among them were John Quamine and Bristol Yamma. It was possible that Wheatley knew of them first through Obour. Members of the Ethiopian Society were drawn from the high proportion of blacks to whites in Rhode Island, one in fifteen, in contrast to one in forty in New England as a whole. "Newport was the center of the New England trade" in slaves. In 1782, "almost one tenth of the population was slave." Obour reported the large number of Christianized "Ethiopians" in her first letter to Wheatley, who replied, "It gives me great pleasure to hear of so many of my nation, seeking with eagerness the way to true felicity. O may we all meet in that happy mansion." Wheatley makes clear to her readers she is African, but it is only to Obour that she refers to "my nation."[42]

She brings the same vision of Christianization—"From dark abodes into fair ethereal light"—to bear on whites, too, in this case referring to "On the Death of a young Lady of Five Years of Age." While this was a conventional usage for Anglophone Protestants, it carried particular connotations for blacks who converted. The same must be said of being "freed from a world of sin" and feeling "the iron band of pain no more," both from the same poem; the metaphor appears throughout her poems. I referred to its significance for literal as well as metaphorical slavery in relation to Quaque's expression of it. Relevant, too, is the synonymous Christian notion of the transcendence of the dead body, when Wheatley writes in "To a Lady on the Death of her Husband":

> Clos'd are his eyes and heavy fetters keep,
> His senses bound in never-waking sleep,

while her "Leonard mounts, and leaves the earth behind."[43]

In that letter to Thornton on her mistress's death, Wheatley presents her as having been equally enslaved in the religious, metaphorical sense, exclaiming to him, "O could you have been present, to see how she longed to drop the tabernacle of Clay, and to be freed from the cumbrous shackles of a mortal Body, which had so many times retarded her desires when soaring upward."[44]

Newport generated antislavery. Grimsted suggests that Wheatley's poem "On Messrs. HUSSEY and COFFIN" was published in 1768, when she was thirteen or so, in the *Newport Mercury* during that year's spectacular revival, because Susanna sent it to Osborn with evident value for evangelical purpose. A few months earlier, Osborn had transmitted Bishop William Warburton's 1766 antislavery and evangelical sermon to the SPG to the same newspaper. "On Messrs. HUSSEY and COFFIN" showed Wheatley's knowledge of classical mythology, as well as her Christian belief. She had overheard two gentlemen visitors describing their escape from a deadly shipwreck off Cape Cod. In printing the poem, the *Newport Mercury* (December 1767) reported that the "lines were by a Negro Girl (belonging to one Mr. Wheatley of Boston)." She had overheard the two men telling their story while "tending Table."[45]

Four years later, Wheatley was baptized by the Rev. Samuel Cooper at the family church, Boston's Old South. Her owners must have been calling her Phillis right after they bought her. For the ceremony, Carretta thinks "she probably sat in the balcony reserved for females of African descent." If not, she felt other racist stings. She planned to publish her book in Boston: the February 29, 1772 issue of the *Boston Gazette* printed "Proposals, for Printing by subscription"—an advertisement to finance the project—"a Collection of POEMS, wrote at several times, by PHILLIS, a Negro Girl, from the Strength of her own Genius, it being but a few Years since she came to this Town an uncultivated Barbarian from Africa." This was to highlight her prodigality in mastery of English. Her poems needed authentification: "The Poems having been seen and read by the best judges, who think them well worthy of the Public View; and upon critical examination, they find that the declared Author was capable of writing them." This advertisement said "small Octavo Volume . . . will contain 200 pages . . . printed on Demy Paper, and beautiful Type." The price to subscribers would be four shillings. Then, uniquely, "It is hoped encouragement will be given to this Publication, as a reward to a very uncommon Genius, at present, a Slave." Did the words "at present" mean Wheatley hoped her feat would lead her to being freed? The advertisement explained that the book would be "put to the Press as soon as the Hundred Copies are subscribed for," subscriptions to be "taken in by E. Russell in Market Street." The advertisement was republished on March 18 and April 18.[46]

One subscriber was Boston lawyer John Andrews, who, in May, wrote to William Barrell, his brother-in-law, in Philadelphia: "Two months since I subscribed for Phillis's poems which I expected to have sent you long ago, but the want of spirit to carry on anything of the kind here has prevented it, as they are not yet published." Robinson calls this sitting on hands a "rejection," then quotes another letter from Andrews to Barrell, describing why and how Wheatley gave up on the Boston printers: "Friends . . . led her to expect a large emolument if she sent the copy home [i.e., England] which induc'd her to remand [the manuscript of the poems] from the printers & also of Capt. Calef who could not sell it by the reason of their not crediting the performances to be by a Negro, since when she has had papers drawn up & sign'd by the Gov., Council, Ministers & most of the people of note in this place, certifying the authenticity if it; which Capt. Calef carried last fall" to Archibald Bell in London. Andrews added that "it is supposed the copy will sell for 100 pounds sterling."[47]

In September 1772, Andrews sent Barrell Wheatley's "A POEM on the Death of C.E. [Charles Eliot] an Infant of Twelve Months," which Andrews wrote was "addressed to the father on this melancholy occasion; and which I think is a masterly performance." Barrell was Charles's mother's brother, and it seems that Wheatley had given a copy of the poem to Ruth Barrell Eliot. Again we can see it charged with the meaning Wheatley had given being enslaved and brought to America. The poem describes the baby flying through the empyreal skies, welcomed by angels to the seat of God, which he thanks for rescuing him—"E'er vice triumphant had possess'd my heart"—and before he has been tempted by the variety of sins besetting older people, he says,

> But, soon arriv'd at my celestial goal,
> Full glories rush on my expanding soul.

So the poet asks the parents,

> Say, parents, why this unavailing moan?
> Why heave your pensive bosoms with the groan?
> To *Charles*, the happy subject of my song,
> A brighter world and nobler strains belong.

And she concludes,

> To you bright regions let your faith ascend,
> Prepare to join your dearest infant friend
> In pleasures without measure, without end.[48]

4

Wheatley Gains Huntingdon's Patronage

An African Genius in America

Wheatley first brought herself directly to the countess's attention by sending her a copy of her elegy "On the Death of the Rev. Mr. GEORGE WHITEFIELD, 1770." John C. Shields calls it "the most pivotal publication of Wheatley's career," because it connected her to Lady Huntingdon.[1]

> HAIL, happy saint, on thine immortal throne,
> Possest of glory, life, and bliss unknown;
> We hear no more the music of thy tongue,
> Thy wonted auditories cease to throng.
> Thy sermons in unequall'd accents flow'd,
> And ev'ry bosom with devotion glow'd;
> Thou dids't in strains of eloquence refin'd
> Inflame the heart, and captivate the mind.

Whitefield distinguished himself theologically and in other ways from his Anglican roots, but here Wheatley describes the psychophysiological effects of his preaching. These effects had been propounded by generations of Anglican preachers, now refreshed and exemplified in the Great Awakening, reaching out to thousands of new believers, notably among them women and the poor, including black people. Whitefield spent years in America.

> He pray'd that grace in ev'ry heart might swell,
> He long'd to see *America* excel;
> He charg'd its youth that ev'ry grace divine
> Should with lustre in their conduct shine.[2]

There can be little doubt that Susanna Wheatley, "originally converted by Whitefield," took her young slave to his services, including perhaps the one in Boston he preached before his sudden death in Newburyport. One of Wheatley's editors suggests Whitefield "may well have resided briefly at the Wheatley mansion."[3]

In Whitefield's voice, the poet adjures the wretched to take "the Saviour"

> . . . for your only good,
> Take him ye starving sinners for your food;
>
> . . .
>
> Ye preachers, take him for your joyful theme,
> Take him my dear *Americans*, he said,
> Be your complaints on his kind bosom laid:
> Take him ye *Africans*, he longs for you,
> *Impartial Saviour* is his title due:
> Wash'd in the fountains of redeeming blood,
> You shall be sons, and kings, and priests to God.

She turns from African men's prospects of spiritual elevation to the Countess of Huntingdon: "Great Countess," footnoting this with, "the Countess of *Huntingdon*, to whom *Mr. Whitefield*, was Chaplain."

> Great *Countess*, we *Americans* revere
> Thy name, and mingle in thy grief sincere;
> *New England* deeply feels, the Orphans mourn,
> Their more than father will no more return.

Wheatley includes her African, female self with "we Americans," in keeping with Christ's impartiality.[4]

Her elegy was published as a broadside in Boston, Newport, New York, and Philadelphia in 1770, then in London, early the following year. It was published, too, in the *New Hampshire Gazette*, on October 19, 1770, the paper noting it was written "by a native of Africa, and would have done Honor to a Pope or Shakespeare." The advertisement for it in the *Massachusetts Spy* announced that the broadside was "Embellished with a Plate, representing the position in which the Rev. Mr. Whitefield lay before and after his interment at Newbury–port." It told its readers to buy the plate, followed by "An Elegant Poem on the death of that celebrated Divine and eminent Servant of Jesus Christ, the reverend and learned GEORGE WHITEFIELD, Chaplain to the Right Honourable the Countess of Huntingdon &c & &. Who made his Exit from this transitory state, . . . 30th September, 1770, when he was seiz'd with a fit of the Asthma at Newbury-port, near Boston, New England." The ad describes the poem's inclusion of "a consolatory Address to her truly noble benefactress the worthy and pious Lady Huntingdon; and the Orphan children in Georgia, with many thousands, are left, by the death of this gentleman, to lament the loss of a father, friend and benefactor. By PHILLIS, a Servant girl of seventeen years of age, belonging to Mr. J. Wheatley of Boston, she has been but nine years in this country from Africa."[5] The *Boston Journal* reprinted the advertisement in its three subsequent issues, and it was published twice in two other Boston papers, as well as in papers in Pennsylvania and New York.

Wheatley, then, was identified as a poet, a prodigy, an African, an American, and implicitly, a slave. That identity was repeatedly linked to Whitefield and to the Countess of Huntingdon. She had chosen to link herself to them by her poem, and it must have been Susanna, with her husband and clerical connections, who implemented the publication. The link was fundamental to Wheatley's fame, comparable to Sancho's connection to Sterne in England, existing because of Sancho's initiative in 1766, although not made public until 1775.[6]

Wheatley's letter to the countess, dated October 25, 1770, sent with her Whitefield poem, addressed her as "Most Noble Lady," and as in the case of Sancho in writing to Sterne, apologized for thus breaking hierarchical propriety but, unlike him, unequivocally. "The Occasion of my addressing your Ladiship will I hope apologize for my boldness in doing it; it is to enclose a few lines on the decease of your worthy chaplain, the Rev'd Mr. Whitefield, in the loss of whom I sincerely sympathize with your Ladiship but your great loss which is his greater gain, will . . . I hope, meet with infinite reparation in the presence of God, the Divine Benefactor, whose image you bear by that imitation."

Wheatley was one of those Africans, her poem tells her readers, for whom Whitefield had longed. She concluded, "The Tongues of the Learned are insufficient, much less the pen of an untutor'd African, to paint in lively character, the excellencies of this Citizen of

Zion!" This was to elevate Whitefield in the same terms as her poem. The sincerity of sympathy transcended learning, a view she had expressed in "To the University of CAMBRIDGE, in NEW ENGLAND" in 1767. We can juxtapose that with Wheatley's calling herself "an untutored African."

> WHILE an intrinsic ardor prompts to write,
> The muses promise to assist my pen;
> 'Twas not so long since I left my native shore
> The land of errors, and *Egyptian* gloom;
> Father of mercy, 'twas thy gracious hand
> Brought me in safety from those dark abodes.

She reiterates her traumatically charged theme of being brought from Africa as she characterizes a privileged Harvard student's exposure to modern science, and her poems show her admiration for Newton.[7]

She expresses, too, her moral superiority to students who (like their contemporaries at Oxford and Cambridge) were notoriously immoral and irreligious.[8] In 1783, Abigail Adams described her apprehensions in sending her sons there, worried about the dangerous effects of their reading Voltaire, Hume, and Mandeville; her near son-in-law sired a child on a serving woman while at Harvard.[9] Wheatley adjured the students,

> Let sin, that baneful evil to the soul,
> By you be shunn'd,

and she concluded,

> Ye blooming plants of human race divine,
> An *Ethiop* tells you 'tis your greatest foe;
> Its transient sweetness turns to endless pain,
> And an immense perdition sinks the soul.

She had opened another poem, "An Address to the Deist," also written in 1767 (and not included in her 1773 book), with the same ironic authority.

Must Ethiopians be imploy'd for you
Greatly rejoice if any good I do[,]

asserting the divinity of Christ and the Trinity, and that,

The vilest prodigal that comes to God
Is not cast off, but bro't by Jesus Blood.

Here, as elsewhere, Wheatley adapts literary and religious conventions, the prodigal son and the "fortunate fall," to her own experience, dramatically as an Ethiopian, brought from her Pagan land, as she was in her poem to Cambridge students.[10]

Conversion to Christianity conferred equality on souls, as well as superiority to unbelievers, one resource for women of sensibility, denied university education, but enabled to group dissolute students with other unreformed men.[11] This had still further value for Africans, for black people, and we can read Wheatley's calling herself an "untutor'd African" in light of the last two lines of "On being brought from AFRICA to AMERICA," soon after this one addressed to the Harvard students.

Remember *Christians*, *Negroes*, black as Cain,
May be refin'd and join the angelic strain.

Wheatley declared her Africanness that same year in "America," after three lines referring to New England's settlement in "the wilderness."

Thy Power, O Liberty makes strong the weak
And (wond'rous instinct) Ethiopians speak
Sometimes by Simile, a victory's won.

The simile is Wheatley's representation of "Britannia" as the mother of "Americus." Americus's liberty was at issue, but the revolutionary context had more immediate, more literal meaning for enslaved Ethiopians who, her parenthesis exclaims, shared that innate human instinct for liberty. To paraphrase the poem, while the son grew up "virtuous," his mother feared his strength, so laid taxes on him, promising to remove them if he mended his "manners." But Britannia's motherly "Sympathy and

Love" was merely "seeming," and she scourged "the Best of Infants" till he cried. At first insensitive but eventually "awaken'd by maternal fear," she asked her son why he wept. He begins to answer, "My dear mama," but falls "Prostrate at her maternal feet." "What ails the rebel, great Britannia Cry'd." He asks her why she treats him this way, saying,

> . . . what no more English blood?
> Has length of time drove from but English veins
> The kindred tie he to Great Britannia deigns?

This was a charge—familial betrayal—Jefferson was to include in his Declaration of Independence.

Then Wheatley reproduces American republicans' slavery rhetoric again:

> Tis thus with thee O Brittain keeping down
> New English force thou fear'st his Tyranny and thou didst frown
> He weeps afresh to feel his Iron chain
> Turn, O Brittania claim thy child again

although the unusual reversal, America's potential tyranny, pre-empted by Britannia's, suggests meaning for the enslaved Ethiopian, who has told us she is inspired by the call for Liberty. The "monstrous inconsistency" is at play in whatever Wheatley writes of white Americans' call for liberty from British slavery.[12]

This poem was not published, but by February 1773, Wheatley had published enough to become emblematic to whites of African "negro" capacities, that is, before the publication of her book. That month, Dr. Benjamin Rush, the leader of enlightened reform in Philadelphia, "was coaxed into the antislavery struggle by Benezet." He did so anonymously, however, in giving Granville Sharp permission to reprint his "Address to the Inhabitants of the British Settlements in America upon Slave Keeping."[13] Rush's chief argument was a religious one, based on Biblical, Christian texts. In challenging those who suppose "Negroes . . . to be inferior to those of the inhabitants of Europe," an allusion to Hume's view, perpetuated that year in the wake of the Mansfield decision, Rush declared that travelers' accounts of "their ingenuity, humanity, and strong attachment to their parents, relations, friends and country, show us they are equal to the Europeans." In fact, he declared, "We have many well attested anecdotes of as sublime and disinterested virtue among them as ever adorned a Roman or a Christian character." He illustrated with two references in the accompanying footnote the first: "See S P E C T A T O R, Vol. I No. 11," the story of Yarico's selfless love for Inkle, who sells her into slavery, and he then notes, "There is now in the town of Boston a Negro Girl, about eighteen years of age, who had been but nine years in the country, whose singular genius and accomplishments are such as not only do honour to her sex, but to human nature." The latter distinction reflects the view that women were distinct—and implicitly inferior—in their accomplishments, with Rush here asserting that Wheatley transcended conventional definitions of gender, too.[14]

To call her a singular "genius," one honoring "human nature," invoked the eighteenth century's development of a word with ancient, classical connotations, one of its meanings an inborn "intellectual power of an exalted type," one coming to be "attributed to those who are esteemed greatest on any form of art," with "extraordinary capacity for imaginative creation, original thought." In his *Lives of the Poets* (1777), Dr. Johnson described "accidents" which "produce that particular designation of mind, and propensity for some certain science or employment, commonly called genius. The term genius is a mind of large general powers, accidentally determined to some particular direction." It was high praise from Rush, a founding father and signer of the Declaration of Independence, the opposite of Jefferson's contemptuous dismissal of Wheatley's poetry.[15]

In the same document, Rush observed the effect of the 1772 Mansfield decision: "a late decision in favour of a Virginia slave in Westminster Hall has raised the Clamors of the whole Nation" against slave trading merchants. Another context to which Rush appealed was the dawning American Revolution: "Ye men of S E N S E and V I R T U E—Ye Advocates for American Liberty—rouse up and espouse the cause of Humanity and general Liberty!" The "negro girl" was a part of that double cause, linked to it by her human nature and the claim to liberty she shared with the enslaved black people whose liberty Rush was advocating. Further context for his praise was his taking pains, in Christine Levecq's words, "to establish the equality of blacks and whites, despite their differences in skin color, and interestingly he ventures into the realm of aesthetics." Rush intended "to defuse the white repugnance at the appearance of black skin."[16]

Rush's pamphlet outraged Richard Nisbet, a planter from Nevis living in Philadelphia. He repeated Hume's argument that the natives of Africa "are a much inferior race of men," adding that they were characterized by "beastly customs and gross stupidity." In the face of Benezet as well as Rush, he said Africa was "totally over-run with barbarism"; its inhabitants lack "letters, manufactures, and everything which constitutes civilized life." Nisbet saw no sign they had even "the most distant idea of a supreme Being." Africans "seem unacquainted with friendship, gratitude, and every tie of some kind." So "contrary to those who have taken pains to give a high colouring to the affecting scenes between relations when parted at sale, these creatures are separated from their nearest relations without looking after them, or wishing them farewell."

It is in the context of declaring that Africans lack the capacity for human ties and do not care about being separated from their nearest relations, "at the disposal of a cargo," that Nisbet refers to Wheatley. "A few instances may be found, of African negroes possessing virtues and becoming ingenious," but those instances do not contradict their general character. He writes that the author of an "'Address . . . upon Slave Keeping' gives a single example of a negro girl writing a few silly poems, to prove that the blacks are not deficient to us in understanding."[17]

Wheatley's Prospects

Wheatley had ended her October 25, 1770, letter to Lady Huntingdon accompanying her Whitefield poem, "I beg an interest in your Ladiship's Prayer," signing it, "and am With great Humility your Ladiship's most obedient Humble Servant Phillis Wheatley." The next letter we have of hers was to John Thornton, about whom Wheatley knew because of his sponsorship of Samson Occom, a Christianized Mohegan who often stayed with the Wheatleys, through whom Thornton transmitted money for Occom's mission.

Occom had spent five years under the wing of the Rev. Eleazor Wheelock, who intended that he and other Indians spread the Great Awakening to their peoples, founding "Moor's Charity School" in Lebanon, Connecticut, for that purpose. The fall of Canada seemed to open a door to the "back nations" of America, and Wheelock entered it with a driving vision of "tawny souls blanched by the Bible." Occom was converted to evangelical Christianity and partially to English ways and went on to preach in poverty to the Montauk Indians on Long Island. Wheelock drew some Iroquois and others from British conquests, but failed to rid them of their Indianness, pride above all. He complained at length to the Rev. Whitefield about their linguistic insufficiencies— "they are as unpolished and uncultivated within as without"—and in his 1771 *Narrative* of the school to that date, many were "sunk down into as low, savage and brutish manner of living as they were before any endeavours were used to raise them up."[18] Implicit was Wheelock's purpose, the same as that embarked upon by Puritan forbears (when they did not massacre and enslave the native peoples), to turn them into an inferior kind of Englishman or Englishwoman.[19] Like preceding and contemporary SPG missionaries, Wheelock believed "it is necessary to civilize Savages before they can be converted into Christianity." Quaque had been processed this way, and he followed the Rev. Thompson at Cape Coast in their efforts to convert Africans from the 1750s on. The influential opponent of the slave trade, the Rev. James Ramsay, illustrated the same view prevailing among those who would Christianize enslaved Africans in the West Indies. The title of his *Essay on the Treatment and Conversion of Slaves in the British Sugar Islands* (1784) represented the sequence.[20]

Wheelock failed despite his self-promotion. "When Hezekiah Calvin, a Delaware, and one of Wheelock's former schoolmasters to the Iroquois, opted out of the Doctor's 'Design' in 1768, he let it be known that the inmates of Moor's School were not one big happy family." The racism of the school ("the English Boys . . . despise them & treat them as Slaves") was integral to the failure. "Wheelock's cultural and theological assumptions were as ethnocentric and racist as those of his neighbors." Some "gentlemen" confessed, "They could never respect an Indian, Christian or no Christian, so as to put him on a level with white people on any account, especially to eat at the same table—no—not with Mr. [Samson] Ocham himself, be he ever so much a Christian or ever so Learned." (Most governors of Cape Coast Castle excluded Quaque from the white officers' table as well.) Wheelock "frequently referred to his 'Black' children, especially his 'black son,' Samson Occom, and to the 'Black Tribes' on the frontier who need his help." He owned slaves most of his life.[21]

Wheelock shifted his earlier goals as popular support for such "Grand Designs" evaporated. He sent Occom to Britain where he became a celebrity from dark places, preaching "his way across Britain from February 1766 to July 1767," and raised twelve thousand pounds. Some of it was contributed by the Earl of Dartmouth and Thornton. Occom met the king, whom Wheatley would be scheduled to meet in 1773. Lady Huntingdon said she considered Occom "one of the most interesting and extraordinary characters" she had met, and she also donated to his fund.[22]

It was Occom's metropolitan success that allowed Wheelock "to sever all ties with the missionary societies on which he had long depended." Occom's intention had been to raise money for the Indian school, but Wheelock applied it to the founding of the college in Hanover, New Hampshire. He claimed it was "primarily for Indians," because that was what his benefactors believed was their donations' purpose, and Wheelock made it appear that the English youth were merely a secondary addition. He named it after the Earl of Dartmouth, although Dartmouth refused to give it his financial support. Indians were subordinate, attending Moor's Charity School, which had moved to New Hampshire under the shadow of Dartmouth College. "Wheelock proceeded to exhaust his ample treasury—over the protests of his English trustees—on a . . . college that graduated only three Indians in the eighteenth century and eight in the nineteenth." Occom wrote Wheelock, "Your having so many White Scholars and so few or no Indian Scholars, gives me great Discouragement . . . I am very jealous that instead of your Semenary Becoming alma Mater, she will be too alba mater to suckle the Tawnees . . . your present Plan is not calculated to benefit the poor Indians." He continued to preach to Native Americans and Thornton continued to support him.[23]

On February 16, 1771, Occom suggested Wheatley might be sent as "a Female Preacher to Africa." "Please to remember me to Phillis, and the rest of your Servants. Pray madam what harm would it do to send Phillis to her Native Country as a Female Preacher to her kindred, you know Quaker women are alow'd to preach and why not others in an extraordinary Case." He had written the idea on the back of a letter to Susanna Wheatley—Phillis was now seventeen or eighteen, and presumably they had been discussing her future.[24]

Already publishing individual poems, she and Susanna had not found a publisher in Boston for a collection. This was the context for her correspondence with Thornton, initiated by Wheatley, likely in collaboration with Susanna. Whether or not Occom communicated his idea to Thornton about Wheatley's returning to Africa to preach cannot be said. Wheatley wrote, "Hon'd Sir, I rec'd your instructive fav'r of Feb. 29 for which, return you ten thousand thanks. I did not flatter myself with the tho'ts of your honouring me with an Answer to my letter, I thank you for recommending the Bible to be my chief study," so we can see what Thornton must have written her. Her posture is that of one deficient, so far, and in need of such adjuration from this powerful associate of Lady Huntingdon. "O that my eyes were more open'd to see the real worth . . . of the word of truth, my flinty heart soften'd with the grateful dew of divine grace and the stubborn will . . . and the vitiated palate may be corrected to relish heav'nly things." She tells Thornton she has been very sick and is "still very weak & the Physicians, seem to think there is danger of consumption." She hopes "God would be her strength . . . forever," then praises Thornton for his father-like care: "You could not, I am sure have express [*sic*] greater tendencies and affection for me than by being a welwisher to my soul," bearing "some resemblance to the father of spirits and . . . partakers of his divine Nature." She concluded with more deference, "I can't expect you to answer this." Evidently she hoped for his help. Thornton and Lady Huntingdon must have been in touch about this untutored, suppliant African, living with one of their Connexion and in correspondence with Occom.[25]

Wheatley Proves Herself

Lady Huntingdon asked other Bostonian followers about her. In May 1772, one of them, Richard Carey, testified she was "the Negro girl of Mr. Wheatley's by her virtuous Behaviour and conversation in Life, of Divine Grace, of an extraordinary Genius, and in full communion with one of the Churches. . . ." The "family & girl was affected at the kind enquiry your ladyship made after her. . . ."[26]

On February 20, 1773, Susanna Wheatley wrote Lady Huntingdon to report on "the safe arrival of the rev'd Mr. Page," one of Huntingdon's ministers, and gave her "Ladiship" her opinion that Page was "a very serious good man & one who has the interest of the true religion at heart." She had heard on authority that Page preached "the Doctrines of Grace," according to Whitefield's theology, remarking "we have need of such faithful ministers." Susanna welcomed and encouraged Lady Huntingdon's contribution to revivalism in the American colonies. "I sincerely hope that your Ladiship's endeavors for the interest of religion in this part of the World will be crown'd with great success." She expressed her "great astonishment that someone of her Ladiship's situation & distinction in life," a widow and an aristocrat, should with "disinterestedness, unwearied diligence, and delight . . . [spread] the blessed gospel in those corners of the world which still remain in Darkness & the shadow of eternal Death."[27]

Susanna called her "a Mother in Israel," and wrote, "I wish you much of the preference of God to strengthen your heart, and carry your Ladiship thro', with such a great & laudable undertaking." Her vision here of Lady Huntingdon's efforts to extend the gospel to the dark corners of the world matched that of Whitefield's successor as her chaplain, the Rev. Shirley, in his interest in the world Christ had not reached, and the promise in Gronniosaw's conversion.[28]

In her February 1773 letter to the countess, Susanna told her how she could help spread the gospel to New England, in her own, womanly way; she had expected another minister, the Rev. Mr. Mead, and disappointed, assured the countess "that I shall bid him [Page] a hearty welcome to my House as his home, and any other Itinerant Preachers which your Ladiship may please to send this way. I shall think myself highly honour'd in entertaining those who are devoted to the cause of Christ." On March 13, 1773, Lady Huntingdon wrote to send thanks to "Mrs. Wheatley for her hospitality extended to the countess's evangelizing ministers who might travel to Boston; also asks to be remembered to 'your little poetess' . . . Many the Lord keep her heart alive with the fire that never goes out. . . ."[29]

In that February 1773 letter to Lady Huntingdon, Susanna had added, "I have reason to hope that Phillis has chosen the better part," that is, to follow the proper "Doctrines of Grace," "and I have a great deal of comfort in her." This speaks to the kind of relationship Wheatley herself described. "Begging an interest in your Ladiship's prayers" for Phillis and herself, Susanna concluded with deference comparable to that Gronniosaw and Wheatley expressed in their dedication. A postscript reinforced the invitation her letter contained: "When your Ladiship finds any of those gentlemen this way please to direct them to John Wheatley Merchant, in King Street Boston."

The following month, Bernard Page finally arrived. He wrote to reiterate Susanna's solicitation to her Ladyship, in which she was joined by John Wheatley, that "if you will honor them with any of the itinerant Ministers taking up their abode at their house when in Boston," and that they asked him to convey their "interest in your Ladyship's Prayers at the Throne of Grace." Page singled out Susanna "as a real Child of God" so that "a better house in Boston . . . a Gospel Minister can't desire." Page devoted the rest of his letter to Phillis Wheatley. Evidently he had gone to Boston to inspect her because of the questions raised by the publication of sophisticated and, above all, religious poetry published under her name. "I have dined at Mr. Wheatley's and seen Phillis, whose Presence and Conversation demonstrate the written performances with her Signature, to be hers." He conveyed to Lady Huntingdon that "Phillis heartily desires That her Duty together with her Request whether Mr. Whitefield's Elegy hath been only received, might be humbly presented to your Ladyship." Then he returned to the subject of the authenticity of her poetry. "Since I wrote thus far, I have again seen Phillis, who showed me a Letter from a Minister to her and her Answer to the same." This may well have been a letter to Samson Occom, which the introduction to her *Poems* would publicize as an expression of her prodigality, written, John Wheatley's biographical notice of her said, in 1765, when she was eleven.[30]

Page offered the countess the same kind of eyewitness evidence that was elevated in the Anglophone Puritan tradition to which the Huntingdon Connexion was heir, in the context of the new science. "And I myself saw her write several lines and then took the opportunity to watch her narrowly, by which I found she wrote a good & expeditious hand." We can imagine Wheatley herself, conscious of this authority and knowing his purpose, herself expressly desiring *his* patron's patronage, demonstrating what he called "written performance," necessarily self-conscious in a way or ways he was not, implementing a talent he did not have, with further capacities in reserve.[31]

"She frequently made use of a quarto Dictionary," this, too, a deliberate part of her performance, showing Page she could read and knew the alphabet, in case he thought otherwise. He gave his approval, "and well she deserves the use thereof": authoritative whites could withhold that usage from those they judged undeserving. He explained, "For I'll delineate her in a few words: Her aspect, humble serene & graceful; her Thoughts, luminous & sepulchral, ethereal & evangelical and her Performance most excellent, yea almost inimitable. A WONDER of the Age indeed!" The adjectives corresponding to Wheatley's presentation of feature and posture, along with what she said, had specific religious connotations, ones we must assume appealed to Page and Huntingdon, as well as to Susanna Wheatley. We can think of "performance" (which Richard Bushman has described as a general feature of eighteenth-century politeness) in its meaning to Page and other authoritative whites, and to the enslaved female poet herself.[32]

It can be assumed that Page's account of Wheatley's "Thoughts" referred to Wheatley's "Thoughts on the Works of Providence," which she wrote shortly before his visit. Those "several lines" he watched her write in all likelihood were from that poem, which celebrates the Newtonian universe as the Book of Nature, the combined religious and scientific interpretation that Page's eyewitness of the truth also expressed. That she quoted her "Thoughts" is further endorsed by Page's concluding exclamation, "A WONDER of the Age, indeed!," because its third stanza reads:

> Almighty, in what wond'rous works of thine,
> What *Pow'r*, what *Wisdom*, and what *Goodness* shine?
> And are thy wonders, Lord, by men explor'd,
> And yet creating glory unador'd!

Wheatley was very capable of humorous irony; here she could represent this intrusive religio-scientific investigator's encounter with herself, embodying and articulating a power beyond his imagining and, at the same time, supplying him with the word to describe her to the power (next to "the Throne of Grace"), who could advance her towards personal freedom, as well as in publishing her art. Whether or not Wheatley wrote the lines from "Thoughts" for Page, her writings make clear her creation of a poetic *persona* described by Charles Scruggs.[33]

There was another Englishman who sent an eyewitness account of Wheatley's composing to his noble employer. On his appointment in 1772 to Lord North's cabinet as Secretary of State for the Colonies and First Lord of Trade, William Legge, 2nd Earl of Dartmouth, sent Thomas Wooldridge to America to get a first-hand report on the state of the mainland colonies. In November 1772, Wooldridge wrote that, in New York, he had heard of "a very Extraordinary female slave" because she "had made some verses on our mutually Dear deceased friend." This was Whitefield. Dartmouth was "a devoted lay follower and personal friend" of the Countess of Huntingdon, so much so that in 1767, when she was seriously ill, her followers looked to Dartmouth to assume her work. A fellow peer criticized Dartmouth for having "too much humanity, too much religion."[34]

The context for Wooldridge's errand was the worsening relations between metropolitan Britain and her white American colonists. The Treaty of Paris, kicking the French out of North America, loosened the American colonies' military dependence on Britain, which tried to get colonists to pay the debt the war with France had incurred. In 1763, Massachusetts lawyer James Otis challenged Parliamentary power in a pamphlet repeatedly asserting it threatened to make "slaves" of white colonists, but challenged the enslavement of Africans, too, a crucial link as we have seen. The first liberty pole was erected in 1766. The Townshend Acts, the Parliamentary response to colonial assertion, were passed in 1767, and in that same year, some Bostonians were massacred.[35] (Wheatley wrote about one of them, "On the Death of Mr. Snider, Murder'd by Richardson"—"the first martyr for the cause"—a poem she chose not to include in her *Poems* to be published in London.[36]) Dartmouth helped in the Parliamentary repeal of the Stamp Act. In gratitude, Americans sent animals for his private menagerie. American evangelicals were especially pleased with his appointment on Secretary of State for the Colonies because of his relationship with Lady Huntingdon.[37]

Wooldridge had been under the impression that the author of the Whitefield elegy was a fraud, but he was able to report to Dartmouth that "he found by conversing with the African, that she was no Impostor"; he had put her to the test. "I asked if she could write on any Subject; she said Yes; we have just heard of your Lordship's appointment." He continued, "I gave her your name, which she was well acquainted with." "She"—and nowhere does Wooldridge give this "very Extraordinary female slave" a name—"immediately wrote a rough copy of the enclosed [poem] & letter which I promised to convey or deliver." Wooldridge's astonishment was combined with virtual disbelief. "I was astonish'd and could hardly believe my own Eyes." He repeats the proof that she was no impostor. "I was present while she wrote, and can attest that it is her own production." Wheatley knew the importance of the countess to Dartmouth: she "shew'd her letter to Lady Huntingdon, which I dare say, Your Lordship has seen." Wheatley had kept a copy of that October 25, 1770, letter with which she had accompanied her elegy on Whitefield's death.[38]

Wheatley's ability to write poetry spontaneously could be an amusing party trick for whites. In 1774, "Mrs. Dickerson and Mrs. Clymer and Mrs. Ball with some other ladies were so pleased with Phillis and her performances that they bought her books and got her to compose some pieces for them . . . I thought it could be very agreeable." Of course, prodigality alone was provocation to audiences to test, as for example, the child musicians Wolfgang and Nannerl Mozart were tested, "with unknown places to read at sight or improvised on." Moreover, literate young people, like these Boston ladies, engaged in the spontaneous writing of rebuses (riddles in verse) in party-like gatherings of an evening: Wheatley published one in 1773. In her case, however, it was combined with the racially inflected investigatoriness—and her own playing with that.[39]

In his letter to Dartmouth, Wooldridge also enclosed "the account signed by her master of her Importation, Education & these are all wrote in her own hand." Actually signed by the Wheatleys' son, "Nath. I. Wheatley Boston New England Oct. 12th 1772" (two days after Wooldridge witnessed Wheatley writing it), it was a briefer version of the one signed "John Wheatley" and dated "Boston, Nov. 14, 1772," one of those prefatory documents written "for all original editions of the book [*Poems*] except the first English edition." The earlier manuscript version quoted by Wooldridge included the fact that Wheatley, "in 1765, wrote a letter to the rev'd Occom while in England." Again, this referred to the relationship between Wheatley and the Huntingdon Connexion's evangelization of people under the imperial aegis.[40]

A Particular Love of Freedom

In the letter dated October 10, 1772, which accompanied her poem "To the Right Honourable WILLIAM, Earl of DARTMOUTH, His Majesty's Principal Secretary of State for North America, &c.," Wheatley told him that the "Joyful occasion"—the partial repeal of the Townshend Acts which had punished the colonists for their opposition to them—"will I hope Sufficiently apologize for this freedom from an African." This was a loaded phrase; Wheatley knew Dartmouth knew she was a slave, but all the same she, "who with the (now) happy America exults with equal transport, in the view of one of its greatest advocates. Presiding with the Special Tenderness of a Fatherly Heart over that Department."[41]

If Wheatley's terms here resemble those she had addressed to Thornton, her poem to Dartmouth expands on the meanings of equality and freedom, as well as fatherhood:

> Hail, happy day, when, smiling like the morn,
> Fair *Freedom* rose *New England* to adorn:
> The northern clime beneath her genial ray,
> *Dartmouth*, congratulates thy blissful sway:

his more lenient rule,

> With pleasure we behold
> The silken reins and Freedom's charms unfold,

because "she"—Freedom—is now supreme, so "hated faction dies." The poem looked back to the previous years of conflict from the perspective now offered by his appointment.

> No more America in mournful strain
> Of wrongs and grievances complain,

alluding to the train of protests between 1764 and 1770, including the "Declaration of Rights and Grievances," adopted by the Stamp Act Congress in 1765.

> No longer shalt thou dread the iron chain,
> Which wanton *Tyranny* with lawless hand
> Had made, and with it meant to t'enslave the land.

This was to reproduce the same melodramatic and overdetermined characterization by American rebels that Wheatley assumed in her poem "To the King's Most Excellent Majesty," as well as in "America," and illustrated by James Otis, for one, pointing out the inconsistency in American slaveholders' opposition to their own purported enslavement.

She then tells Dartmouth that this hyperbolic metaphor used by white, American proto-revolutionaries has particular meaning for her:

> Should you, my lord, while you peruse my song,
> Wonder from whence my love of *Freedom* sprung,
> Whence flow these wishes for the common good,
> By feeling hearts alone best understood,
> I, young in life, by seeming cruel fate
> Was snatch'd from *Afric's* fancied happy seat;
> What pangs excruciating must molest,
> What sorrows labour in my parent's breast?
> Steel'd was that soul and by no misery mov'd
> That from a father seiz'd his babe belov'd.

This dramatically reverses the perspective on her enslavement presented in "On being brought from AFRICA to AMERICA." It may be that Wheatley maintains that poem's religious values with the words "seeming" and "fancied" (she erased that qualification in a later poem's description of Africa), but now, uniting the sensibilities of "feeling hearts" with the inspiration of the American Revolution's opposition to slavery, Wheatley directly admits the terrible pain to herself and her parent caused by being torn from him, which elsewhere she has poetized in sympathy for whites' loss of a beloved child to death. Sondra

O'Neale writes, "There are perhaps no more moving lines in the entire Wheatley canon," and Helen M. Burke notes that this is "the most self-revelatory passage in her writing."[42]

In direct contrast to the person who had torn the child from her parent in Africa, from her father there, Dartmouth has a "Special tenderness," Wheatley tells him in her letter, "a feeling heart," along with the evangelical Christianity he shares with her. He is capable of understanding her love of freedom, rooted in her experience of being torn from her actual father in being enslaved.

She ends this passage in the poem with exquisite ambiguity.

> Such, such my case. And can I then but pray
> Others may never feel tyrannic sway?

Her enslavement was and is still "the case," not merely the hyperbolic apprehension by whites (many of whom were slaveholders), but all other enslaved Africans and African Americans in Britain's transatlantic colonies.

Wheatley's words to Dartmouth anticipated a twentieth-century poem by Langston Hughes: words like freedom and liberty

> almost make me cry
> If you had known what I knew
> You would know why.
> [These lines are from "Words Like Freedom."]

The political significance of Wheatley's poem to Dartmouth was emphasized by its publication in the New York Journal on June 3, 1773, while Wheatley was in England, meeting with him. It was accompanied by a paraphrase of Wooldridge's letter to him, describing how he had her prove she was no impostor, an issue we see her poem addressed.[43]

Lady Huntingdon decided to serve as the untutored African slave's patron for the publication of Wheatley's poems in book form. A week before Wheatley left for London, Susanna wrote Lady Huntingdon. Her letter began with news of the Connexion's ministers' comings and goings: "Mr. Carey tells me that the Rev'd Mr. Piercy has settled the affairs in Georgia," referring to the Orphanage, its slaves and the large acreage Whitefield had left Lady Huntingdon. "He is to come this way and I am almost impatient for his coming, for I hear he is an excellent Preacher, and we want some Whitefield here."[44]

The main subject was Wheatley's crossing the Atlantic to London. David Grimsted suggests that one purpose was to "promote the evangelical-reform Anglo-American alliance."[45] Susanna presented a mixture of reasons, the first that Phillis was "in a poor State of Health, the Physicians advis[d] . . . the Sea Air," and "as my Son is coming to England upon Som Business and as so good an opportunity presented I tho't it my duty to send her." Susanna refers to Lady Huntingdon's patronage and Wheatley's chief purpose, the publication of her book, "& as your Ladiship has condescended to take so much notice of my Dear Phillis as to permit her Book to be Dedicated to you, and desiring her Picture in the Frontispiece; I flatter'd my Self that your good advice and Counsel will not be wanting. I tell Phillis to act wholly under the direction of your Ladiship." We can imagine Wheatley's own feelings about this transatlantic voyage, its purpose, the publication of her poems, fruit of her coming to terms with America and mastering the writing of poetry in English, in utter contrast to her first, traumatic, transatlantic voyage as a child.

Susanna was concerned about the circumstances of a young, female subordinate in the, at best, more complex, at worst, more dangerous social conditions of London. Lady Huntingdon's "direction" included what the young female slave poet should wear: Susanna added in her letter to her, "I did not think it worth while nor did the time permit to fit her out with cloaths: but I have given her money to Buy what you think proper for her, I like She should be dress'd plain." The plainness, along with Wheatley's moral conduct, would serve the exemplary, evangelical purpose of her trip, in contrast to the stereotype of the nature of a "black wench," which we shall see it provoked. Susanna followed her expression of concern over Wheatley's clothing with: "Must beg the favour of your Ladiship to advise my son to Some Christian House for Phillis to board at." This was to be Thornton's. She concluded, "And as you are so dispose'd to promote the good of souls I hope you will not be wanting in your advice to my Dear Son."[46]

There is a record of how Lady Huntingdon first responded to Wheatley's assemblage of poems, a conversation with its publisher reported in a letter from Robert Calef to Susanna Wheatley. Calef captained the *London Packet,* the ship with which John Wheatley "conducted most of his transatlantic and coastal trade." Calef had brought the manuscript of Wheatley's poems to London, arriving there the December preceding Wheatley's journey. He wrote Susanna to describe the countess's reception of them from Archibald Bell, the London bookseller specializing in evangelical publications, to whom Calef had delivered the manuscript. (We recall Wheatley's ensuing book was subtitled *On Various Subjects, Religious and Moral.*) Bell told Calef, "He had waited on the Countess of Huntingdon with the Poems who was greatly pleas'd with them, and pray'd him to read them: and often would break in upon him and say, 'Is not this, or that very fine? Do read another,' and question'd him much, whether she was *real,* without a deception." Bell "convinced her," Susanna wrote, "by bringing my name in question," that is, to answer the countess's doubts. Wheatley sent Occom Captain Calef's account of Bell's meeting with Lady Huntingdon.[47]

Calef added, still reporting on what Bell had told him, that "I had like to forget to mention to you, she is fond of having the book dedicated to her, but one thing she desir'd which she said she hardly thought would be denied her, that was, to have Phillis's picture in the frontispiece. So that if you would get it done, it can be engraved here. I do imagine it can be easily done, and think it would contribute greatly to the sale of the book." In short, the frontispiece was to be yet another attestation that the author was really "a Negro girl," testifying, too, to the potential in converting Africans.

In fact, the original frontispiece was made by Scipio Moorehead, an African owned by the Rev. John Moorehead, one of the reverends whose names were included in the *Poems* to attest to their authenticity.[48] If it shows her to be African, in no sense is it a racist stereotype: it shows her at her writing desk, quill in hand, eyes raised apparently to inspiration, perhaps to God. Only the words added to frame the picture tell of her color and formal subordination: "Phillis Wheatley, Negro Servant to Mr. John Wheatley, of Boston," and she is dressed as a maidservant. We can see the picture itself as the expression of the painter Scipio's respect for her art, that of an African, and his equivalent of her expression of respect for him in "To S.M. a Young African Painter," discussed in the next chapter.

The Publication of Wheatley's *Poems on Various Subjects, Religious and Moral*

Framing Wheatley's Book

Archibald Bell implemented the "prepublication marketing" of Wheatley's *Poems* in London newspapers in April and May 1773, before she sailed from Boston. Her presence was intended to accompany the book's publication there. The marketing included those three documents to be printed in most of her *Poems*' first editions, following the Dedication to the Countess of Huntingdon quoted earlier. Then came a "PREFACE" by Wheatley. According to convention, she said that her "Poems were written originally for the Amusement of the Author, as they were the Products of her leisure Moments." This speaks to the publisher's identification on the title page as "NEGRO SERVANT to Mr. JOHN WHEATLEY of BOSTON," and the latter's endorsement of her. Slaves could be called servants; Wheatley, in the book so far, was not called a slave. She had time to herself, with the power to write and to publish or not. "She had no Intention ever to have published them; it was at the Importunity of many of her best, and most generous Friends; to whom she considers herself, as under the greatest Obligations." These must have included the Wheatleys, Susanna above all. Then there were the attestations to her authenticity, already an issue for those visitors to the Wheatleys' home, including agents of Huntingdon and Dartmouth. It is evident that Wheatley herself was determined to publish her poems in book form.[1]

Wheatley's "Preface" continued, "As her Attempts in Poetry are now sent into the World, it is hoped the Critic will not severely censure their Defects; and we presume they have too much Merit too be cast aside with Contempt, as worthless, and trifling Effusions." They are, in Wheatley's own view, meritorious. The critic's severity should be tempered anyway, by her book's dedication to the Countess of Huntingdon, signifying her endorsement. "As to the Disadvantages she has labored under, with Regard to Learning, nothing needs to be offered, as her Master's Letter in the following Page will sufficiently show the Difficulties in this Respect she has had to encounter."[2] Of course, in Bell's and other publicists' presentation of her, Wheatley was an "unassisted genius," untutored in her own ambiguous word, "genius" there perhaps meaning "natural capacity" or "special endowment," rather than the emerging meaning of exalted, unique power.[3]

The next introductory document is headed "a Copy of a LETTER sent by the Author's Master to the Publisher," although Carretta writes, "It was actually dictated by Nathaniel, not John, to Phillis," and we can surmise her input. "Phillis was brought from *Africa* to *America* in the Year 1761, between Seven and Eight Years of Age." She was a child and spoke no English: "Without any Assistance from School Education, and by only what she was taught in the Family, she in sixteen months Time from her Arrival"—so she was less than nine—"attained the English Language to which she was an utter stranger before." Wheatley used the same metaphor a year later, in explaining why she refused to return to Africa to help Christianize "the Natives," "being an utter stranger to the language of Anamaboe." Its point was the same as Bell's: she was a natural genius, a prodigy, but a type recognizable in the Anglophone literary world. The letter continued, "[She learned the English language] to such a Degree as to read any, the most difficult Part of the Sacred Writings, to the great Astonishment of all who heard her." That they heard her meant she read such Biblical passages aloud to them, in scenes perhaps comparable to her demonstration of her literary abilities to the emissaries of Lady Huntingdon and Lord Dartmouth, whose "astonishment," so frequently witnessed by Wheatley, she knew expressed racist and sexist expectations of a young, black female. Did she initiate her first reading aloud?

The letter further explains the prodigy to the chiefly white, astonished audience: "As to her WRITING, her own curiosity led her to it; and this she learnt in so short a time that in the year 1765"—her readers can reckon she was then fifteen—"she wrote a letter to the Rev. Mr. Occom, the *Indian* Minister, while in *England*." As noted, Occom had preceded her there, connecting up with Lady Huntingdon and

John Thornton, as well as the Earl of Dartmouth. Occom's "sincerity and eloquence impressed English crowds drawn by curiosity to see an American native preach Christianity." While there, a mezzotint was made of him, resembling the one Lady Huntingdon wanted made of Wheatley, although he wore clerical garb and was seated by a wall on which hung an arrow. Alan Taylor remarks that Occom's popularity and the print's publication "attests to the fascination of pious Anglo-Americans with the prospects of converting natives to their culture." This was the prospect raised by the Huntingdon Connexion's sponsorship of Gronniosaw's *Narrative*. The reference to Occom published in the front matter of Wheatley's *Poems* was to remind readers of his impact and significance.[4]

This prefatory letter concluded, "She has a great Inclination to learn the Latin Tongue, and has made some Progress in it," another mark of prodigality and of her aspiration to higher reaches of literary culture, but her last sentence reminds its reader that she is in fact a slave, brought from Africa. "This Relation is given by her Master, who bought her, and with whom she now lives, JOHN WHEATLEY."

The front matter of the book included a third document. Because "Numbers would be ready to suspect they were not really the writings of PHILLIS," her publisher "has procured the following Attestation from the most respectable Characters in Boston, so that none might have least ground for disputing their Original." This time, in contrast to the *Proposals* advertised in Boston in 1772, when the authentication had been left vague ("the best judges"), eighteen names were specified: "We whose Names are under-written, do assure the World, that the POEMS specified in the following Page" (here a note added that this alluded "to the Contents of the Manuscript Copy, which are wrote at the back of the . . . Attestation"), "as we verily believe were written by PHILLIS, a young Negro Girl, who was but a few Years hence, brought an uncultivated Barbarian from *Africa*, and has ever since been, and now is, under the Disadvantage of serving as a Slave in a Family in this Town." It resembles part of the Rev. Shirley's introduction of Gronniosaw—"through born under every outward Disadvantage, and in regions of Grossest Darkness, and ignorance," Wheatley's manuscript of poems "has been examined by some of the best judges, and is thought qualified to write them." One of the signatories was

Richard Carey, who had examined Wheatley and her poems on Lady Huntingdon's behalf, reinforcing the evidence of her influence in getting the Christian, African girl's poems published, once their authenticity was beyond doubt. One can imagine that Bell wrote this in consultation with Lady Huntingdon and/or the Rev. Shirley, who had declared in his preface to Gronniosaw's *Narrative* that "his character can be well attested . . . by many creditable Persons in London and other Places."[5]

Henry Louis Gates, Jr., imagines this document as the result of a formal "trial of Wheatley" before "an astonishingly influential group of the colony's citizens" (each identified by Gates), assembled to "interrogate" the young African slave, to "determine whether [she] was truly the author of the poems she claimed to have written. These gentlemen were relatives and rivals, friends and foes." Most saliently they were divided over resistance to Britain. But this was a moment for the expression of common ground, publicly stating a degree of respect for African achievement, which could be seen as a counter to metropolitan Britain's claims to moral superiority in freeing James Somerset the year before, characterizing American colonials as barbarians with their slave culture.[6]

African-British writer and composer Ignatius Sancho commented on the names of this attestation. This was in a letter dated January 27, 1778, to an American Quaker, probably Philadelphian Jabez Fisher, thanking him for some antislavery books, and expressing his horror for slavery and the slave trade. The books must have included Wheatley's *Poems*, which he praised: they "do credit to human nature—and put art—merely as art—to the blush."[7] "Human" here he uses inclusively, as did those African American petitioners in 1773, a value Wheatley expressed in her poems on Wheatfield and the University of Cambridge. Sancho calls Wheatley a "Genius" in the same paragraph, so his praise of her poems also resembled Benjamin Rush's. That it was "Genius in bondage" meant it was an unnatural trammeling of a transcendent human power that should be free.

Sancho's letter had turned to the names preceding Wheatley's *Poems*: "That list of splendid—titled—learned names, in confirmation of her being the real authoress—alas! should show how very poor the acquisition of wealth and knowledge are—without generosity—feeling—and humanity." These were the qualities of sensibility to which abolitionists appealed and which Sancho's letters displayed throughout. One of them would draw the celebrity novelist Lawrence Sterne into antislavery.[8] Sancho continued, "These good great folks—all know—and perhaps admired—nay, praised Genius in Bondage—and then, like the priests and the Levites in sacred writ, passed by—not one good Samaritan amongst them." The allusion was not only to Luke 10:30–37 but also to one of Sterne's famous sermons on that parable, "Philanthropy recommended" describing a "settled principle of humanity."[9]

Most of these "Boston notables . . . owned black servants or slaves," notes William H. Robinson, Helen M. Burke adding that this and the other prefatory documents show Wheatley "existed as a speaking subject only within the boundaries of a hegemonic culture." She and other scholars have described the challenges to that culture that Wheatley made through her poetry and letters, breaking and entering those boundaries.[10]

At the same time, writers and preachers on this list, together with other New England clergy, provided Wheatley with some of the intellectual resources on which she could draw. James Levernier writes, "She could hardly have escaped the thorough immersion in Enlightenment theological, philosophical, and political theories on the 'natural rights' of human beings to liberty and justice."[11]

The attestation's first signer was the loyalist "His Excel'ency, THOMAS HUTCHINSON, GOVERNOR," of course, deeply politically connected with the metropolitan officials Wheatley was to meet in London, including one of Massachusetts's chief agents there, Israel Mauduit. Hutchinson, those agents, and other governmental officials were adamantly opposed to the "liberty" Wheatley celebrated in "America." The second signer, also opposed, was Hutchinson's brother-in-law "the Hon. ANDREW OLIVER, Lieutenant Governor." The *Poems* included Wheatley's "To His Honour the Lieutenant-Governor, on the Death of his Lady, March 24, 1773." As usual, Wheatley consoled the bereaved:

> But cease they strife with *Death*, fond *Nature*, cease;
> He leads the *virtuous* to the realms of peace;
> His to conduct to the immortal plains,
> Where heav'n's Supreme in bliss and glory reigns.

The poet assures the Lieutenant Governor, "illustrious Sir," that his "beauteous spouse" sits in heaven, enjoying the rewards of virtue. Wheatley also reminds the reader that she is African:

> Nor canst thou, Oliver, assent refuse
> To heav'nly tidings from the *Afric* muse,

apprehending his resistance to or dismissal of her poem because she is African, because she is black. Her artistic gift authorizes her to transmit consolation from a power superior to his. Here, as elsewhere, her religious message is conveyed in sentimental terms.

> As soon may change thy laws eternal fate,
> As the saint miss the glories I relate;
> Or her *Benevolence* forgotten lie,
> Which wip'd the trickl'ing tear from Mis'r'y's eye.

And Wheatley refers to further, devastating, family loss and Mrs. Oliver's Christian resignation:

> Whene'er the adverse winds were known to blow,
> When loss * ensu'd and woe to woe,
> Calm and serene beneath her father's hand
> She sat resign'd to the divine command.

The poet's asterisk referred the reader to a footnote: "Three amiable Daughters who died when just arrived to Woman's Estate." His wife's resignation was a lesson the African muse teaches the Lieutenant Governor:

> No longer then, great Sir, her death deplore,
> And let us hear the mournful sign no more.

She tells him:

> Nor let thy wishes be to earth confin'd,
> But soaring high pursue th' unbodied mind.

However, she concludes by reminding him of her temerity, asking Oliver to

> Forgive the muse, for give th' advent' rous lays,
> That fain thy soul to heav'nly scenes would raise.[12]

After those of the Governor and Lieutenant Governor, the names of the other attestators were set out in two columns, on the left, those "Hons," of the Governor's Council, but including John Hancock, who was at daggers drawn with Hutchinson, and declined to serve. James Bowdoin was also an opponent of Hutchinson but a rival of Hancock. In the same column were the names of Joseph Green, a prominent and aged Boston literary figure; a Tory; and Richard Carey, Lady Huntingdon's emissary.

The right column was made up of ministers' names, along with that of John Wheatley, headed by Charles Chauncy, "venerable pastor of the Boston First Church," and opponent of the slave trade, although as a young man he had attacked revivalism "because it allowed women and girls; yea Negroes—to do the business of preachers." Second on this list was Matthew Byles, a probable tutor of Wheatley, himself a distinguished poet and correspondent of Alexander Pope, whom Wheatley revered. Then came Samuel Cooper, who had baptized Wheatley and whose encouragement she acknowledged in her poem on his death. His views illustrate the clerical sympathy for the revolution described by Levernier, who quotes his 1776 election sermon: "All Men are entitled to . . . the Rights that belong to human Nature." His congregants included Hancock, as well as John and Samuel Adams and Joseph Warren. Another signer was the "Rev. Ed. Pemberton," an apparent typo for "Eb," because Ebeneezer Pemberton "appended Wheatley's poem to his published sermon [and] was courier for some of the letters from Wheatley to [Obour] Tanner and [the Rev. Samuel] Hopkins." A copy of Pemberton's elegy-sermon on Whitefield was reprinted with Wheatley's elegy at the time of his death; later, Pemberton would help in the distribution and sale of Wheatley's *Poems*. A fifth minister was John Moorhead, an Irish immigrant and the first pastor of the Federal Street Presbyterian Church, who was with Occom, one of Susanna's best friends in Boston. He owned Scipio Moorehead.[13]

Crossing the Atlantic Again

Three days after Susanna's letter to the countess about Wheatley's coming to England and five days before she sailed, Carey also wrote Lady Huntingdon about the trip, his letter to be delivered to her in person by Wheatley. We saw the year before that Carey had reported Wheatley's "virtuous behavior and Conversation," and testified to her "piety." Now his May 1773 letter identified her as "Phillis the Christian Poetess, whose Behaviour in England I wish may be as exemplary as it has been in Boston." The poem Wheatley placed second in her collection after a tribute to her patron was "On Virtue," calling on that "queen" who was leading "chastity alone" to "attend me, thro' my youthful years!" The letter Wheatley carried declared that the Christian poetess was "remarkable for her Humility and spiritual mindedness." In light of his having read at least some of the poems—with their references to politics, their complex presentation of Africanness, their variety and freedom, all despite their being carefully edited and shaped for Wheatley's metropolitan and religious audiences—Carey added, "As she grows older and had more experience I doubt not her writings will run more in Evangelical strain. I think your Ladyship will be pleased with her."[14]

Wheatley's departure was announced in at least eight newspapers in Massachusetts, Connecticut, Rhode Island, Pennsylvania, and New York, some picking up their wording from others. The first announcement in the *Massachusetts Gazette and Boston Weekly News Letter* (May 3, 1773), the Saturday before the scheduled departure of "London, Capt. Calef," listed among the passengers "Mr. Nathaniel Wheatley, Merchant; also Phillis, servant to Mr. Wheatley, the extraordinary Negro poet, at the invitation of the Countess of Huntingdon." So the extraordinariness of Wheatley as a "Negro poet" was coupled with her relationship with the metropolitan aristocrat, known to many New Englanders for her evangelical leadership. A week later, however, the same paper declared that the inclusion of the phrase "at the invitation of the Countess of Huntingdon" "was a mistake." Of course she had already been publicly identified with the countess at Wheatley's and colonial newspapers' initiatives, but not with her permission. I have referred to her touchiness in this, and her American agents were on the job.[15]

Four of the announcements were accompanied by Wheatley's poem "Farewell to America/To Mrs. S-W." The *Massachusetts Gazette and Boston Post Boy* introduced the poem— "The following lines, wrote by Phillis (Mr. Wheatley's Negro girl) just before she sailed for England, we have been desired to publish: 'To the Empire of AMERICA beneath the Western Hemisphere'"—as did two of the other American printings, a title omitted in its London printings. It was published separately in the *London Chronicle* (July 1–3, 1773), as well as towards the end of Wheatley's book. The phrase "we have been desired to publish" in the American printings suggests to Julian Mason that "clearly it was part of a publicity campaign in anticipation of Phillis's book, which finally was published there in early September, after she was back in Boston." The version published in the book was changed by the poet on board the "London Packet" from its continuous arrangement to "the less classical four line stanza." There were some changes in wording, too.[16]

Wheatley's "Farewell to America" could have given Nisbet pause in his denial that Africans ever said "farewell." Wheatley's was to her mistress, the woman she came to see as her virtual mother. It began by reiterating what Susanna Wheatley had written Lady Huntingdon (and Phillis, too, in her own letter to her), that she voyaged to England for her health, concluding it in pastoral and sentimental terms, the latter particularly appropriate given the combination of pain and pleasure in leaving someone whom one loved. On her deathbed the following year, Susanna's last words were "farewell, farewell," having prayed for an "easy and quick passage." Partings, on the dock especially, potentiated finality more in those days. If Wheatley's expression of the "dominant theme of loss" was profoundly inflected by her childhood trauma, it can be imagined that her saying farewell to her adoptive mother to recross the Atlantic was similarly charged.[17]

Having bid adieu to New England's smiling, springtime meads in her first stanza, Wheatley continues:

> In vain for me the flow'rets rise,
>   And boast their gaudy pride,
> While here beneath the northern skies
>   I mourn for health deny'd

Her necessary leaving brings pain to the poem's addressee:

> SUSANNA mourns nor can I bear
>> To see the crystal show'r,
> Or mark the tender falling tear
>> At sad departure's hour;

Wheatley responds with expressions of the pain her mistress's causes her:

> Nor unregarding, lo! I see
>> Thy soul with grief oppress't:
> But let no sighs, no groans for me,
>> Steal from her pensive breast.

The poet cannot bear to see Susanna's tears, but here she wishes to restrain her own sighs because they will add to Susanna's pain. The poet cheers up with the prospect of "Health . . . celestial Dame!" delighting her soul. As yet veiled and distant, the word "charms" perhaps invokes the magnetism of the metropolis for so many in Britain and her colonies, which held particular attraction for young women, in shopping, fashions, and entertainment, in the new heterosocial opportunities that worried Wheatley's sponsors.[18]

> For thee, *Britannia*, I resign
>> *New England's* smiling fields;
> To view again her charms divine
>> What joy the prospect yields!

In the first, American version, this stanza had expressed Wheatley's pain right before she left, rather than the anticipation of return:

> For thee Britannia, I resign
>> *New England's* smiling Face,
> To view again her Charms divine,
>> One short reluctant Space!

This illustrated the poet's meticulousness in registering the immediate feelings, expressing the sensibility that was characteristic of her poetry.

> But thou Temptation, hence away,
>> With all thy hated Train
> Of Ills,—nor tempt my Mind astray
>> From Virtue's sacred Strain.

Is the temptation giving in to reluctance, dwelling on New England's charms and having to give them up, yearning to be restored to Susanna's "Armes"? Or are the "Charms" of London its temptation?

> Most happy: who with Sword and Shield
>> Is screen'd from dire Alarms,
> And fell *Temptations* on the Field
>> Of fatal Pow'r disarms!

The final stanza, published in the *Massachusetts Gazette and Boston Post Boy* but omitted from *Poems*, adds to the possibilities: the poet is tempted to withhold compassion from her mistress,

> But cease thy Lays, my Lute forbear;
>> Nor frown, my gentle Muse
> To see the secret, falling Tear,
>> Nor pitying look refuse.

This, then, elaborates the lines

> Ah! Curb the rising Groan from me,
>> Nor Sighs disturb thy Breast!

because the poet's expressions of pain at parting further upset Susanna, a bind of the mutuality idealized by cultivators of sensibility.[19]

For Vincent Carretta, however, the "Temptation" was that offered Wheatley by the Mansfield decision once she reached London, where "she will face the opportunity to resurrect herself from the social death of slavery."[20] One might well say she had passed through the social death of enslavement in her African capture and the Middle Passage, in her own view to be resurrected by Christianity, under the care of a second mother. Carretta quotes reports of the Mansfield decision in the 1772 Boston newspapers familiar to Wheatley, including the *Gazette*.[21] She might have had that option of running away in mind. Other possibilities can be imagined, leaving aside the poet's feelings in saying farewell to Susanna. Wheatley was intent on getting her poems published in book form, able to capitalize on Huntingdon's patronage, surely thinking of the meaning for the sense of self she had perforce remade. While Carretta is likely right in suggesting Wheatley was conscious of Britain's identification with the Mansfield decision, this poem more convincingly invokes its own, sentimental subject. Wheatley's hopes were combined with her reluctance at leaving her virtual mother, to cross the Atlantic again, although this time able to return. In any case, the voyages to England and home resulted in Wheatley being freed.

Wheatley in London

Wheatley had hoped to meet her patron in London: she wrote her on June 27, 1773, "to acquaint your Ladiship of my safe arrival in London after a fine passage of 5 weeks in the Ship London with my young master," Nathaniel Wheatley. She added to this, "(advised by my physician for my Health)," repeating Susanna's nominal explanation for the voyage, and it seems deferential to the propriety of not mentioning its chief purpose directly to her aristocratic patron. She continued, "Have Brought a letter from Richd. Carey Esqr." She was, she told the countess, "Disappointed by your absence, of the Honour of waiting on your Ladyship with it." Lady Huntingdon had gone to her missionary school in Wales. "I would have inclosed it but was doubtful of the Safety of the conveyance."[22]

Wheatley added, "Should think my self very happy in seeing your Ladyship, and if you was so desirous of the Image of the Author as to propose it for a Frontispiece, I flatter myself that you would accept the Reality." This referred to what Captain Calef had reported of Bell's conversation with Lady Huntingdon, charged therefore with Wheatley's awareness of the countess's doubts as to the authenticity of an African girl writing poetry.

Wheatley concluded by telling the countess of her gratitude, admiration, and dependence, also in terms resembling those her mistress had expressed, "thanking your Ladyship for permitting the dedication of my poems to you; and am not insinsible that under the patronage of your Ladyship, not more eminent in the Station of Life than in your exemplary piety and virtues." She follows that praise with self-deprecation: "My feeble efforts will be shielded from the severe trials of unpitying Criticism and being encourag'd by your Ladyship's Indulgence, I more feebly resign to the world these Juvenile productions, and am Madam with greatest Humility, your Dutiful Huml Sev't, Phillis Wheatley."[23]

Her patron had left London before Wheatley arrived but, in addition to knowing she was to stay with Thornton, Lady Huntingdon must have arranged for Wheatley to meet, as she recorded, "Lady Cavendish and Lady Carteret Webb," sisters, and close friends of the countess, active in her Connexion. Wheatley lists her meeting them and others in London in a letter she wrote "Col. David Worcester" (David Wooster) the month after her return from London. Mukhtar Ali Isani judges it to be "the most notable item in her extant correspondence," describing this "climactic year of her literary career," and illustrating that Wheatley was, at nineteen, "an ambitious and worldly-wise woman. . . . capable of unabashedly representing her own interests."[24]

She would also have to resist the pressure later brought on her by John Thornton. His had been the "Christian home" where she stayed for some of her time in London, to satisfy the concern for the young woman's morals that Susanna and Carey had expressed, sharing that with both Lady Huntingdon and Thornton himself. Given Thornton's habit of "pious pontification" and the nature of their correspondence, it is possible that their conversations were one-sided and condescendingly religious, although Wheatley showed herself fully capable of self-assertiveness, with him in particular.[25]

She did not mention her stay with him specifically in her letter to Wooster, telling him, "I was receiv'd in England with so much kindness Complaisance and so many marks of esteem and real Friendship as astonishes me in the reflection for I was no more than 6 weeks there." Because of her poem to him, and her connection with Lady Huntingdon, she "was introduced to Lord Dartmouth and had near half an hour's

conversation with his Lordship with whom was Alderman Kirkman."
This must have been at Dartmouth's London house. (Kirkman was a city
merchant, elected Sheriff of London in 1766, married to the daughter
of the Governor of the Bank of England, and to be elected MP for the
City in 1780.) Most likely their half an hour's conversation referred to
the countess, to their common ground in religion, and perhaps to the
reconciliation between Americans and the British government, which
her poem to him expressed. With that in mind Wheatley omitted the
title "To the Empire of AMERICA" and the poem "America" from the
manuscript to be published in London. Similarly, she omitted poems
identifying herself with the first armed resistance to Britain in 1770, including "On the Death of Mr. Snider, Murder'd by Richardson," Snider
being a lad Wheatley's poem called "the first martyr for the common
good." He was shot by "an informer on Americans' circumventing British taxation," whom Wheatley calls a "Tory chief." She also omitted the
poem, now lost, on the Boston Massacre, "on the Affray in King Street,
on the Evening of the 5th of March."[26]

Conversely, she chose to include her previously unpublished "To the
King's MOST Excellent Majesty, 1768," and placed it fourth:

> Your subjects hope, dread Sire—
> The crown upon your brows may flourish long,
> O may your sceptre num'rous nations sway,
> And all with love and readiness obey!

While those "nations" included Britain's recent conquests, Wheatley's
second stanza brings the American mainland colonies particularly to
mind:

> But how shall we the *British* King reward!
> Rule thou in peace, our father, and our lord!
> Midst the remembrance of the favours past,
> The meanest peasants most admire the last.

The "last favor" meant the repeal of the Stamp Act, as we saw, but her
poem's publication in Britain meant readers could appreciate it as a conciliatory expression of gratitude, of deferential monarchism:

> May *George*, belov'd all the nations round,
> Live with heav'ns choicest blessings crown'd!

But the last two couplets can be read as at least ambiguous, at most, admonitory:

> Great God, direct, and guard him from on high,
> And from his head let ev'ry evil fly!

"Ev'ry evil" can be read vaguely, but in light of the reference to the repeal of the Stamp Act (along with the passage of the Declaratory Act), it could be seen to refer to the imposition of arbitrary, even tyrannical laws on his American colonies:

> And may each clime with equal gladness see
> A monarch's smile can set his subjects free!

Most apparently that would be freedom from those laws white Americans characterized as threatening enslavement but, as her poem to Dartmouth makes plain, she has enslavement of Africans in mind, too. This would also resonate differently in post-Mansfield Britain, especially in antislavery circles. The two poems go together; the name of Dartmouth's new post is significantly given in the poem's title, "His Majesty's Principal Secretary of State for the Colonies." Wheatley added "1768" to the title "To the King," backdating her loyalty, and obliquely replacing "America," which she had written in that year.[27]

In her letter to Wooster, Wheatley separated her account of that conversational meeting with Dartmouth from her later writing that "the Earl of Dartmouth made me a gift of five guineas," so she could purchase "the whole of Mr. Pope's Works, as the best he could recommend to my perusal, tis I did." It is possible that they met again and Dartmouth's gift reflected that Wheatley had told him of her admiration of Pope during their earlier conversation. She said she "got" the Pope, together with "Hudibras, Don Quixot, & Gay's Fables." "Quixot" was *The History and Adventures of the Renowned Don Quixote*, in four volumes (London: W. Strahan and F. Rivington, 1770). On the fly leaf of volume one was inscribed, "To Phillis Wheatley by the Earl of Dartmouth, London, July 1773." She added, "Was presented with a Folio Edition of Milton's Paradise Lost, printed on a Silver Type (so call'd for its elegance, I suppose) by Mr. Brook Watson Mercht, whose Coat of Arms is prefix'd." He was a baronet, and like Dartmouth, was believed to be sympathetic to Americans, presumably why Wheatley was formally acknowledged in this way, although he was in America when Wheatley was in London. Watson, born in England in 1735, went to live with his uncle in Boston as a child and worked for him as a sailor (he lost a leg to a shark in Havana Harbor—an episode later painted by John Singleton Copley). He was a commissary in the British army in the war with the French in Canada, thereafter returning to London, making his fortune as a transatlantic merchant between London and Boston (and Montreal), combining private and governmental business. He travelled to New York and Boston prior to the outbreak of the revolution. He professed to be a Whig, sympathetic to the revolutionaries, but in fact, he "ingratiated himself with many leading Americans, obtained as much information on their designs as he could, and transmitted it to his chosen masters." He was in touch with General Thomas Gage, commander of the British troops who perpetrated the Boston Massacre.[28]

So Wheatley hid her sympathy for its victims, while Watson's connection with Gage was not known, each at that point representing the reconciliation that her poems (including the one addressed to Dartmouth) nominally expressed, as did the list of conflicted attestators. But Dartmouth believed fundamentally in Parliamentary supremacy; he had coupled his repeal of the Stamp Act with his advocacy of the Declaratory Act. Two days after Wheatley had sailed from Boston, Parliament passed the Tea Act, provoking the famous political frolic of December 16, 1773, when white Bostonian men, dressed as Mohawks, threw tea into Boston Harbor, the assertion of liberty for themselves. And the year after Wheatley had her conversation with him in London, when he faced rebellious colonies' attempts to curtail the slave trade, Dartmouth asserted, "We cannot allow the colonies to check or discourage in any degree a traffic so beneficial to the nation."[29]

Among other London contacts Wheatley listed to Wooster was a dissenting minister who had also written a poem on the death of Whitefield. Another was Joshua Reynold's sister. Wheatley was flattered that Lord Lincoln (Sir Henry Clinton the Elder, an American-born general with service in America) visited "me in my own Lodgings," bringing with him "the famous Dr. Solander who accompan'd Mr. Banks in his late expedition round the world."[30] Perhaps the rationale for Lincoln's coming to see Wheatley was his Americanness, but the scientists? David Solander, a Swedish disciple of Linnaeus, had joined English naturalist Joseph Banks on Cook's first voyage, becoming Banks's secretary on their return. While they were principally botanists, one cannot help suspecting they shared that orientation towards Africanness expressed by other gentlemen scientists. Wheatley met two more of them, Israel Mauduit and Benjamin Franklin, each of whom she identified as "FRS," that is, a Fellow of the Royal Society. Franklin told a Boston correspondent, "Upon your recommendation I went to see the Black Poetess and offer'd her any Services I could do her."[31]

Wheatley also told Wooster she had met "Greenville Sharp Esqr." Inspired by his correspondent, Benezet, Granville Sharp was the leading British opponent of slavery, and supporter of Somerset in organizing his *habeas corpus* case that Mansfield had recently judged in Somerset's favor. Sharp was, with Thornton and Dartmouth, "close to the Countess," sharing "her evangelical and reform enthusiasm," although he was opposed to Huntingdon and Dartmouth's view of slavery. He had written Dartmouth the previous year to express his concern over the British military campaign in St. Vincent, warning it would "occasion the withdrawing of God's blessing from the King's family, and the Kingdom" because of its extension of slavery.[32]

Wheatley told Wooster that Sharp "attended me to the Tower & show'd the Lions Panthers, Tigers, & the Horse Armoury, Small Armoury, the Crowns, Sceptres, Diadems for Christening the Royal Family." Because her list of the other places she visited immediately follows, it was probably Sharp who "attended" her when she "saw Westminster Abbey, British Museum[,] Coxe's Museum, Saddler's wells, Greenwich Hospital, Park and Chapel, the royal Observatory at Greenwich, &c. &c.," crossing the Thames for the latter places. That Sharp took this now famously accomplished but enslaved African poet around must have linked to his fundamental concern, one that had climaxed personally for him the previous year. Sharp's showing Wheatley the Tower and the emblems of monarchy was literally political, and both Grimsted and Carretta have imagined what Sharp and Wheatley talked about while viewing "caged African animals." Sharp gave Wheatley one of his religious works, and maybe others, attacking slavery. It is with this extensive personal meeting in mind that Carretta discusses Wheatley's "temptation" to use the Mansfield decision to free herself. It seems she already had good reason to think she would be emancipated on her return, a subject it appears she discussed at the time with her host, John Thornton, very possibly referring to her conversation with Sharp.[33]

On July 17, 1773, three weeks after her letter to Lady Huntingdon announcing her arrival, Wheatley wrote to decline her invitation to visit her in South Wales. Susanna was mortally ill, and Wheatley had to return—"the Ship is certain to Sail next Thursday." She said she was "extremely reluctant to go without seeing your Ladiship. It gives me great satisfaction to hear of an African so worthy to be honoured with your Ladiship's approbation & Friendship as him you call your Brother." Wheatley thus paired Lady Huntingdon's patronage of Gronniosaw with that of herself, perhaps verging on telling Lady Huntingdon that she could be called "your Sister," as Wheatley called Obour a sister in Christ. Her letter continued, "I rejoice with your Ladiship in that Friend of Mental Felicity, which you cannot but be possessed of, in consideration of your exceeding great reward." There is further assertion of spiritual equality, it seems, in Wheatley's stating, "My great opinion of your Ladiship's goodness, leads me to believe I have an interest in your most happy hours of communion, with your most indulgent Father and our great & common Benifactor." She may have shared Christian kinship with her patron and been able to hope Lady Huntingdon would pray to God for her, but she also acknowledged the proper social distance by signing this, "with greatest humility I am most dutifully Your Ladiship's obed't sevt. Phillis Wheatley."[34]

Publication

Wheatley's *Poems* was published on September 16, 1773. Editions that year included the documents designed to prepare its audience to read the contents sympathetically, if not admiringly, leaving cruel criticism aside, and to persuade readers of their authenticity. Bell's accompanying advertisement for his first edition, published in the *London Chronicle* the day the book came out, made the same points those documents made.

Bell describes the book, "adorned with an elegant engraved likeness of the Author," identifying Phillis Wheatley as the title page did as "Negro Servant to Mr. John Wheatley of Boston," where it was published, too. "The Book here proposed for publication displays one of the greatest instances of pure, unassisted genius, that the world ever produced."[35]

We have seen that Benjamin Rush had called Wheatley a natural genius, and Ignatius Sancho would do so later. Charles Scruggs takes as his starting point for understanding Wheatley's London reception, the contemporary "fascination for poets who illustrate the principle of 'natural genius,'" first popularized by the *Spectator*, which defined them as "artists who by their natural parts, and without any assistance of art or learning, have produced works that were the delight of their own times and the wonder of posterity." This was in contrast to those artists "who formed themselves by rules and submitted the greatness of their natural talents to the . . . restraints of art." Wheatley would say of herself that she had the art "which art itself could ne'er acquire," in "THE ANSWER" (discussed in my next chapter). This was the same evaluation of her poetry Sancho gave, in effect a refutation of the frequent labelling of her as a Negro genius, both in the colonies (Lathrop wrote a friend, "The famous Negro Phillis . . . is a singular genius") and especially in London during her visit and on the publication of her *Poems* there. It was usually invidious, as Robinson points out, presenting Wheatley as "a black oddity who read English and Latin, and wrote acceptable poetry," or any poetry at all. At midcentury the notion was "given a . . . democratic twist" by the English literary elite. Scruggs's examples are Stephen Duck, the "Thresher Poet"; James Woodhouse, the "Shoemaker Poet," encouraged by Lord Littleton; Henry Jones, the "Bricklayer Poet"; and in the 1790s, Ann Yearsley, the "Milkmaid Poet" who, to her eventual annoyance, was patronized by Mrs. Montagu and Hannah More, themselves called "Bluestockings." To these might be added John Keats, "the Cockney Poet."[36]

Bell's advertisement of *Poems* by the "Negro Servant" continued, "The Author is a native of Africa, and left not that dark part of the habitable system till she was eight years old." Bell wrote this after Wheatley had been in London, so was able to add, "The writer while in England a few weeks since, was conversed with by many of the principal Nobility and Gentry of this Country . . . signally distinguished for their learning and abilities, among whom was the Earl of Dartmouth . . . and others who unanimously expressed their approbation of her genius, and their amazement at the gifts with which infinite Wisdom has furnished her." This was followed by the attestation from American gentlemen.[37]

The first of the poems in Wheatley's book was "To Maecenas," the patron of Virgil (whom, like Dante, Wheatley calls "Maro" and "the Mantuan poet") and of Horace, who had addressed Maecenas in his first "Ode." It was one of Wheatley's longer, "particularly polished and sophisticated poems," written with her metropolitan audience in mind. Cynthia J. Smith writes that it "played a pivotal biographical role." In flattering her own patron, "the Negro servant identified herself with these great classical predecessors, doubly so, because her poem refers most extensively to Pope," her favorite author, who had written a number of "imitations of Horace."[38]

In "To Maecenas," Wheatley addresses Pope directly, comparing his language to that of the Latin poets Maecenas had supported:

> Does not your soul possess the sacred flame?
> Their noble strains your equal genius shares
> In softer language, and diviner airs.

These last two lines are immediately amplified by Wheatley turning to Pope's translation of Homer, in this case, the *Iliad*, on which she among a much larger audience, notably including women, could draw, after centuries of being denied it.

> . . . As the thunder shakes the heavenly plains
> A deep-felt horror thrills through all my veins.

Pope, "Great sire of verse," can do this, but he is able to have another emotional effect on this reader's sensibility:

> When gentler strains demand thy graceful song,
> The length'ning line moves languishing along.
> When great *Patroclus* courts *Achilles'* aid,
> The grateful tribute of my tears is paid;

> Prone on the shore he feels the pangs of love,
> And stern *Pelides* tend'rest passions move.

Wheatley assumes readers know these lines.

> Meantime *Patroclus* to Achilles flies;
> The streaming Tears fall copious from his Eyes;

and she shows herself to be a poet of sensibility, but she cannot rival Pope. If so,

> . . . the same beauties should my mind adorn,
> And the same ardors in my soul should burn
>
> . . .
>
> But here I sit, and mourn a grov'ling mind
> That fain would mount and ride upon the wind.

Cynthia Smith judges that "the emphasis should be placed on 'here I sit,'" adding emphasis to "here," "meaning here I sit in the eighteenth century, rather than in the time of Virgil and Maecenas." Moreover, the "grove'ling mind" refers to the limits placed on her by race, by slavery, and by gender, rather than being self-deprecatory, capable of writing poetry that soars. This is expressed in a metaphor virtually quoted from Pope's "Essay on Man," a passage considering the value of ambitious passion:

> Reason the card, but Passion is the gale;
> Nor God alone in the calm storm we find,
> He mounts the storm and walks upon the wind.[39]

According to Wheatley, Pope's "bosom" is "the *Muses*['] home":

> They fan in you the bright immortal fire,
> But I less happy, cannot raise the song,
> The faulting music dies upon my tongue.

> The happier *Terence* all the choir inspir'd,
> His soul replenish'd, and his bosom fir'd.

Her asterisked footnote: "He was an *African* by birth." Why should not this writer, Phillis, "brought from *Africa* to *America*," the reader has learned, not be inspired by the Muses, too?

> But say, ye Muses, by this partial grace,
> To one alone of Afric's sable race;
> From age to age transmitting thus his name
> With the first glory in the rolls of fame?

This then was self-assertion by an African poet, who identifies herself, too, with the tradition exemplified by Pope, by Virgil, and, as Smith points out, by Horace. Wheatley's work will survive, the poet suggests, like Terence's, together with that of other great classical and contemporary poets. Terence's cognomen, "Afer" means Africa because he was brought to Rome from North Africa as a slave. Impressing his master with his literary abilities, he was freed. His six plays "were a standard part of the Latin curriculum of the neo-classical period." John Adams recommended him to his son in 1780. "Terence is remarkable for his good morals, good taste, and good Latin . . . His language has simplicity and an elegance that makes him proper to be accurately studied as a model." It was probably Wheatley's poem and footnote that led Jefferson to assert Terence was white in the same place he dismissed all of her poetry.[40]

That footnote identifying Terence as an African was on page three of Wheatley's *Poems*, the first of only three in the whole book. It was close to that sentence "Phillis was brought from *Africa* to America" in the front matter, but also to the publisher's title pages identifying her as a "negro" servant to John Wheatley. But "Negro" was a word Wheatley used only once, choosing to identify herself with Ethiopia and Africa.[41]

Wheatley declares to Pope, enshrined in heaven, the triumphant artist she yearns to emulate:

> While blooming wreaths around thy temples spread,
> I'll snatch a laurel from thy honour'd head[.]

She asks,

> Then grant, Maecenas, thy paternal rays,
> Hear me propitious, and defend my lays[,]

having opened this prayer referring again to Pope by way of his famous house on the Thames at Twickenham. She told her patron that she hoped her Dedication to her would defend her poems against London critics.[42]

Wheatley also appeals to the muses in "An HYMN to HUMANITY." Its opening invokes Milton and Newton:

> Lo! for this dark terrestrial ball
> Forsakes his azure-paved hall
>   A prince of heav'nly birth!
> Divine *Humanity* behold.
> What wonders rise, what charms unfold
>   At his descent to earth!

While "the prince"—Christ—viewed the "bosoms of the great and good / With wonder and delight," God asked,

> Each human heart inspire:
> To act in bounties unconfin'd
> Enlarge the close contracted mind,
> And fill it with thy fire.

All hearts should be as opened as Wheatley's had been to make poetry, even to escape the confinement of the slave ship, the contraction of enslavement.

> For when thy pitying eye did see
> The languid muse in low degree,
>   Then, at thy desire
> Descended the celestial nine;
> O'er me one thought they deign'd to shine,
>   And deign'd to string my lyre.

Her next and last stanza expresses her gratitude, asserting, too, that each "human heart" includes Africans':

> Can Afric's muse forgetful prove:?
> Or can such friendship fail to move
>   A tender human heart?

Humanity is identifiable with tenderness, with openness and connectedness with others. Celebrants of such humanity challenged contracted minds, in Wheatley's case the racists who refused to believe "an African girl" could write poetry.[43]

More Return of the Repressed?

I have suggested that all the poems on the death of children and the bereavement of parents were indirect expressions of Wheatley's childhood trauma of being torn from her parents, made direct in her poem to Dartmouth. She visited him in London, where surely they talked about the poem and the subject of her letter to him accompanying it, as he showed her around his mansion. (Dartmouth then giving Wheatley five guineas to buy the works of Pope, the poet she most admired and emulated, could indicate his real sympathy for her work.) It was there she may well have seen one of the four versions of Richard Wilson's "The Destruction of Niobe's Children."[44]

Even if the picture Wheatley viewed was made from a popular engraving of Watson's work by William Woollett, as some scholars think[45] (although she specified "a painting"), it must have been close to the time of that memorable meeting with Dartmouth that Wheatley wrote "NIOBE in Distress for her Children slain by APOLLO, from *Ovid's* Metamorphoses, Book VI, and from a View of the Painting by *Richard Wilson*."[46]

Wheatley's decision to change the title to focus on Niobe's feelings is significant, as well as that she chose to precede it with a poem that invoked the same scene of a father's loss of a daughter that had been the poignant, autobiographical focus of her Dartmouth poem. It was "to the Honorable T. H. Esq.; on the Death of his Daughter." T. H. was Thomas Hubbard, who had once licensed "the Tory patronized Admiral Vernon's head" across the street from the Wheatley home, and who had also signed the attestation published with her poems. His own death soon after had preceded that of his wife, to whom Wheatley wrote "To a Lady on the Death of her Husband," but she placed it much earlier in the collection.[47]

She opened the former by telling the father,

> While deep you mourn beneath the cyrpress-shade
> The hand of Death and your dear daughter laid
> In dust, whose absence gives your tears to flow,
> And racks your bosom with incessant woe,
> Let *Recollection* make a tender part,
> Assuage the raging tortures of your heart,
> Still the wild tempest of tumultuous grief,
> And pour the heav'nly nectar of relief:

The picture resembles that of her African father's "excruciating pangs" when his daughter was torn inexorably from him. But he could not know the consolation she offered Mr. Hubbard:

> Divinely bright your daughter's *Virtues* shone:
> She is in the Christian heaven:
> She unreluctant flies to see no more
> Her dear-lov'd parents on earth's dusky shore:
> . . .
> She leaves her earthly mansion for the skies,
> Where new creations feast her wond'ring eyes.

This might be seen as a version of "On being brought from AFRICA to AMERICA."

But Wheatley's view of being "brought" in her Dartmouth poem had an opposite perspective. Placing this dyad immediately before "Niobe" meant "Niobe" could have referred to the same slave raid when the babe who became Wheatley was first seized. Lucy Hayden has suggested she could have been "drawing subliminally on her African past . . . when she faced the challenge of recreating Ovid's passionate story of Niobe." Niobe can be seen to represent her African mother enduring the same loss. Wheatley sets her picture of the mother-in-distress in distant mythological time and place, presenting it in a form she had mastered under the aegis of a second mother, by her recreated self, still consciously African. That word, Africa, always inevitably connoted her enslavement when a child. This was, by definition, no simple memory; its expression was centrally indirect.[48]

Wilson's painting showed the grieving Niobe surrounded by the corpses of her fourteen children, slaughtered by Apollo and Diana (Phoebus and Phoebe), because Niobe had offended their mother, the Titaness Latona, emblem of motherhood, by boasting of her superior fecundity. Ovid gives the action that the painting cannot.[49] Wheatley calls on the Muse to sing of "APOLLO's wrath to man the dreadful spring / Of ills innum'rous," to "Inspire" her

> . . . with glowing energy of thought,
> What *Wilson* painted, and what *Ovid* wrote.
> Muse! lend thy aid, nor let me sue in vain,
> Tho' last and meanest of the rhyming train!

This is apparently more self-deprecation, but she is in the great classical tradition:

> O guide my pen in lofty strains to show
> The Phrygian queen, all beautiful in woe.

Proud Niobe has reviled "celestial deities" because they fail to pay her tribute, despite the fact that "Round me what a large progeny is spread!," in contrast to the very small number of children Latona has borne. Niobe boasts,

> No frowns of fortune has my soul to dread.
> What if indignant she decrease my Train
> More that Latona's number will remain?

This was hubris. Niobe tells Latona's nymphs no longer to honor her by observing her rites. Outraged, Latona calls on Phoebus/Apollo to kill Niobe's sons:

> Wrap them in the shades of death
> To punish pride and scourge the rebel mind.

Their father, Amphion (the equivalent, perhaps, of Wheatley's African father she describes suffering excruciating pangs by his loss of her),

> . . . with grief oppress'd,
> Had plung'd the deadly dagger in his breast.

Niobe then

> Weeps, nor weeps unpity'd by the foe
> On each pale corse the wretched mother spread
> Lay overwhelm'd with grief, and kiss'd her dead,
> Then rais'd her arms,

crying to Latona,

> If I've offended, let these streaming eyes,
> And let this sevenfold funeral suffice.
> Ah! take this wretched life,

In her outburst, though, she reminds Latona of the superiority that had provoked her:

> Tho' I unhappy mourn these children slain,
> Yet greater numbers to my lot remain.

Niobe has, then, "By her distresses more presumptuous grown." Latona's rage is now directed at Niobe's remaining seven daughters, each of whom is struck dead by an arrow, until,

> Only one daughter lives, and she the least
> The queen close clasp'd the daughter to her breast
> "Ye heav'nly pow'r ah spare me one," she cry'd,

this line most resonant of all, if this was Wheatley's closest approach to such a traumatic memory, along with being seized from her father's arms.

In vain she begs, the Fates her fruit deny
In her embrace she sees her daughter die.[50]

The queen of all her family bereft
Without or husband, son, or daughter left
Grew stupid at the shock,

And she turns to stone,

A marble statue now the queen appears.
But from the marble steal the silent tears.

Wheatley's title represents the outcome of Niobe's *lese majeste* (to which Ovid devoted much greater attention), that is, her "distress," an emotional condition of central importance to cultivators of sensibility.[51]

Lucy Hayden suggests that Ovid's Niobe is "militant, aggressive, boastful and provocative," whereas Wheatley makes her "more soft and tearful, more pathetic and conciliatory, more self-sacrificing and heroic." Christine Levecq suggests this enhances "the horror of the tale" to create "a character not too far removed from Sethe in Toni Morrison's *Beloved* . . . Niobe's feelings, like Sethe's seem to belong to a world of infinite pain hardly comprehensible to the sedate reader." Sethe had killed her daughter. Jennifer Thorn observes that while throughout Wheatley's "oeuvre, and especially in her many elegies, death is represented as a blessing the . . . heavenly reward for virtue." In "Niobe," Wheatley renders it as "the gloomy mansions of the dead."[52]

To this can be added David Grimsted's view that Wheatley was "evoking the objects of darkest dreams," and "the extraordinary bloodiness" of Niobe and her other "poems drawn from classical-biblical sources suggests . . . subterranean anger which the gentle young woman expresses only when it was sublimated in distant settings and in religious truisms about God's terrible wrath." Anger, yes, least indirect in her self-revelatory poem to Dartmouth, where her anger toward the steely-hearted, African slave-catcher was coupled with profound sympathy for her parent's shock and grief.[53]

Wheatley followed this account of the effect on her of painting with another expressly linked to Africa, and to her own artistry, the latter a subject both of "To Maecenas" and "NIOBE in Distress," as well as elsewhere—in short, asserting and demonstrating that Africans can master the cultural standards of the culture in which they live, and thereby change them. This was the poem she addressed to Scipio Moorehead, the slave belonging to the Rev. Moorehead, another of the gentlemen who condescended to attest to the authenticity of the poems written "by a young Negro girl."

It was entitled "To S.M. a young *African Painter*, on seeing his Works." He may first have been taught by the Rev. Moorehead's wife, Susanna, "who enjoyed a local reputation as an instructor of art to Bostonians," as Wheatley first learned English from Susanna Wheatley. Wheatley's poem's title was in telling contrast to the apparent reference to him in a January 3, 1773, advertisement in the *Boston News-Letter*: "A Negro man whose extraordinary genius has been assisted by one of the best masters in London; he takes faces at the lowest rates. Specimen's of his Performances may be seen at said place." This was in a shop not far from where Wheatley lived and may have been where she viewed his works. The advertisement's account of him is comparable to Wheatley being termed a Negro and therefore an extraordinary genius.[54]

In contrast to her poem's response to Wilson's painting of Niobe, Wheatley barely mentions any of "the Works" of the title of this poem, instead concentrating on the African painter himself. Her calling "S.M." an African was also a clue to S.M.'s name: the Roman general after whom the young African was named (with conventional racist irony) was called "Africanus" because of his victories in North Africa. Furthermore, Scipio Africanus was an intimate of Terence, so Wheatley's calling S.M. "African" signified the personal link between these two artists, identified and celebrated as Africans in the same book.[55]

Wheatley presents S.M.'s African interiority to her audience, intending

> TO show the lab'ring bosom's deep intent,
> And thought in living characters to paint,

> When first thy pencil did those beauties give,
> And breathing figures learnt from thee to live.

Then she couples that with her account of her own:

> How did those prospects give my soul delight,
> A new creation rushing on my sight!

Her next line exhorts him to continue his pursuit of immortality, suggesting that they mutually inspire each other in that pursuit:

> Still, wond'rous you! each noble path pursue,
> On deathless glories fix thine ardent view:
> Still by the painter's and the poet's fire
> To aid thy pencil and thy verse inspire!

Watching Phillis Wheatley perform a poem in his investigation of her authenticity on behalf of Lady Huntingdon, Bernard Page had exclaimed, "A WONDER of the Age indeed!" But Wheatley's words written directly to the young African painter, "wond'rous you," expressed direct admiration for his art, without the racist shock Page seems to have felt.

She ascribes her own artistic inspiration to Scipio:

> And may the charms of each seraphic theme
> Conduct thy footsteps to immortal fame!

Echoing her own elation in looking heavenwards (depicted in Scipio's picture of her), she paints a picture of Jerusalem, that is, of the Christian heaven:

> High to the blissful wonders of the skies
> Elate thy soul, and raise thy wishful eyes.
> Thrice happy, when exalted to survey
> That splendid city . . .
> Celestial Salem. . . .

His being African suggests that he (and therefore she) endured particular temporal conflicts and pains:

> May peace with balmy wings your soul invest!
> But when theses shades of time are chas'd away,

"peace" also connoting Scipio's being named after a Roman warrior. Her subject becomes explicitly "we," inspired African artists:

> And darkness ends in everlasting rest
> On what seraphic pious shall we move,
> And view the landscapes in the realms above?

The next lines then address each of them, exchanging their chosen genres:

> There shall thy tongue in heav'nly murmurs flow,
> And there my muse with heav'nly transport glow.

No picture by Scipio Moorehead survives, except that of Wheatley, but her next lines suggest that he painted two classical subjects:

> No more to tell of Damon's tender sighs,
> Or rising radiance of Aurora's eyes,

no more, though, in heaven to depict such figures,

> For noble thence demand a nobler strain,
> And purer language on th' ethereal plain.

Damon, the name of a singer-shepherd in Virgil's *Eclogues*, was adopted as a sentimental figure in eighteenth-century English pastoral poetry.[56] Thus Wheatley shows this African artist putting a piece of classical Western culture to use, just as she had in the ambitious opening poem "To Maecenas," to put her untutored African genius in the great tradition of Western poetry. The terms of her response to the "won'drous" artist, Scipio, painting Damon, resemble the opening lines of "To Maecenas," invoking eighteenth-century pastoral, too:

> Maecenas, you, beneath the myrtle shade,
> Read o'er what poets sung and shepherds play'd

one of them, Damon—

> What felt those poets but you feel the same?
> Does not your soul possess the sacred flame?
> Their noble strains your equal genius shares
> In softer language, and diviner airs.[57]

Hayden suggests Wheatley was drawing subliminally on her African past in "GOLIATH OF GATH. I SAM Chap. xvii," as she was in "NIOBE in Distress," both of them, incidentally, the only poems in epyllion (short epic form).[58] It was also another from "classical-biblical" sources that Grimsted suggests drew on her "subterranean anger": "The dreadful scenes of toil and war I write," two armies arrayed against one another, the setting for the familiar story of David's killing of the apparently invulnerable Goliath, saving Israel from being enslaved. The story is analogous to the one implicit in "To Dartmouth," when American revolutionaries and herself, especially, resist their enslavement by Britain.

Her monstrous figure of Goliath is encased in metal:

> A brazen helmet on his head was plac'd,
> A coat of mail his form terrific grac'd,
> The greaves his legs, the targe his shoulders prest:
> Dreadful in arms high-tow'ring o'er the rest
> A spear he proudly wav'd whose iron head
> . . . six hundred shekels weigh'd.

This was close to the description in *Samuel*, but it takes on another meaning when we recall that the pitiless slaver who seized Wheatley when a babe from her African father had "steel'd his soul" to do so. The massive, metallic figure of Goliath brought terror, dread, and chilling horror to "Jacob's race."

Challenging Israel to find a hero, Goliath promises,

> . . . he who wins, in triumph may demand
> Perpetual service from the vanquish'd land.

This, too, sticks closely to *Samuel* but can be read differently in the 1773 poem written by an enslaved, African, young woman. The "wond'rous hero," David, a stripling in the Bible, Wheatley also calls a "beardless youth." Laying aside the armor he is offered, David is confident his omnipotent God will defeat the would-be enslaver.

In keeping with Grimsted's suggestion that the bloodiness of such scenes in Wheatley's poetry is over-determined, her version of David's killing of Goliath and its consequences is notably more violent than her source. In *Samuel*, David's pebble stuns Goliath, so he finishes him off by decapitating him. In Wheatley's, however,

> Just o'er the brows the well-aim'd stone descends,
> It pierc'd the skull and shatter'd all the brain,

so decapitation is overkill. David

> . . . HEW'D THE GHASTLY HEAD
> The blood in gushing torrent's drench'd the plains
> The soul found passage through the spouting veins.

In *Samuel's* account, it is the Israelites who pursue the fleeing Philistines, wounding some. In Wheatley's, however,

> . . . the conqu'ror, swift pursu'd
> What scenes of slaughter and what seas of blood!
> . . .
> And David there were thy ten thousand laid:
> Thus *Israel's* damsel's musically play'd.

On his return with Goliath's head and armour, King Saul asks his commander-in-chief, "Say who is this amazing youth?," the question that the prodigious Wheatley routinely provoked, and answered with more poetry.

David destroyed Goliath,
That all earth's inhabitants may know
That there's a God who governs all below.

Thereby he gained "Freedom" for his house in Israel. In a letter written the following year, and widely published, Wheatley identified herself— and enslaved Africans—with "the Israelites," battling slave owners she represented as Egyptians for civic and religious freedom, declaring that "the same Principle lives in us." Frances Burney presented herself in the dedication to *Evelina* (1778) as a "hero," taking the "field of battle" against the male literary establishment in a context where transgressive women were conventionally called Amazons.[59]

Reactions

Wheatley's publication of several individual poems in American magazines made her known before the London publication of her *Poems*, so both her departure and her return were newsworthy. *Poems* (published in September 1773) was widely advertised in New and Old England, but chiefly reviewed in Britain.[60] Frank Shuffleton writes that by that autumn, "Wheatley had become a figure of public note in Boston and London," making "an almost triumphant visit to the imperial capital," and Sondra O'Neale notes that her "contemporary reception was phenomenal . . . perhaps recognized even more in England and Europe than in America." (Voltaire praised her "très-bon vers anglais.") The frequently reprinting of her *Poems* makes it clear that the book was extremely popular in America, too, from the Revolutionary through the Early National Periods, and, writes Phillip M. Richards, Wheatley's broadside verse met "an eager reception."[61]

Notices invariably pointed out that she was a "Negro," "one born in the wilds of Africa," and therefore her "poetical Genius" was "extraordinary." The *Critical Review* of London declared her "a literary phenomenon," and, reprinting "To Maecenas," said it was "extraordinary, considered as the production of a young Negro who was but a few years since, an illiterate barbarian," a paraphrase of the gentlemen's attestation.[62]

The *Gentleman's Magazine's* reviewer added emphasis, capital letters, and an exclamation mark to its paraphrase of the attestation included in Wheatley's *Poems*, signed by the Governor, Lieutenant-Governor, several clergymen, and "others eminent for station and literature," and her master: "This poor girl was brought an *uncultivated barbarian* from Africa, and *ever since* been and *now* is—A SLAVE!" The *Scots Magazine* reprinted this, adding, "disgraceful as it may have been to all that have signed it," a comment to be echoed by that 1778 letter of Ignatius Sancho's.[63]

Several seem to reflect the moral superiority metropolitan Britons assumed after the recent Somerset decision, especially in the current light of American claims to liberty, writing, "We are much concerned to find that this young woman is yet a slave" and coupling it with the inconsistency of white Americans now identifying themselves with liberty. The London *Monthly Review* quoted a lengthy extract from Wheatley's address to Dartmouth, including,

> I, young in life, by seeming cruel fate
> Was snatch'd from Afric's fancied happy seat:
> . . .
> . . . from a father seiz'd . . .

then remarked, "The people of Boston boast themselves chiefly on their principles of liberty. One such act as the purchase of [Wheatley's] freedom, would . . . have done them more honour than hanging a thousand trees with ribbons and emblems."[64]

Another London reviewer implied that both Wheatley's particular "genius" and "the rights of nature" required her to be free. "Youth innocence, and piety, united with genius, have not yet been able to restore her to the condition and character with which she was invested by the Great Author of her being. So powerful is the custom in rendering the heart insensible to the rights of nature and the claims of excellence!" This was an appeal to the heart, to sensibility, as well as to the head.[65]

A "London correspondent of the *Pennsylvania Chronicle*," evidently aware of the growing antislavery sentiment of Quakers (led by Benezet), held that the sensibility Wheatley's poetry expressed intensified her "claim to the rights of humanity." It "is hoped (though it is not so expressed) that the profits of this publication will in the first place be applied towards purchasing the freedom of the author; and if so, it is not doubted that every friend to the rights of humanity will liberally contribute to an emancipation of both mind and body [from a condition] always dreadful, but felt with double poignancy by genius and sensibility." According to this view, Wheatley has demonstrated that an African is capable of the most praiseworthy expressions of being an eighteenth-century, English-speaking human being. It was this, along with "the rights of humanity" that justified her being freed, not any claim to princely rank (that was confined to males anyway).[66]

"Alexis," an apparently black and Christian poet, publishing "Wrote After Reading Some Poems Composed by Phillis Wheatley, an African Girl," in the *Sentimental Magazine* (London), praised Wheatley, but added that all blacks should claim freedom:

> Why stand amaz'd at Afric's muse
> Why struck with sacred awe!
> One God our genius did infuse
> Our colour's nature's law.[67]

Quoting these reviews, her biographer Robinson observes it "would hardly be surprising then that, back in Boston, very shortly after her return, Phillis Wheatley . . . was finally manumitted," implying a connection. Among the reviews' readers were Thornton, Huntingdon, and Dartmouth, apparently decisive in freeing Wheatley, although expecting they could put her to their own use.[68]

In a dramatic contrast, the *Monthly Review* (which we just saw relished its moral superiority over white American slaveholders) began its remarks on Wheatley's poetry with the assertion that "proximity to the Sun" enfeebles the powers of the mind "in proportion as it enervates the faculties of the body." Hence the tropical regions are "remarkable for nothing but the sloth and languor of their inhabitants, their lascivious dispositions, and their deadness to invention." It dismisses the "poems written by this young negro as merely imitative."[69]

That review in the *Critical Review* had begun, "The Negroes of Africa are generally treated as dull, ignorant, and ignoble race of men, fit only to be slaves, and incapable of any considerable attainments in the liberal arts and sciences." The writer does not challenge this generalization, going on to say, "A poet or poetess among them, of any tolerable genius, would be a prodigy." Phillis Wheatley was that "literary phenomenon."[70]

Wheatley had been called "the Negro girl" from her first publication, through the attestation printed with her *Poems*, in the frequent reprintings as abolitionism gained increasing momentum, and by subsequent writers throughout the century, the phrase coinciding with Sterne's ubiquity of influence. One way or another the phrase came to refer to Sterne's "Negro girl, the tender Tale" of whom, he wrote in reply to Sancho's letter to him (calling on Sterne to raise his influential voice on behalf of his "miserable black brethren . . . in our West Indies"), he intended to weave into *Tristram Shandy*. He did so in volume IX, published in 1767, the year after Sterne wrote him, changing Sancho's "brethren" to a sister, "a poor negro girl with a bunch of white feathers tied to the end of a long cane flapping away flies—not killing them." She shares that vital expression of compassion (with Sterne's inevitable tongue-in-cheek) with the sentimental Uncle Toby, who would not kill a fly: "'Tis a pretty picture! said my uncle *Toby*—she had suffered persecution, *Trim* and had learnt mercy—She was good an' please your honour from nature as well as from hardships."[71]

Trim asks Uncle Toby several questions about her, including, "A Negro has a soul?," implicitly seeing her as one of all "negroes," male as well as female. "I am not much versed, Corporal, quoth my uncle Toby, in things of that kind, but I suppose, God would not leave him without one any more than thee or me." One clear illustration of the relation between Sterne's influence and Wheatley was an unpublished "Conversation between New York Gentleman & Phillis Wheatley." It was "probably the 'dialogue'" mentioned by John Andrews (whom we met earlier as one who took a keen interest in Wheatley), which he wanted to send to his brother-in-law in 1773. The "gentleman" asks "Wheatley," "Do you think that a Woman has a soul, Phillis?" "Phillis" gives a persuasive answer, as had Uncle Toby.[72]

In addition to reprintings of *Tristram Shandy*, the popularizing *The Beauties of Sterne: Including All the Pathetic Tales, and Most Distinguished Observation on Life, Selected for the Heart of Sensibility* was published in 1782. Such hearts belonged to "the *chaste* lovers of literature," who had "complained so loudly of the obscenity which taints the writings of Sterne"—we can infer women readers especially, included the tale of the poor negro girl. Alan Howes suggests it was in the *Beauties* that "Sterne's work was most frequently read during the 1780s. . . . It reached a seventh edition within a year and a half, and a twelfth by 1793." In his 1808 *The History of the Rise, Progress, and Accomplishment of the Abolition of the African Slave Trade*, Clarkson wrote, "Sterne, in his account of the Negro girl in his Life of Tristram Shandy, took decidedly the part of the oppressed Africans. The pathetic, witty, and sentimental manner, in which he handled this subject, occasioned many to remember it, and procured a certain portion of feeling in their favour."[73]

Samuel Foote also connected Sterne with Wheatley, the year after her stay in London, though this time in a ribald, racist farce: "The Cozeners," of 1774. Of course, Sterne was notorious for his sexual *double entendres*. Foote (1720–77) was "eighteenth-century London theater's most notorious figure."[74] Three years after Foote produced this, another male writer stereotyped Wheatley as a lusty black wench, part of his satire of English women writers, published in three issues of the London *Public Advertizer*, in June, July, and August 1777. The *Monthly Review* had associated Wheatley with the "lascivious dispositions" of Africans.[75]

The anonymous writer in the *Public Advertizer* had been provoked by Mary Scott's *The Female Advocate: A Poem, Occasioned by Reading Mr. Duncombe's Feminead* (1774).[76] Duncombe's book was one of a *genre*, catalogues of notable women published continuously from the latter seventeenth through the eighteenth century, manifesting their rise and their literacy, expressed in literature and art but in other respectable public activities, too. Originally very markedly aristocratic, they became increasingly middle-class. Scott expanded and updated Duncombe's 1754 celebration of what in her prose introduction she called "only a small number of Female Geniuses," in the face of "the illiberal sentiments of men in general in regard to our sex," in explanation of her title, "and prompted by the most fervent zeal for their privileges, I took up the pen with the intention of becoming their advocate." In the first section of her poem itself, Scott writes,

> . . . LORDLY MAN asserts his rights divine,
> Alone at wisdom's sacred shrine;

> With tyrant sway would keep the female mind
> In error's cheerless dark abyss confined.

She had anticipated that last phrase in her prose dedication that even if "the sentiments of all men of sense relative to female education are now more enlarged than ever they were," generally they "are still very contracted." Although, as Gae Holladay writes in her introduction, it "treads but cautiously over convention, it is an early feminist document, defending the rights of women to explore and develop their minds."[77] We saw in "An HYMN to HUMANITY," Wheatley had God tell Christ in his descent to earth,

> Each human heart inspire:
> To act in bounties unconfin'd
> Enlarge the close contracted mind,
> And fill it with thy fire.

Scott's insistence on liberating the female mind is powerful; at the same time she insists in women's "virtue":

> For sure alone in Virtue can ye find,
> Enjoyments suit'd to th' immortal mind.[78]

Reassuringly, women's public accomplishments were not at the expense of such traditional qualities. Wheatley had placed her poem, "On Virtue," second only to the acknowledgement of her patron in the first poem.

> . . . O my soul, sink not into despair,
> Virtue is near thee and with gentle hand
> Would now embrace thee, hovers o'er thine head.

But as was so often the case, Wheatley's expression of this routine defense takes on further significance in the face of the racist stereotyping of African women as lusty black wenches:

> Auspicious queen, thine heav'nly pinions spread,
> And lead celestial *Chastity along;*

Lo! now her sacred retinue descends,
Array'd in glory from the orbs above.
Attend me, *Virtue*, thro' my youthful years![79]

Tyranny had long been a preoccupation among republicans on both sides of the Atlantic. Scott had followed her praise of Wheatley with that of historian Catherine Macaulay, who had recently published the fifth of her "magisterial eight-volume *History of England*," the "Whig answer to David Hume's influential Tory *History of Great Britain*." It is Macaulay's political perspective Scott praises, consistent with her own opposition to tyranny. Macaulay's name was

to ev'ry son of freedom dear,
Which patriots yet unborn shall long revere.

American revolutionaries, including "Sons of Liberty," celebrated Macaulay, inheriting the republican tradition she articulated. Scott adds:

O Liberty! Heav'n's unblest gift below,
Without thee life were but one scene of woe.

In that previous stanza, Scott illustrates the application of the term "tyranny" to men's oppression of women, anticipating the systematic application of republicanism to that relation in Wollstonecraft's *Vindication of the Rights of Woman* (1792).[80]

Wheatley joined her white American revolutionary contemporaries in her republicanism, employing the term "tyranny" in her political poems, as her "To Dartmouth" illustrated. She may well have witnessed riots and demonstrations in Boston's streets, Robinson notes, calling her "a Whig or American patriot," but evidently of a non-racist kind. Her "wishes for the common good," she said, were by "feeling hearts best understood." Christine Levecq has highlighted that relationship between republicanism and sensibility. In Wheatley's case, it was combined with her liberal, individual voice. She wanted all feeling hearts, female and male, black and white, to be free.[81]

6

Married in Africa or Free in America

Wheatley's Third Transatlantic Crossing and Manumission

By the time Wheatley's *Poems* was published, she was on-board a ship for Boston, arriving there on September 20, 1773. Her arrival was announced in the *Massachusetts Gazette and Post Boy* as that of "Phillis the extraordinary Negro poetess servant to Mr. John Wheatley." She was freed almost immediately. In her letter to Wooster, written a month after she landed, and following her description of the edition of *Paradise Lost* she had been given in London, she wrote, "Since my return to America my Master, has at the desire of my friends in England given me my freedom. The instrument is drawn so as to secure me and my property from the hands of Executus[,] administrators, & of my master, and secure whatever should be given me as my Own. A Copy is sent to Isra. Mauduit, Esqr. FRS."[1] Mauduit, a pamphleteer and lobbyist in London, where we saw Wheatley met him, was a front-man and fixer for the government headed by Lord North, and, with his brother, Jasper, the colonial agent for Massachusetts. He presented the province's case against the Sugar and Stamp Act of 1764, operating with Dartmouth.[2]

Most likely the letters she carried, asking that she be manumitted by her formal owner, were from Dartmouth and Thornton. They may have had in mind Wheatley's serving their evangelical purpose as Samson Occom did, in his case as a missionary to Native Americans. It is feasible they already knew of the Rev. Hopkins's plan for her, or that Occom had mentioned his idea.

Wheatley adds to her letter to Wooster announcing she had been freed, "I found my mistress very sick on my return." Despite being free, she stayed with Susanna until she died the following March (1774). (Nathaniel Wheatley did not return to Boston until September that year, bringing an English bride, then returning to spend the rest of his life there.)[3]

The next part of this letter tells us why it was to Wooster, a Connecticut merchant, to whom Wheatley wrote about being freed. To her, the corollary of freedom was being able to support herself in her own way. She told Wooster that the copies of her book to be sold in America "will arrive in 8 or 10 days." She sent him her proposal for a second collection, asking him to encourage "Gentlemen & Ladies of your acquaintance to subscribe also, for the more subscribers there are, the more it will be for my advantage as I am to have half the Sale of my Books." It must have been while in London that she had made arrangements for the books to be sent to her at the Wheatleys' address in Boston.

She continues, "Tho I am the more solicitous for, as I am now upon my own footing and whatever I get by this is entirely mine, & it is the Chief I have to depend on." This was "the Property" her instrument of manumission was drawn to secure to her "as my Own." She continues with these instructions to Wooster, requesting him to stop New Haven printers from reprinting her book, "as it will be of great hurt to me, preventing any further Benefits that I might receive from the Sale of my Copies from England. The price is 2/6d Bound of 2/- Sterling Sewed." Before returning to Boston, Wheatley had taken the precaution of signing every copy. "If any should be so ungenerous as to reprint the genuine Copy may be known, for it is sign'd in my own hand-writing." Noting that "Phillis's autograph was written on the back of the title page of many of the copies," a writer in the Massachusetts Historical Society's journal *Proceedings* suggests that the publication of her *Poems* was so far along when Wheatley was in London that she had been able to sign them there. She had anticipated being on her own footing, further evidence that she knew she would be freed by the time the book was published, and had then talked to those "dear friends" about that.[4]

We recall that part of John Andrew's explanation for Wheatley's withdrawing her collection from the Boston printer was the hope of substantial "Emolument" to be gained from its publication in London. He sent her *Poems* to Barrell early in 1774, and wrote him, "After so long a time have at last got Phillis's poems in print," adding, "These don't seem to be near all her productions—she's an artful jade, I believe, & intends to have the benefit of another volume."[5]

Wheatley wrote Obour twelve days after her letter to Wooster, telling her of her experience in England, but only after encouraging Obour in her sense of "our dependence on the Deity." Her diction is by and large very different from that in her Wooster letter. She had a cold and since her return had been suffering from asthma. "I can't say but my voyage to England has conducted to the recovery, . . . of my health." On the other hand, the "friends I found there among the nobility and gentry, their benevolent conduct towards me the unexpected civility and complaisance with which I was treated by all fills me with astonishment. I can scarcely realize it." That benevolence had been extended to letters arranging for Wheatley to be manumitted, but she was not explicit about that to her fellow enslaved African.[6]

Instead, she continues, "This"—the benevolence—"I humbly hope has the happy effect of lessening me in my own esteem," an issue raised by Thornton: if one were to phrase it "not wanting to act above myself," one might see it as a very muted reference to being freed by London benevolence, and not wanting to esteem herself above her still enslaved sister. "Your reflections on the sufferings of the Son of God & the inestimable price are immortal souls, plainly demonstrate the sensations of a soul united to Jesus." This elevation was something she told both Lady Huntingdon and Thornton they could expect and that she wanted. She elaborates on this transcendent religious status with the perhaps overdetermined metaphor of buying and selling: "What you observe of Esau is true of all mankind who, (left to their own devices) would sell their heavenly birth rights for a few moments of sensual pleasure, whose wages at least (dreadful wages) is eternal condemnation." Wheatley emphasizes their common ground in this, in fact, that they had the power to sell themselves, metaphorically. "Dear Obour, let us not sell our birthright for a thousand worlds, which would indeed be as dust upon the balance." Her pleasure is relief. "The God of the seas and dry land has graciously brought me home in safety. Join with me in thanks to him for so great a mercy." This was to confine herself to the motive for returning, reaching home, although the context—the transcendent value of being Christian—and the direction of this voyage to another being "brought home" to Susanna, superseding the issue of her enslavement or manumission, invokes the meaning of her "On being brought from AFRICA to AMERICA." Wheatley reiterates their common ground. "Join me in thanks to him . . . that it may excite me to praise him." Obour can help Wheatley in this superordinate responsibility, "so that my heart may be fill'd with gratitude."[7]

She promised a more detailed account of her voyage and signed the letter, "I am Dear friend, Most affectionately ever yours Phillis Wheatley." She added a postscript about "my mistress" being very sick, and then, "I enclose Proposals for my book," asking Obour to "use your interest to get subscriptions." (Obour sold copies of her *Poems* for her.) She had written on the same subject to Wooster, in his case, connecting it to her literally being freed, but here she leaves that aside, subordinating it to the shared birthright she had realized as Obour had, their metaphorical freedom in Christ.

She had written Thornton on December 1, 1773, most apparently on the evangelical belief they shared, but Wheatley could be as subtly self-assertive in her prose as she was in her poetry. Here she first tells him "of the goodness of God in safely conducting my passage over the mighty waters, and returning me in safely to my American friends." This, too, echoes "On being brought from AFRICA to AMERICA," and those American friends included her Christian family, the Wheatleys, who had rescued her from the trauma of being enslaved, and her dearest friend, Obour. Her safe return to Boston was an "amazing Mercy, altogether unmerited by one," which leads her to consider what she can expect at the end of her final voyage when "Paul tells us the wages of sin is death," all sin being hateful to God, who is "essential Purity." She asks Thornton, "Should we not sink, hon'd sir, under this sentence of Death . . . were not this blessed Contrast"—God's essential Purity—be "annexed to it." She quotes Paul to say that "the Gift of God is eternal life through Jesus Christ," who took a load from the sinner's shoulder. This was a sublime mystery, to be searched eternally. "This Eternity how dreadful, how delightful! Delightful to all those who have an interest in the Crucified savior, who has dignified our Nature, by seating it at the Right Hand of the Divine Majesty." This was the nature implicitly shared by all believers in this mystery, here, by Wheatley and Thornton, transcending such invidious categories as "untutored African" and "Negro Servant." In fact, she dismisses them and asserts equality, against those whom she had written in the poem on the voyage she has successfully re-iterated, who "view our sable race with scornful eye" to the prospect of joining "the angelic train." A believer has "Cause to rejoice even on the brink of that Bottomless Profound" she had crossed.

She tells Thornton, "I doubt not (without the least Adulation)"—the disclaimer, and perhaps unconscious revelation—"that you are one of that happy number." Of course, only God could know. Wheatley herself must live with uncertainty, asking Thornton, "O pray that I may be one also, who shall join with you in songs of praise at the Throne of him, who is no respecter of Persons, being equally the great Maker of all." This removes the sentence's earlier distinction; the African poetess and the gentleman philanthropist are on an equal footing.

But Wheatley was anticipating her next sentence, an adjuration: "Therefore disdain not to be called the Father of Humble Africans and Indians," a reference, surely, to Thornton's support of Occom's mission and perhaps, to the prospect of another to Africans, certainly to his support of her. She continues to link Africans and Indians, "though despised on earth on account of our colour, we have this Consolation, if he enables us to deserve it. 'That God dwells in the humble & contrite heart.'" She does not have that adequately: "O that I were more & more possess'd of this inestimable blessing: to be directed by the immediate influence of the divine spirit in my daily walk & Conversation." She identifies Thornton with the divine spirit. Was she resisting his urging to go on a mission like Occom's, even to Africa, saying she was not yet qualified? She would soon say that explicitly.

She insists on her point by way of that adulatory contrast between them: "Do you, my hon'd sir, who have abundant Reason to be thankful for the great share you possess of it, be always mindful in your Closet, of those who want it, of me in particular."

Another reason she will shortly make explicit for not complying with Hopkins's ambition for her African mission, one which Thornton shared (although one cannot say when he joined in it), was the health of Susanna Wheatley. Wheatley had cut short her visit to England to be with her dying mistress. When she first arrived home, she told Thornton that Susanna was "not expected to live above two or three days" and "remains in a very weak & languishing Condition." Begging an interest in Thornton's prayers, Susanna asks Wheatley to tell him "that she may be only prepar'd for that great Change which she is likely soon to undergo." She asks him, too, to counsel Nathaniel, in fact to be "a spiritual father to him." Similarly, Thornton watched over Phillis at Susanna's request.

"She thanks you heartily for the kind notice you took of me while in England."

Wheatley asks Thornton "please to give my best Respects to Mrs. & miss Thornton, and masters Henry and Robert who held with me a long conversation on many subjects which Mrs. Drinkwater knows very well." She concludes by asking him to remember her to the whole family: "I thank them for their kindness to me begging still an interest in your best hours." In a postscript, she tells Thornton, "I have written to Mrs. Wilberforce, sometime since please to give my duty to her, since writing the above the Rev'd Mr. Moorhead has made his exit from this world, in whom we lament the loss of the Zealous and Pious & true Christian."[8]

She does not mention her manumission, which it seems Thornton had been instrumental in bringing about. Was this because he had linked it to his African plan for her, one she wished to postpone at least? Certainly in his reply he makes her future as a free woman his business. He warns her, "Many a good man is often a snare by too openly commending his good qualities, and not aware how under-signedly he spreads a net at the feet of his friend." Thornton will not trap her this way. "Your present situation," by which he means her being now free, "and the kindness you meet with from many good people, and the respect that is paid to your uncommon genius, extorts this friendly hint from me. I have no reason to charge you with any indiscretion of this kind: I mean only to apprize you of the danger." Not only was she free, she was in the land of liberty, in contrast to being enslaved and under Thornton's roof. Moreover, she had enjoyed the public triumph in London, which perhaps forced the Connexion's hand in having her freed. "I feared for you when here, least [unless] the notice many took of you should prove a snare."[9] To what does he refer? Most evidently, it was putting her literary ambition above her commitment to the religious purpose defined by the Huntingdon Connexion, the subject Wheatley was careful to emphasize in her letters to Thornton. There were other possibilities now confronting this brilliant and celebrated young black woman. He well may have raised such issues while Wheatley stayed with him: Thornton described that stay later to the Rev. William Richardson, emphasizing her prodigality in learning "conversant" with "Scripture very humble and teachable," but he failed to mention her poetry.[10]

Wheatley's Prospects of a Fourth Transatlantic Crossing

The next letter of hers we have, dated February 9, 1774, two months after that letter to Thornton, was to the Rev. Samuel Hopkins, whom we met because of his correspondence with Quaque at Cape Coast Castle. Wheatley had probably heard him preach (and perhaps Whitefield, too) at Boston's Old South, the Wheatley family's church.[11]

Hopkins had received his first reply from Quaque in September 1773, and dated his own reply December 10 of that year. He must have made his proposal to Wheatley around the same time, because her reply to him was dated February 9, 1774. He had sent her a copy of his and Stiles's circular, together with the proposal that she marry one of the two African men—either would do—in order to accompany them to Africa. They were to enter the unchristianized, "pagan" world, where sexual, matrimonial customs were essentially different, and therefore grist for white fantasy, shot through with the kind of moralism registered by Quaque, who had warned Hopkins of the "Debaucheries" to which his two protegés inevitably would be "enticed." Not only should Quamine and Yamma be Christianized adequately to control themselves, but to exemplify their religious values to the natives, one of them should model Christian marriage. We recall that both the Revs. Thompson and Johnson had urged Quaque to marry an African publicly because it would contribute to the success of his mission and, perhaps, because of the sexual behavior they generally ascribed to Africans.[12]

The first subject of Wheatley's February 9 reply to Hopkins is the marketing of her books in Newport. Her own first batch had finally arrived from London and she was sending "package 17 for you and 2 for Ms. Tanner, and one for Mrs. Mason and only wait for you to appoint some proper person, by whom I may convey them to you. I received some time ago 20s sterling upon them, by the hands of your son, in a letter from Abour Tanner." This was her priority. Hopkins was "privately on record as loathing all kinds of poetry."[13]

She then turns to the Hopkins-Stiles memorial. "I received a paper by which I understand there are two negro men, who are desirous of returning to their own country, to preach the Gospel." Leaving implicit the particular connection with her life Hopkins had proposed in his letter, she continues, "But being much indisposed by the return of my asthmatic complaint besides the sickness of my mistress, who . . . is not expected to live . . . all these things render it impracticable for me to do anything at present with regard to that paper[.]"

After declining the proposal or, rather, postponing a decision in response to it, Wheatley promises to do what else she could, "influencing my Christian friends to promote this laudable design, shall not be wanting," and then includes the passage which we saw Hopkins quoted to Quaque. To that can be added that in her elegy on Whitefield's death, written four years before, Wheatley had Whitefield say,

> Take him ye starving sinners, for your food
>
> . . .
>
> Take him, ye Africans he longs for you,

which can be compared to this passage to Hopkins: "Europe and America have long been fed with the heavenly provision, and I fear they loath it, while Africa is perishing with spiritual Famine." The Europeans have more of an opportunity than Africans in this regard, but they have actively rejected it: "O that they could partake of the previous crumbs which fall from the table of these distinguished children of the Kingdom." Her next and last paragraph could be read as a positive response to "that Question that has perplex'd the Minds of so many serious Persons viz. in what Manner will God deal with those benighted Parts of the World where the Gospel of Jesus Christ hath never reach'd?," which the Rev. Shirley hoped Gronniosaw's *Narrative* would help to solve. Wheatley writes that African "minds are unprejudiced against the truth, therefore 'tis to be hoped they would receive it with their whole heart. I hope that which the divine royal Psalmist says by inspirations is now on the point of being accomplished, namely, Ethiopia shall soon stretch forth her hands unto God." Wheatley is quoting Psalm 68:31, "Princes shall come out of Egypt; Ethiopia shall soon stretch out her hands unto God." She notes, "Of this Abour Tanner and I trust many others within your knowledge are living witnesses. Please give my love to her."[14]

Two days after Wheatley's reply to Hopkins, Occom wrote her about "the Preachers or Ministers of Jesus Christ . . . who keep Negroe Slaves." "The Gospel," he says, "is a Dispensation of Freedom and Liberty, both Temporal and Spiritual," countering such preachers as Whitefield who justified their enslavement of Christian blacks with precisely that distinction, or more evidently for him, Eleazor Wheelock. "If preachers are True Liberty men, let them preach Liberty for the poor Negroes . . . and those ministers who have Negroes set an example before the People by freeing their Negroes."[15]

Evidently his words touched Wheatley in the context of the subject of her correspondence with Hopkins, and perhaps she recalled Occom's earlier proposal that Wheatley herself become a preacher, like himself and Sarah Osborn, rather than the wife of one. She answered him the day she received it (February 11). "I have this Day received your obliging kind Epistle, and am greatly satisfied with your Reasons respecting the Negroes, and think highly reasonable what you offer in Vindication of their natural Rights." Hopkins threatened hers by proposing she subordinate herself to a husband. "Those that invade them," she continues, "cannot be insensible that the divine Light is chasing away the thick Darkness which broods over the Land of Africa, and the Chaos which has reign'd so long is converting to beautiful order, and reveals more and more, the glorious Dispensation of civil and religious Liberty, which are so inseparably Linked that there is little, or no Enjoyment of one without the other." Two days earlier, she had praised the Hopkins-Stiles "Design" for Africa in very similar terms. Further to illustrate the relationship between civil and religious liberty (manifest in the natural rights of "Negroes" and a dawning of Christianity in Africa), Wheatley continues to Occom, "Otherwise, perhaps the Israelites had been less solicitous for their Freedom from Egyptian Slavery. I do not say they would have been contented without it, by no Means for in every human Breast," that is, regardless of religion, "God has implanted a Principle, which we call Love of Freedom," not just white male frolickers claiming to resist "enslavement" by British taxes. As Wheatley had recently written in her poem to Dartmouth, she might be even better attuned to the "Love of Freedom" because of her experience of being literally enslaved, snatched from Africa, and shipped to America, where, having found the resources to recreate herself, she was now in the process of separating her own civil liberty from the prospect of doubly subordinating herself to the project of the religious "liberation" of all Africans. Wheatley asserted the principle of liberty in her own breast. She had declared its universality in her "HYMN to HUMANITY," published in her *Poems* the previous year.[16]

She continues in this letter to Occom, the "Principle which we," female and male, black and white, real Indians and American revolutionaries, "call love of Freedom, is impatient of Oppression, and pants for Deliverance"; and here she does address the enslavement of Africans: "And by the Leave of Modern Egyptians I will assert that the same Principle lives in us." She has made it clear this means regardless of religion, regardless of being Christianized. "God grant Deliverance in his own way and Time."[17] In her "To the University of CAMBRIDGE, in NEW ENGLAND," written in 1767, the year before she wrote "On being brought from AFRICA to AMERICA," Wheatley represented herself as having been brought from her "native shore / The land of errors and *Egyptian* gloom," the latter, though, not explicitly slavery but "those dark abodes," whence "the Father of mercy" has rescued her. Here she expands that analogy; the Egyptian are the slave masters of Christians' Biblical forbears, the Israelites, with whom Wheatley identifies herself, expressing a tradition to be salient in nineteenth-century African American culture, foreshadowed by Wheatley's celebration of David killing Goliath, one wherein Moses leads his people to promised freedom. Quaque had made this analogous to the enslavement of Africans.[18]

The year after Hopkins proposed to send John Quamine, Bristol Yamma, and Phillis Wheatley to Africa, the Countess of Huntingdon sent the black David Margate as a missionary to her slaves in Georgia. Having already stirred up enslaved Africans during a visit to New York, Margate returned to Georgia, where the Rev. Piercy (sent to sort out Bethesda after Whitefield's death and to travel back to England via the Wheatleys' home) reported to Lady Huntingdon, "The Devil put it into his [Margate's] head that he was sent here to be a second Moses, & should be called to deliver his people from slavery." Margate's circumstances, like Wheatley's, included white, male, American revolutionaries' calling for the same delivery. "We have been under a continual apprehension of an Insurrection among the Slaves from his conduct & discourses among the negroes." Piercy's brother wrote the countess that Margate "compared their State to that of the Israelites during their Egyptian bondage," and he was shipped back to England before he could be lynched.[19]

But Wheatley was a generous Christian in her hopes for American slaveowners, the modern Egyptians, from whom she seized leave to speak. She asks God to "get him honour upon all those who Avarice impels them to countenance and help forward the Calamities of their Fellow Creatures." To "countenance," as well as "help forward," cut a very wide swathe among contemporary, white Egyptians; to attribute such actions to "Avarice," at the expense of those she asserts are "Fellow Creatures," was characteristic of antislavery argument.

With further Christian forbearance, Wheatley writes, "This"—God working his righteous will on avaricious enslavers—"I desire not for their Hurt, but to convince them of the strange Absurdity of their Conduct whose Words and Actions are so dramatically opposite." Her next sentence spells this out: "How well the Cry for Liberty and the reverse Disposition for the Exercise of oppressive Power over others agree. —I humbly think it does not require the Penetration of a Philosopher to determine." This was to echo Occom's language back to him. Robinson observes that while this letter was "restrained and genteel," it was "an unequivocal indictment of the colonial Christian hypocrisy that justified human slavery . . . all the more biting for its assumed stance of humility, its deft use of Biblical analogy, its politely ironic scoring of patently absurd Christian racists."[20]

Wheatley asked Thornton to forward this letter to Occom, then ministering to Native Americans in Mohegan territory. We have seen that Thornton was in touch with Occom's mission (including through Susanna Wheatley)—he was a trustee and Treasurer of the Indian Charity (a body patronized by Huntingdon and Dartmouth)—and that Wheatley urged him not to disdain being called "the Father of Humble Africans and Indians." Whether or not she intended Thornton to read the letter to Occom, it was soon published in the *Connecticut Gazette* (where her Hussey and Coffin poems had been published in the interests of antislavery), among "almost a dozen New England newspapers," including the *Massachusetts Gazette and the Boston Post Boy and Advertizer* of March 21, 1774, introduced in terms that could imply she was still a slave.

"The following is an Extract of a letter from Phillis, a Negro Girl of Mr. Wheatley's of this Town, to the Rev. Samson Occom, which we are desirous to insert as a specimen of her Ingenuity."[21]

Susanna Wheatley died on March 3. Phillis wrote her dear African friend and co-religionist Obour Tanner, the letter of March 21. I quoted in chapter three of the tenderness of "a Parent, Sister, or Brother . . . united in her." She did not want to forget this second phase of her childhood, so utterly distinct from the first. "This I hope ever to keep in remembrance. Her exemplary life was a greater monitor than all her precepts and instruction," example being a much greater force than instruction. She told Obour that Susanna's death alleviated the family's sorrows, representing it as "we," having "the satisfaction to see her depart in inexpressible raptures, earliest longings, & impatient thirstings for the upper courts of the Lord."[22]

She asked Obour to pray for them, told her of her own recovery of health, and concludes, "I shall send the 5 books"—copies of her *Poems*— "you wrote for, the first convenient opportunity; if you want more, they shall be ready for you." Even in her profound grief, Wheatley kept this central feature of her life in mind, perhaps taking on still more practical value now she had to pursue it without Susanna's help.

She ends this letter, "I am very affectionately your friend Phillis Wheatley," and began her letter to Thornton, eight days later, "Much Honoured Sir," then gave a far longer, highly elaborate and less personal account of Susanna's death, in terms she believed would conform to his wishes and expectations of her piety (Robinson notes "her subtle and adroit handling of the pontification of the millionaire philanthropist"[23]). She tells him that the "mournful Occasion" for her letter "is the death of Mrs. Wheatley." After a protracted illness, "she has at length took her flight from hence to those blissful region, which need not the light of any, but the sun of Righteousness. O could you have been present to see how she long'd to drop the tabernacle of Clay, and to be freed from the cumbrous shackles of a mortal Body, which had so many Times retarded her desires when soaring upward." This had been the view of death with which Wheatley had consoled others, evidently of particular meaning to the enslaved, but writing about it now when she was free, able if she wished, to place a higher value on her temporal existence, at issue in her correspondence with Thornton.

She then incorporates Thornton into her story, flattering him even: Susanna "has often told me how your Letters have quicken'd her in her spiritual course: when she has been in darkness of mind they have rais'd and enliven'd her insomuch, that she went on with clearfulness and clarity in the path of her duty." Then a great deal more, paraphrasing Susanna's expressions of faith in her salvation, and a very detailed description of her last half hour of life on earth, opening her arms, crying for "an easy and quick Passage," then at last "'fare well, fare well' with a very low voice . . . I sat the whole time by her bed side, and saw with Grief and Wonder the effects of sin on the human race." Then still more, with hopes her prayers "for her son & for me will be answer'd." Wheatley entreates Thornton "for the same Interest in your best thoughts for me," and that Susanna's prayers for peace (in the war between Britain and her American colonies) be answered, "on my behalf."

The Wheatleys' mediatorship between Thornton and Occom had continued. In this letter on Susanna's death, Phillis reported they had forwarded Thornton's letter to Occom authorizing twenty-five pounds for his mission—"He has not the least shelter for his Creatures to defend themselves from the inclemencies of the weather, and he has lost some already for the want of it." She tells Thornton that Occom "said Mrs. Wheatley and the rev'd Mr. Moorhead were his best friends in Boston. But alas! they are gone." She thanks Thornton "for your kind Letters to my Mistress it came above a fortnight after her Death." She asks for his prayers and signs, "I am hon'd sir with dutiful respect ever your obliged and devoted Humble servant Phillis Wheatley."[24]

On May 6, 1774, she combined mutual piety with thanks to Obour Tanner for remitting the proceeds from the sale of Wheatley's *Poems*. "I have rec'd the money you sent for the five books & [2 pounds six pence] for another, which I now send & wish safe to hand." Mr. Pemberton "brings the book you write for."[25]

The same day she wrote Hopkins, from whom Pemberton had brought a letter the previous evening. She tells him right off, "I have also rec'd the Money for the 5 books I sent Obour, & 2/6 more for another." Only then does she turn to the subject of Philip Quaque. "I am very sorry to hear that Philip Quaque has very little or no apparent success in his mission. Yet, I wish that what you hear respecting him may be only a misrepresentation." Hopkins must have written Wheatley of the great difficulties Quaque described, although they had not inhibited him from urging Wheatley to go to Africa. Here she continues, "Let us not be discouraged, but still hope that will bring about this great work tho' Philip may not be the instrument in the Divine Hand, to perform this work of wonder, turning the Africans from darkness to light." She has a suggestion, though: "Possibly if Philip could introduce himself properly to them (I don't know the reverse), he might be more Successful and in setting a good example which is more powerfully winning than Instruction."

Hopkins apparently had not given up on the idea of Wheatley's marrying Yamma or Quamine and accompanying them to Africa, because Wheatley adds, "I Observe your Reference to the Maps of Guinea and *Salmon's Gazette*, and will consult them." But she reminds Hopkins of her own priority by concluding, "Rec'd . . . from London 300 more Copies of my Poems, and wish to dispose of them as soon as Possible. If you know of any being wanted I flatter myself you will be pleas'd to let me know if, which will be adding one more to the many Obligations confer'd on her, who is with a one Sense of your kindness, Your most humble and Obedient servant Phillis Wheatley." Far from being obedient to Hopkins's wishes for her, she is asking him to help maintain her on her own footing.[26]

Five months after this, her letter to Thornton (October 30, 1774)[27] showed that he supported the idea that she return to Africa married to a Christian African. He may have originated the idea—certainly it was consistent with the Huntingdon Connexion's vision of missionary possibilities. More likely, he had found out about Hopkins's proposal (perhaps through Granville Sharp), and then thrown his particular weight behind it. Wheatley writes as if it was Thornton's proposal, but first describes the effects of Susanna Wheatley's death on her in the more personal terms she had used in her letter to Obour. She feels herself to be in the same state she had been "as a poor little outcast," seized from her African parent, one can add. "By the great loss I have sustain'd of my best friend I feel like one forsaken by her parent in a desolate wilderness, for such the world appears to me, wandr'ing thus without my friendly guide." She comes close to describing the vulnerability about which Thornton recently had warned her: "I fear lest every step should lead me into error and confusion." She tells him that Susanna had used "unwearied diligence to instruct me in the principles of true religion." But she declines Thornton's offer that "in these respects you could supply her place," an expression of his sense of authority to control Wheatley morally, as he may have tried to do in London at Susanna's behest, and when she was still a slave. She had flattered him as "the Father of the Humble African." But this, she continues, meaning supplying Susanna's place, "does not seem probable from the great distance of your residence," foreshadowing her still more dramatic refusal of his more dramatic proposal to marry her off and send her to Africa.

She continues, diplomatically, "However I will endeavour to compensate it by a strict observance of hers [Susanna's precepts and instructions] and your good advice from time to time which you have given me encouragement to hope for," but reminding this powerful, white, male authority, "what a Blessed source of consolation that our greatest friend is an immortal God," then surely with tongue-in-cheek, "it almost hinders a commendable self-estimation (at times) but quite beats down a boldness of presumption."

Wheatley follows this with her deliberate misreading of Thornton's warning against the indiscretion she might commit because of other people's kindness and respect for her, once she was free; she tells him, "I find exactly true your thoughts on behavior of those who seem'd to respect me while under my mistress's patronage, you said right, for some of them have already put on reserve"—in no wise way was this provoked by her, as Thornton had suggested—"but I submit while God rules; who never forsakes any till they have ungratefully forsakes him." This is to reiterate that her only master now was God.

The train of thought leads to "My old master's generous behavior in granting me freedom," specifying he had done so "about three months before the death of my deer mistress & of her desire, as well as his own humanity." This misrepresents the date—it had been six months before Susanna's death—but perhaps they had agreed it would take effect after that dreadful event. Perhaps, too, it reflects the fact that Thornton had written to John Wheatley urging him to free Wheatley. It is only now, once she is free of all earthly authority, Wheatley tells Thornton that if John had not freed her, "I hope I should willingly submit to servitude to be free in Christ.—But since it is this—Let me be a servant to *Christ* and that is the more perfect freedom."

This—telling Thornton she was free and that she wished to serve Christ—Wheatley follows immediately with, "You propose my returning to Africa with Bristol Yamma and John Quamine, if either of them upon strict enquiry is such, as I dare give my heart and hand . . . to." She tells Thornton that he saw her marriage as the corollary of her being freed. Her word "dare" connotes real risk, even reservations. "I believe they are either of them good enough if not too good for me, or they would not be fit for Missionaries." As the Hopkins-Stiles circular explained, they were not yet fit for missionaries. On the other hand, Wheatley was known and tested by her sponsors for her piety and learning. Thornton could read her sentence as irony, the kind of subtle self-assertion Wheatley showed earlier in this letter.

No longer can Wheatley give Susanna's illness as the reason not to accept Thornton and Hopkins's proposal. She asks Thornton, "Why do you hon'd sir, wish those poor men so much trouble as to carry me so long a voyage? Upon my arrival, how like a Barbarian shou'd I look to the Natives"; of course, she had come from a different part of West Africa, not Anomabu. The result of her traumatic leaving of what she called her "native shore," a place of "dark abodes," and a *"Pagan* land," had been her transformation into an Anglophone Christian. But this was witty irony, written to one who shared a view of Africans with, say, those eighteen gentlemen attestators to the authenticity of Wheatley's poetry in English, saying that the African child had been an "uncultivated Barbarian." Nisbet told Rush in connection with his published denigration of her poetry that Africa was a land of barbarianism, but it became a typical characterization of slave traders by their opponents.

Here Wheatley adds, "I can promise that my tongue shall be quiet for a strong reason indeed being an utter stranger to the language of Anamaboe." This is further evidence that Hopkins had shown Wheatley more of his correspondence with Quaque, addressing the condition of the place where Hopkins planned on sending the Quamine–Yamma–Wheatley mission. She may have been referring, too, to the requirements of Christian wifehood that she would be expected to demonstrate amidst the sexuo-racial complexities of the slave coast Quaque registered.[28]

Wheatley begins her next sentence in this letter to Thornton, "Now to be serious," implying jest in what she has just said, or said so far about

Yamma and Quamine having so much trouble in taking Wheatley with them to Africa. "This undertaking appears to be hazardous, and not sufficiently Eligible to go [she refers to herself]—and leave my British & American Friends," denoting family (the surviving Wheatleys, John, Mary, and Nathaniel); her "sister," Obour Tanner; her church's ministers; in fact, all those with whom she had become a Christian American after her childhood trauma, as well as Lady Huntingdon, Dartmouth, and Thornton himself. This must be read in the light of what she has told Thornton in the selfsame letter of the meaning of Susanna's very recent death, to prepare him for this refusal.

The sentence continues, "I am also unacquainted with these Missionaries in Person," her ignorance of these men denoting the physical consequence of the marriage she invoked again, although with the significant omission of "I am" before the phrase "not sufficiently Eligible." Her terms combine risks in marriage with those of a transatlantic crossing from America to Africa, the latter fraught with the prospect described so dauntingly by the returned Christianized African Quaque, whom she saw as a failure.

Hopkins, moreover, was badgering her: "The reverend gentleman who under[ta]kes their [Quamine and Yamma's] Education has repeatedly inform'd me by Letters of their prospect in Learning, also an account of John Quamine's family and [Kingdom? Letter torn]," obviously to enhance his attractiveness and qualifications to be Wheatley's husband. She concludes, "Be that as it will. I will resign it all to God's all wise governance. I thank you for your generous offer." This was a refusal. One could again see irony in her last sentence.

Metropolitan writers of fact and fiction, of private letters and sentimental novels, had long represented marriage as potential and actual slavery, a powerful source for women's particular interest in the enslavement of Africans.[29] Implicitly, Wheatley saw her civil liberty at stake in this "proposal" made by two powerful white men, to one of whom she was indebted, it seems, for playing a decisive role in her being freed from slavery. She shared vital religious values with them, values her beloved Susanna had imparted to her. How could she say no? But it bears repeating that their proposal was that Wheatley give control of her body and her life to a man she had never met, an agent on a mission Quaque represented as near hopeless. It would entail a return Middle Passage to a "Pagan Land," where she had first been enslaved by Africans and endured a voyage fraught with further trauma.

Conversely, her tongue would be made quiet. The proposal almost certainly would mean giving up her literary life, expressed in the poems her reborn self had made and was still making, and including the contacts for publishing, which Wheatley now needed to pursue herself.

Exuberant Freedom

Along with her direct, prose expression of herself to Thornton (presented partly in jest and with some irony), Wheatley put on her poet's *persona* to address her hypothesized husband's leaving her to go to Africa. This was in three poems published in the *Royal American Magazine*. The first was dated October 30, 1774, the same day she dated the letter to Thornton rejecting his proposal.[30]

The magazine introduced it in a paragraph probably written by Wheatley herself: "By particular request we insert the following Poem by Phillis (a young African of surprising genius) to a gentleman of the navy with his reply." The identification is not the invidious "a Negro poetess," but rather simple assertiveness, in keeping with the introduction's attack on racism and slavery, leaving aside religious values, consistent with her Occom letter's dramatic distinction, and with the ensuing poems' playfulness. "By this single instance may be seen the importance of education—Uncultivated nature is much the same in every part of the globe. . . . It is probable Europe and Africa would be alike savage or polite in the same circumstances; though, it may be questioned, whether men who have no *artificial* wants, are capable of becoming so ferocious as those, who, by faring *sumptuously every day*, are reduced to a habit of thinking it necessary to *their* happiness, to plunder the whole human race." The equivalence of Europe and Africa as "savage or polite," and the description of enslavers as "ferocious," can be seen as a version of the exclamation in her letter, "how like a Barbarian shou'd I look to the Natives" and in giving the motive of slavers as "Avarice." European slavers' nature was as degraded as they asserted Africans' was, by the luxury that the slave system produced.[31]

The first of the poems is entitled "To a Gentleman of the Navy," his name, "Rochfort." The poet adds a second naval gentleman

("Greaves deserves my lays"), going on to celebrate their relationship. Vincent Carretta has identified "Rochfort" and "Greaves" as sailors who served on the Royal Navy's ship *Preston*, one of twenty-two ships commanded by Vice Admiral Samuel Graves in the summer of 1774, enforcing the Boston Port Act, Britain's punitive response to the Tea Party. There were three men named Graves on the fleet, Third Lieutenant John Graves, a nephew of the admiral, and his brother, Thomas. "Greaves," Carretta notes, was "a phonetically accurate alternative spelling of "Graves." Carretta takes at face value that "Rochfort" wrote the second poem, "THE ANSWER [BY THE GENTLEMAN OF THE NAVY]," December 2, 1774, to Wheatley's first poem; Carretta remarks that "none of the historical context finds its way in to the poems exchanged between Wheatley and John Prime Iron Rochfort . . . an able seaman on the *Preston*." Just how Wheatley settled on these names has not been explained. In any case, I suggest that Wheatley wrote all three poems in playful response to the Thornton-Hopkins design to send her to Africa with Quamine and Yamma; the proposal and her declining it were the poems' very immediate context.[32]

The proposed voyage was also the occasion for Wheatley to emulate Pope's *Iliad* again, throughout asserting she is a poet, not a missionary's wife. She tells the embarking heroes,

> Had you appear'd on the Achaian shore
> Troy now had stood, and Helen charm'd no more.
> The Phrygian hero that resign'd the dame
> For purer joys in friendship's sacred flame,
> The noblest gift, and of the immortal kind,
> That heightens, dignifies the manly mind.

Leaving Wheatley behind, Quamine's and Yamma's relationship would be unsullied by sexuality, expressing superior manliness, appropriate to their religious mission.

They sail off:

> Strange to relate! With canvas wing they speed
> To distant worlds; of distant worlds the dread.

The trembling natives of the peaceful plain,
Astonish'd view the heroes of the main,
Wond'ring to see two chiefs of matchless grace,
. . .
The thirst of glory burns each youthful breast.

Quamine had claims to being a chief, but more evident is the relation between these lines and Wheatley's coincident sentence "how like a Barbarian shou'd I look to the Natives." They bring to mind the boy Gronniosaw's first sight of a slave ship approaching the African shore and perhaps, a seven-year-old African girl's, too.

But her heroes are not classical Greek pagans, let alone slave traders, but missionaries:

In virtue's cause, the muse implores for grace,
These blooming sons of Neptune's royal race;
Cerulean youths! Your joint assent declare,
Virtue to rever'nce, more than mortal fair,

The two heroes' promise of success is in terms conventionally applied to evangelization, combined with that elevated, manly relationship. They prefer to show their virtue in deeply respectful, religious feeling, over the earthly beauties of a woman,

A crown of glory which the muse will twine,
Immortal trophy! Rochfort shall be thine!
Thine too, O Greaves! For virtue's offspring share,
Celestial friendship, and the muse's care.

The muse wishes them "Bon Voyage."

Had Rochfort or Greaves been as accomplished a poet as Wheatley shows herself here, and had they had the appropriate feelings to express, the next poem is what they might have said in answer to her rejection of the proposal to take her with them as a sexual partner. The writer of "THE ANSWER [BY THE GENTLEMAN OF THE NAVY]" puts the poet on a pedestal, rather than allow a white reverend to assign her to his mastery:

> Celestial muse! Sublimest of the nine,
> Assist my song, and dictate every line:
> . . .
> To sing this great, this lovely virgin's praise;
> But yet, alas! What tribute can I bring
> WH-TL-Y but smiles, whilst I thus faintly sing.

Her coinciding letters to Thornton said of her two marital prospects she believed "them good enough if not too good for me," damning them with faint praise and the Hopkins-Stiles circular's wish to raise money to improve their learning. The poem's insistence, too, on Wheatley's virginity hypostasizes her rejection of her sexual union with a potential missionary's person.

The white gentleman officer sees no color line as he brings poetic tribute to the Wheatley he is happy to leave virginal.

> Behold with reverence and with joy adore;
> The lovely daughter of the Affric shore,

the line repeating that the feelings he has for Wheatley are reverential, looking up to her, innocent of sexuality.

She further describes the fantasized venue for the mission, taking the opportunity to reiterate the feelings to be kindled are "divine," nonsexual:

> Where every grace and every virtue join,
> That kindles friendship and makes love divine:
> In hue as diff'rent as in souls above;

It is the young African, Wheatley herself, who is different "in hue"—the symbolic gentleman here implicitly white; but just as the color of souls is irrelevant in heaven, so an African can inspire divine love as well as a white. (Wheatley should not have to settle for marriage to an African because of color.)

> The rest of mortals who in vain have strove,
> Th' immortal wreathe, the muses gift to share,
> Which heav'n reserv'd for this angelic fair.

Wheatley has succeeded in snatching a laurel from the great poet's triumphant wreath, her subjects here, like Pope's Homer's, set on the "Achaian shore." She can join "the angelic train," she has told us, by being brought from Africa to America, not the reverse, and now according to the logic of previous lines, she, too, is "angelic fair."

The next stanza's representation of Africa goes with the idyllic one of Wheatley as a lovely virgin, her origin a place where every grace and virtue join.

> Blest be the guilded shore, the happy land,
> Where spring and autumn gently hand in hand;
> O'er shady forests that scarce know a bound,
> In vivid blaze alternately dance around:

The tropics are, moreover, inspirational, contrary to Hume and the review of Wheatley's poems published shortly before she wrote this:

> Where cancer's torrid heat the soul inspires
> With strains divine and true poetic fires;
> (Far from the reach of Hudson's chilly bay)
> Where cheerful phoebus makes all nature gay;

"Phoebus" has the same power she has described the poet's "imagination" having[33]—

> Where sweet refreshing breezes gently fan;
> The flow'ry path, the ever verdant lawn,
> The artless grottos, and the soft retreats;
> "At once the lover and thee muse's seats."

It was a vision Wheatley shared with James Thomson and other British creators of an Africa intended to counter its denigrators, termed "pseudo-Africa" by Wylie Sypher,[34] but given first-hand authority by Michael Adanson's *Voyage to Guinea*, translated in 1759, one source for Benezet and for lawyer Francis Hargrave's refutation of African barbarism in his defense of James Somerset, before Lord Mansfield.[35] It may be, as Wheatley told Dartmouth to make her political case, that enslavement taught her the meaning of freedom, and that being brought from Africa to America was worth it since it brought her to Christianity. Even in that poem (to which she alludes earlier in this sequence of poems), she had adjured "Christians" to "Remember Negroes black as Cain may be refin'd"—they may already be refined, as well as having the potential she demonstrates. But in this poem, Wheatley is free to think about Africa in this way—to share this idyllic vision with other sympathetic writers, to assert the poetic self she has become, precisely because she is not going back there. She is free to declare Africa was

> Where nature taught (tho's strange it is to tell,)
> Her flowing pencil Europe to excel

emphasizing her further repudiation of the assertion that proximity to the sun enfeebles the mind and deadens invention.[36]

Africa's glory is its capacity to inspire art; Britain's, she writes here, has been manifest in "great Sir Isaac's" scientific exploration of "the sacred depths of nature." Her description of the godlike Newton, who, "on philosophic wings,"

> Rode with the planets thro' the circling rings:
> Surveying nature with a curious eye,
> And viewing other systems in the sky[,]

resembles her representation of poetic imagination, indeed, of poets themselves, again alluding to that line of Pope to which she had referred in "To Maecenas," using the same ten syllable line Pope so frequently used:

> We on thy pinions can surpass the wind,
> And leave the rolling universe behind.

"THE ANSWER" turns from Britain's glory in Newton to Milton:

> Where nature's bard with true poetic lays
> The pristine state of paradise displays.
> And with a genius that's very rare

> Describes the first the only happy pair
> That in terrestrial mansions ever reign'd
> View'd happiness now lost, and now regain'd.

It is tempting to see here a glancing reference to the hazardous coupling Wheatley has just forsworn. But the poet's point is that now, in 1774, Britain, this once "happy land,"

> No more can boast but of the power to kill,
> By force of arms or diabolic skill.

This last phrase is a reference to Wheatley's poem on Tarleton's capture of General Lee during the Revolutionary War. This was metropolitan Britain, attempting to put down the American rebels, the purpose of the fleet blockading Boston in which "Rochfort" and "Greaves" served, but Wheatley's naval gentleman ostensibly writing this has the same view of Britain as the revolutionaries.

The supposed poet's purpose in describing Britain's Goliath-like tyranny is to contrast that with the poet, turning to the figure of Wheatley with relief:

> For softer strains we quickly must repair
> To Wheatley's song, for Wheatley is the fair,
> That has the art, which art cold ne'er acquire
> To dress each sentence with seraphic fire,

The self-emancipated Wheatley can now express the promise of the American Revolution.

The last two lines repeat the contrast between Wheatley's and the supposed Rochfort's poetic ability:

> Her wondrous virtues I could ne'er express!
> To paint her charms would only make them less.[37]

The compliment paid to her in "THE ANSWER" is reversed in "PHILLIS'S REPLY TO THE ANSWER," published three days later in the *Royal Magazine*. Wheatley asks the muse,

For one bright moment, heavenly goddess! Shine,
Inspire my song and form the lays divine.
Rochford attend!

She calls him "Beloved of Phoebus," like Africans, perhaps a clue that she had written his poem, too, giving this reply fine, ironic scope.

Struck with thy song, each vain conceit resign'd,
A soft affection seiz'd my grateful mind,
While I each golden sentiment admire
In thee the muse's bright celestial fire.
The generous plaudit 'tis not mine to claim,
A muse untutor'd, and unknown to fame.

Wheatley is known as "untutor'd" but is famous, more clues that she is the poet who has written Rochford's lines. It was, perhaps, an additional rebuke to Thornton.

"PHILLIS'S ANSWER" continues to contrast her ostensibly inferior, African ability with that displayed by the white gent, and one imagines the pleasure Wheatley took in the irony of her writing his lines for him.

The heavenly sisters pour thy notes along
And crown their bard with every grace of song.
My pen, least favour'd by the tuneful nine,
Can never rival, never equal thine;
Then fix the humble Afric muse's seat
At British Homer's and Sir Isaac's feet.
Those bards whose fame in deathless strains arise
Creations boast, and fav'rites of the skies.

She elaborates on the effects of Rochfort's poem on her, in its depiction of Africa:

Charm'd with thy painting, how my bosom burns!
And pleasing Gambia on my soul returns,
With native grace in spring's luxuriant reign,

> Smiles the gay mead, and Eden blooms again,
> The various bower, the tuneful flowing stream,
> The soft retreats, the lovers golden dream,
> Her soil spontaneous yields exhaustless stores[.]

Scholars have elicited autobiography in her reference to Gambia. But it is in the light of her freeing herself from having to return that one can see Wheatley now able to make her own psychological link, via Milton, to her innocent childhood, before that terrible tearing from an Edenic parental garden by slavers.

She attributes to "Rochford," a figure one can see as one of self-love, the opposite of prejudice to Africanness:

> For Phoebus revels in her verdant shores.
> Whose flowery births, a fragrant train appear;
> And crowns the youth throughout the smiling year.

The poet has reversed that vision of darkest Africa propounded by Quaque and Hopkins, let alone the Rev. Shirley, and others who would civilize and Christianize it, as in some sense she restores herself to her pre-enslaved, pre-Christianized childhood; but her vision is couched in the language she has mastered, and is suffused with its values.

> There, as in Britain's favour'd isle, behold
> The bending harvest ripen into gold!
> Just are thy views of Afric's blissful plain,
> On the warm limits of the land and main.

If earlier in the poem Wheatley has prayed her "Afric muse" be fixed at Milton and Pope's feet, then, writing towards the end, noting that in Milton, "Britain's prophet dies," she asks, "Whence shall other Newton rise?" and concludes by praying,

> Muse, bid thy Rochford's matchless pen display
> The charms of friendship on the sprightly lay.
> Queen of his song,

surely Wheatley herself, inspiring divine love, his muse, but her own, too, as she unites them in emulating Milton,

> . . . thro' all his numbers shine,
> And plausive glories, goddess! Shall be thine.
> With partial grace thou mak'st his verse excel,
> And his glory to describe so well.
> Cerulean bard! to thee these strains belong,
> The Muse's darling and the prince of song.

Was this last phrase a final, playful clue to the representation of Quamine as Rochford, Quamine identified by either himself or Hopkins-Stiles as the Royal African, the Prince of Annamaboe?[38]

The phrase "partial grace," that is, grace biased in favor of, adds to the suggestion that Wheatley wrote his poem, as well as the other two, answering the question posed in "To Maecenas."

> The happier *Terence* all the choir inspir'd,
> His soul replenish'd, and his bosom fir'd,
> But say, ye *Muses*, why this partial grace,
> To one alone of *Afric's* sable race;
> From age to age transmitting this his name
> With the first glory in the rolls of fame?

Wheatley is the African heir of Terence, and of Milton and Pope, but her art, "art could ne'er acquire." Self-emancipated now, she can be the voice of the American Revolution.

Jerome McGann has defined the "poetics of sensibility" as "a revolution in literary style." "The words 'sensibility' and 'sentiment' name a momentous cultural shift whose terms were defined in the eighteenth century."[39] While he upholds Locke's work as the leader in the "disordering of the senses," he emphasizes Newton's, too. McGann shows us that in his absorption and popularization of Locke and Newton, Pope was powerfully influential in generating this shift in literature, toward sensibility. According to McGann, Pope's attention is captured by "how exquisitely fine," how thin the "partitions which sense from Thought divide," phrases from *An Essay on Man*. To this Pope adapts Newton's optics, which, as a trope "recovers, in a distinctively enlightenment idiom, the ancient idea of the power of art as the special privilege of human nature."[40] Wheatley incorporates Africans and women into this vision, into her poetry, her letters, and its exemplification into herself. These poems on "Rochfort" and "Greaves" demonstrate her learning and her art, in implicit contrast to the qualifications of Quamine and Yamma, to be both husbands and to be missionaries, which we have seen she gently called into question in that letter she wrote to Thornton when she began these poems.

7

Freedom and Death

Transformation

The imaginative freedom Wheatley expressed in the trilogy published immediately after her refusal of Hopkins and Thornton's proposal was deployed under dramatically changing circumstances. In 1775, she and John Wheatley were "refugees from British-occupied Boston," and she "found herself in new and unstable ground as she simultaneously lost her first patrons and discovered that the imperial world that had done so well by her was itself being transformed."[1]

That was the setting for her October 1775 poem "To His Excellency General Washington," accompanied by a letter, the combination she used when writing to Dartmouth and in sending her Whitefield poem to Lady Huntingdon. We can assume she had Washington's patronage in mind.[2] Washington was in New England, about to relieve the besieged Boston. When he "arrived in Cambridge . . . to drive the British out of Boston, he was shocked to see armed black men alongside . . . white New Englanders." He had resisted the recruitment of African Americans into his own troops. Some of his own slaves had emancipated themselves by joining British forces. He told Congress he would allow black soldiers to re-enlist out of necessity but discouraged new recruitments.[3]

Wheatley's poem to him opens, "Columbia's scenes of glorious toils I write," and it was in this poem that Wheatley contributed the first "fully developed personification of America," as "Columbia, although it had been used as early as 1761 to designate English America as opposed to Britannica." She continues,

> While freedom's cause her anxious breast alarms,
> She flashes dreadful in refulgent arms.
> See mother earth her offspring's fate bemoan,
> And nations gaze at scenes before unknown.

This sympathizes with all the dead, but the poet's cause is freedom, for which she has a particular love and wish that it be extended to all (as she said in her poem to Dartmouth), because she has been literally enslaved.

> The goddess comes, she moves divinely fair
> Olive and laurel bind her golden hair
> Wherever shines this native of the skies,
> Unnumber'd charms and recent graces rise.

Responses to freedom are irresistible, ubiquitous.[4]

Wheatley addresses her "Muse!" in describing the movement of armies with Homeric similes, before she asks,

> Shall I to Washington their praises recite?
> Enough thou know'st them in the fields of fight.

She continues, Shuffleton remarks, "more peremptorily":

> Thee, first in place and honours,—we demand
> The grace and glory of thy martial band.

This was "a clever shift of reference without any sense of disruption from addressing the Muse to imploring Washington's aid," to make Washington "a mythic spirit presiding over the American enterprise." Her address to him had direct bearing on the current debate among the white leadership over "enlisting black soldiers in the Continental armies besieging Boston," at the time occupied by British troops.[5]

She demands Washington,

> Fam'd for thy valour, for thy virtues more,
> Hear every tongue, this guardian and implore!

Washington, famed especially for his virtue, should not ignore the tongue of "the famous *Phillis Wheatley*, the African poetess," as she was called "when the poem was published the following spring in Williamsburg and Philadelphia." Wheatley's "'we' in 'we demand / the grace and glory of thy martial band' is simultaneously a patriotic we," including herself as she did, identifying with all American patriots, "and a specifically black collective," on behalf of black soldiers' demand for re-enlistment.[6]

Wheatley prayed to Washington to vent his "fury" on

> . . . whoever dares disagree
> This land of freedom's heaven—defended race!
> Fix'd are the eyes of nations on the scales,
> For in their hopes Columbia's arm prevails.

The "race" is made up of all those identifying themselves with freedom; the word did not yet have the narrow denotation it would, although pseudo-scientific racism was crystallizing in this era. Among those who "disgrace" freedom are not only opponents of General Washington, his armies, and fellow revolutionaries, but in Wheatley's view, those "modern Egyptians" denying freedom to slaves, who "Cry for Liberty." She adjures Washington again,

> Proceed great chief with virtue on thy side,
> Thy ev'ry action let the goddess guide.

One action was the enlistment of black troops. Wheatley showed the way, declaring in the first sentence of her letter to the slaveholding general, "I have taken the freedom to address your Excellency in the enclosed poem, and entreat your acceptance." As in the case of her letter to Dartmouth, she gave the occasion: "Your being appointed by the Grand Continental Congress to be Generalissimo of the armies of North America, together with the fame of your virtues, excite sensations not easy to suppress." Reading the announcement, recalling her knowledge of Washington, irresistibly affected her sensibility, so "Your generosity, therefore, I presume, will pardon the attempt." This is playful irony, depending on mutuality of sensibility between this now famous, African poetess and the famous, slaveholding gentleman-general, a man of feeling. "Wishing your Excellency all possible success in the great cause you are so generously engaged in," "generously" because it is on behalf of a principle in all, regardless of color and implicitly, gender. "I am, Your Excellency's most obedient humble servant, Phillis Wheatley."[7]

She dated her letter October 26, 1775, the day she addressed her poem to him. Washington replied early in 1776. He addressed her as "Miss Phillis," explaining he had not received her letter until mid-December, and mentioning "the variety of important occurrences, continually interposing to distract the mind," and explaining his "neglect" was only "seeming." "I thank you most sincerely for your polite notice of me"—politeness was of central value to the American elite but especially to Washington, so Wheatley's "Excellency" and "Generalissimo" hit the spot—"in the elegant lines you enclosed, and however undeserving I may be of such panegyric"—modesty too, was essential to politeness— "the style and manner exhibit a striking proof of your poetical talents," an echo of the widely publicized examination of Wheatley's ability as a "negro poet." His knowledge that she was black was signified by his addressing her as "Miss Phillis."[8]

Washington tells her he "should have published the poem as a tribute justly to you," but did not because, apprehensive "that while I only meant to give the world this new instance of your genius I might have incurred the reputation of vanity." He knew of her "genius." The charge of vanity became a preoccupation as the genteel began to give themselves over to individualism. One can see this, too, as further evidence of Washington's notorious preoccupation with his reputation. He postponed the fallout of publicly associating himself with a black female poet, whose work was already grist for the debate over slavery. To her Washington disingenuously explained, "This and nothing else, determined me not to give it place in the public prints."[9] Washington concluded with an invitation to Wheatley to visit him at his Cambridge headquarters, overseeing his siege of Boston, where, he wrote, "I shall be happy to see a person so favored by the Muses, and to whom nature has been so liberal and beneficent in her dispensations." Perhaps this was inflected with the same racist investigatoriness Wheatley so often endured. She may have visited Washington at his headquarters soon after this—historians differ.[10]

Washington sent Wheatley's letter and poem to Colonel Joseph Reed, his former secretary, back in Virginia, with the suggestion that Reed might "be amused by reading a letter and poem addressed to me by Miss Phillis Wheatley." Washington explained he had come across the two documents accidentally, while sorting through papers to get rid of useless ones. He repeated what he had written Wheatley: "At first, with a view of doing justice to her poetical genius, I had a great mind to publish the poem; but not knowing whether it might not be considered rather as a mark of my own vanity, than a compliment to her, I laid it aside, till I came across it again in the manner just mentioned." Reed, who was Washington's "closest aid," in whom he had "unbounded confidence," read Washington's wishes and so "forwarded Wheatley's letter and poem to the editor of the *Virginia Gazette*, where they were published apparently without Washington's permission," with a note from Reed to the publisher: "Pray insert the enclosed letter and verses written by the famous PHILLIS WHEATLEY, the AFRICAN poetess, in your next gazette." This identified Wheatley as exceptional in the terms in which she had become famous, but perhaps in a way that would not offend slaveholders, although it could also help Washington with opponents of slavery. Kenneth Silverman writes that the "entire episode, occurring while Washington was preoccupied with shaping and maintaining an army, demonstrated a facet of the new commander's personality of which his admirers so far were ignorant. He saw himself as a patron of the arts." Washington's calling her a "genius" conferred honor on his patronage, albeit ambivalently.[11]

The following month, Tom Paine reprinted Wheatley's letter and poem to Washington in his *Pennsylvania Magazine or American Monthly Museum*. It was an exhibit in Paine's goal for the magazine to promote the view "that the future of literature lay with America," and Wheatley's "To To HIS EXCELLENCY GENERAL WASHINGTON" accompanied other "poems and short fiction," in addition to "scientific and technical treaties, engravings, music, and news," in several "fat issues" which had 1,500 subscribers, "a larger circulation than that of any previous American magazine." In May 1776, John Hancock, president of Congress, commissioned Charles Willson Peale to paint a portrait of Washington after his first military victory, driving the British out of Boston. Silverman writes that a "view of Boston appears in the background, with Old South and Christ churches, and smoke from burning Charlestown. Washington is shown as Phillis Wheatley's 'Generalissimo,' the great commander in chief, in buff and blue uniform with epaulettes, green sash, lunge brass buttons, and sword." One imagines both Hancock—one of Wheatley's attestators three years earlier—and Washington recommended Wheatley's now famous poem to the painter, but probably without referring to Wheatley's subtle plea in the matter of black troops.[12]

The year before, in March 1775, Paine had published his influential "African Slavery in America" and in April, Paine became a founding member of the first antislavery society in America. He asked the same question that had originated among Britons' identifying their Protestant nation with liberty, and now powerfully dramatized by the rhetoric of the American Revolution, a question asked by many of the subjects of this book, from Quaque to Wheatley: "With what consistency [Americans] complain so loudly of attempts to enslave them, while they hold so many hundred thousands in slavery; and enslave many thousands more . . . ?"[13]

Wheatley had not reiterated her version of this inconsistency explicitly in her poem to Washington, but she did in her unpublished "Ode on the Death of General Wooster" of July 1778, the Connecticut merchant to whom she had described her activities in London and who had acted as her agent in selling her book. She sent the poem in a letter to his widow, Mary, the sister of a woman whose death in childbirth Wheatley had commemorated in a consolatory poem to her husband, the Rev. Thomas Clap. Mary Wooster had written Wheatley, enclosing her husband's obituary. Wheatley replied, "It was with the most sensible regret that I heard of his fall in battle: the pain of so afflicting a dispensation of Providence must be greatly alleviated to you and all his friends in the consideration that he fell a martyr in the Cause of Freedom."[14] She then writes out her poem:

> From this the Muse rich consolation draws
> He nobly perish'd in his Country's cause
> His Country's Cause, that ever fir'd his mind
> Where martial flames and Christian virtues join'd.

She had said that Washington possessed these virtues, too. Rooted in their reading of the ancients, eighteenth-century republicans, metropolitan and colonial, made "virtue" central to their self-conception, in opposition to the corruption of ministerial government, Sir Robert Walpole's in particular, and then of the imperial government's assertion of control over the American colonies. As we have seen, Wheatley extended this definition to black people and defined virtue to exclude racism. Conventionally, the "martial" virtue was gendered, Jan Lewis listing "strength, courage, self-sacrifice, distinterestedness" to go with it, "comprising the character necessary for a citizen of a republic." While there was some overlap, a woman's virtue was the chastity with which we have seen Wheatley's "On Virtue" identified. That poem also illustrates such a meaning's conflation with the Christianity to which her poem on Wooster's death refers, following biblical prescription, to "guide my steps to endless life and bliss," common ground between the sexes.[15]

The notion also connoted being "a man of feeling," as Wheatley presents Wooster to have been:

> Only serene the expiring hero lies
> And this (while hear inward roll his swimming eyes):

He prays,

> Permit me yet to paint fair freedom's charms
> For her the Continent shines bright in arms,

and Wheatley continues this female personification of freedom, a romantic equivalent to the lady for whom knights quested with martial and Christian virtues:[16]

> By the high will, celestial prize she came—
> For her we combat on the field of fame,

the trope allowing Wheatley to show the fundamental importance of the love of freedom to being virtuous:

> Without her presence vice maintains full sway
> And social love and virtue wing their way.

Wheatley's favorite poet made social love of central value in his "Essay on Man," essential to the balancing of "true Self-Love," which, untrue and unbalanced, could exploit and enslave.[17]

Wheatley's Wooster continues his prayer that the love of freedom would

> ... lead Columbia thro' the toils of war.
> With thine own hand conduct them and defend
> And bring the dreadful contest to an end—
> For ever grateful let them live for thee
> And keep them ever virtuous, brave and free—

The love of freedom is essential to virtuous success in the war, as well as to social cohesion. This is the setting for the hero's rhetorical warning:

> But how, presumptions shall we hope to find
> Divine acceptance with th' Almighty mind—
> While yet (O deed Ungenerous) they disgrace
> And hold in bondage Afric's blameless race?
> Let virtue reign—And thou accord our prayers
> Be victory our's, and generous freedom theirs.

The "we" is uttered by the white, revolutionary officer, speaking for whites like himself. The "disgrace" refers to the revolutionaries who go against God's making the principle of freedom universal, explicit in Wheatley's letter to Occom, implicit in her poem to Washington. The "deed Ungenerous"—withholding freedom from enslaved blacks—is a betrayal of the "social love," the virtue that depends on the love of freedom. Not to free African slaves could lead to defeat, and if not military defeat, then the triumph of the vicious and antisocial, a view very close to Hopkins's and other clergymen's, linking the revolution to antislavery.

Wooster dies, and in her voice (of course, his had been hers, too), the poet follows his abolitionist prayer, provoked by the monstrous inconsistency, with her typical consolation to a widow, although her husband awaits

> ... thy coming to the realms of light
> Freed from his labours in the ethereal skies
> Where in succession endless pleasures rise!

This may seem to take on particular meaning in view of the poet's words on earthly slavery.

To continue with Shuffleton's view of Wheatley's "self-transformation," she was realigning herself with "an imagined revolutionary order in which she hoped to follow other Americans," black and white, in "the passage from subject to citizen." At the same time, a chief purpose of Wheatley's letter was the practical one of getting Mary Wooster to return "to me by the first opy [opportunity] those books that remain unsold and remitting the money for those that are sold—I can easily dispose of them here for 12/Lmo [lawful money] each—I am greatly obliged to you for the care you show me, and your condescension in taking so much again for my Interest"; Wheatley's business with Wooster had been done by mail. "I am extremely sorry not to have been honour'd with a personal acquaintance with you." She added, "If the foregoing lines meet with your acceptance and approbation I shall think them highly honour'd." She asks pardon for the letter's length, giving as the reason a "fondness for the subject & the highest respect for the deceas'd." The former was the cause of freedom, the subject of her letter to Occom and her poem to Washington.[18]

Wheatley's poem to a third general of the revolutionary armies further illustrates Wheatley's reorientation to the new order. "On the Capture of General Lee" relates an episode in the life of Charles Lee, Washington's second-in-command. He is depicted as a patriotic hero who captured by the Iago-like treachery of the verbose British cavalry leader Banastre Tarleton, unnamed in the poem.[19]

"The deed perfidious and the Hero's fate" she presents largely in the form of a dialogue between her contemporaries—real historical figures—in contrast to those between Greek or Roman gods, or the Biblical characters Goliath and David, although, like Goliath, the figure representing Tarleton is a "boaster." Lee replies to him,

> Oh arrogance of tongue!
> And wild ambition, ever prone to wrong!
> Believ'st thou chief, that armies such as thine,
> Can stretch in dust that heav'n-defended line?

Wheatley then presents the American cause against British attempts to defeat them in entirely patriotic terms, referring to the mercenaries whom Britain is employing—"In vain allies may swarm from distant lands," their motives "various." This is in contrast to the Americans represented by Lee: "For plunder you, and we for freedom fight"—freedom for Wheatley always denoting freedom for black people, too—

> Her cause divine with generous ardor fires,
> And every bosom glows as she inspires!

Wheatley's freedom is invariably represented as a female figure. She takes the opportunity again to apostrophize Washington:

> Yet those brave troops innum'rous as the sands
> One soul inspires, one General Chief commands.

Here, the first of a new modern pantheon—

> Find in your train of boasted heroes one
> To match the praise of Godlike Washington[?]
> Thrice happy Chief! in whom the virtues join,
> And heav-taught prudence speaks the man divine!

So the captive Lee is able to implant "Doubt of conquest, on the hostile plain." The war went badly after the fall of Charleston, and American troops were "suffering from serious loss of morale." In June 1780, "The Sentiments of an American Woman," soliciting contributions for the support of American soldiers, was published anonymously in Philadelphia and reprinted in newspapers everywhere. Its author was Esther DeBerdt Reed, wife of Joseph Reed, Washington's secretary who had been instrumental in publishing Wheatley's poem celebrating Washington. The plan was "the mobilization of the entire female population to raise money for the troops." Mary Beth Norton observes that women of significant "social standing undertook the unfeminine task of soliciting contributions . . . from strangers, poor people, and servants," as well as from friends and neighbors. The total was to be sent to Martha Washington but not to replace what Congress or the States supplied: Washington himself insisted that the $300,000 raised should buy shirts. This large-scale and successful effort was, Norton argues, an important move of women into public life because of the revolution. One of the contributors was "an African American woman," whom Sharon M. Harris identifies as probably Wheatley. Joseph Reed may have suggested her to his wife.[20]

"The Sentiments of an American Woman" asserted women's value "for the public good," in terms comparable to, say, Mercy Otis Warren's *History of the American Revolution*, pointing to the patriotism expressed by the action of classical and Biblical heroines. Of particular meaning to Wheatley would have been its statement that women were "Born for liberty," and the celebration of "queens who have broken the chains of slavery, forged by tyrants in the times of ignorance and barbarity." Now, famously, in 1776, Abigail Adams had brought such a vision to bear on the subordination of wives to husbands ("all men would be tyrants if they could"). This was to apply to the potential she saw in revolutionary lawmaking. Marriage, Abigail's sister said, was "the important crisis on which our fate depends." The British feminist writer Mary Scott placed Wheatley in this tradition, aligning her with Catherine Macaulay.[21]

American revolutionaries won the war, and the peace treaty with their former rulers was signed in Paris in 1783. Wheatley celebrated these events in "Liberty and Peace," published under the name Phillis Peters as a broadside in Boston in 1784, the year of the beginning of antislavery legislation in Massachusetts, along with other Northern states.[22] She was able to develop the assertion she had made in her poem to Washington, his cause freedom. She had said, ". . . nations gaze at scenes unknown," and now declares,

> LO! Freedom comes, the prescient Muse foretold,
> All Eyes th' accomplish'd Prophecy behold:

reminding readers of her own prescience by quoting her now well-known poem to Washington:

> . . . She moves divinely fair,
> "Olive and Laurel bind her golden Hair

Wheatley's goddess looks to a peaceful politics and a welcoming country, associating peace with flourishing international trade, as did Ignatius

Sancho, and because both Wheatley and Sancho opposed the slave trade and slavery, they assumed they would not be part of that commerce. Peace would fix her "illustrious line" in Columbia,

> And bids in thee her future Councils shine.
> In every Realm her Portal open'd wide,
> Receives from all the full commercial Tide.

She envisioned the same future Paine was championing in the *Pennsylvania Magazine*:

> Each Art and Science now with rising Charms
> The expanding Heart with Emulation warms.

This had followed vicious civil war, and "Liberty and Peace" is notable for its recollection of the kind of violence Grimsted suggests expressed subterranean anger in the poet:

> On hostile Fields fraternal arms engage,
> And mutual Deaths, all dealt with mutual Rage;
> The Muse's ear hears mother Earth deplore
> Her ample surface smoak with kindred Gore:
> The hostile Field destroys the social Ties,

That political value she also expressed in her poem to Wooster: "And ever-lasting Slumber seals their Eyes." This continued dramatically: Columbia mourns,

> Her Treasures plunder'd and her towns destroy'd
> Witness how *Charlestown's* curling Smoaks arise,
> In sable Columns to the clouded Skies!

The poem refers to one of the worst defeats suffered by the Americans:

> The ample Dome, high-wrought with curious Toil,
> In one sad Hour the savage Troops despoil
> Peace resounding from every tongue.

Peace has come and liberty is established: Britain acknowledges "Freedom's . . . Independent Reign" and Hibernia, Scotia, Spain, and Germania admire

> The generous Spirit that *Columbia* fires
> Auspicious Heaven shall fill with fav'ring Gales
> Where e'er *Columbia* spreads her swelling sails
> To every Realm shall Peace her Charms display,
> And Heavenly *Freedom* spread her gold ray.

This is a transatlantic vision charged for Wheatley as she recalls what her two voyages have brought her, the freedom with which she associates imagination and political inclusiveness, as well as salvation.

These poems represent Wheatley's response to her post-1773 circumstances, "developing a more complex pluralistic sense of audience" than in her first collection. She had edited *Poems* with British sensibilities in mind, omitting pro-revolutionary work. Now war had closed the British market to American authors. But Wheatley did perpetuate one theme her *Poems* had embodied, referring to her most powerful trauma. In 1779 or so, she wrote "To Mr. and Mrs.—, On the Death of Their Infant Son," resonating with her enslavement in her own infancy. It opens, "O Death!" by whom,

> so sweetly blooming once that lovely boy
> His father's hope, his mother's only joy,

was so soon snatched.

> Two moons revolve when lo! among the dead
> The beauteous infant lays his weary head;
> For long he strove the tyrant to withstand
> And the dread terrors of his iron hand;

the terms are close to those of her poem to Dartmouth, opposing the tyranny which had threatened "the iron chain" of slavery, and depicted the steel-souled slaver seizing her parent's beloved babe.[23]

But in this poem and in a familiar sequence, the heavens welcome the child, showing him "scenes unknown before." There, spirits cry to him:

> Hail: thou! Thrice welcome to the happy shore.
> Born to new life where changes are no more.

The virtually orphaned child was welcomed by Susanna Wheatley. The poet acknowledges,

> Mean time on earth the hapless parents mourn,
> "Too quickly fled, ah! never to return."

Marriage, Pregnancy, and Death

If Wheatley's choice of America rather than Africa allowed her to continue her poetic career, it also allowed her to marry a man she knew. Wheatley married John Peters in November 1778. Carretta writes that they did not "rush into marriage," having announced "their intentions to marry" the previous April. In May 1778, she wrote Obour, then living in Worcester, asking her to "write me by every opportunity. Direct your letters under cover to Mr. John Peters in Queen Street" in Boston. Boston had been occupied and left by the British. "The vast variety of scenes that have pass'd before us these 3 years past," since the time she had written to Washington and probably visited him, "will to a reasonable mind serve to convince us of the uncertain duration of all things temporal, and the proper result of such a condition is an ardent desire of, & preparation for, a state and enjoyments which are more suitable to the immortal mind." She was hungry for letters from Obour, who shared such hopes. "You will do me a great favour if you'll write by every opportunity." By then she was living with her future husband. They were married in Boston's Second Congregational Church, by Susanna Wheatley's son-in-law, the Rev. John Lathrop, widower of Mary Wheatley, who had helped teach Phillis English. She had probably gone with them to Providence during the British occupation; Mary died shortly before Wheatley's marriage, aged thirty five.[24]

Phillip M. Richards writes that, in getting married, Wheatley "followed an increasingly popular pattern of domestic life among blacks in the post-Revolutionary period, by marrying, taking the name of her husband and bearing children."[25] They shared the hope expressed by those black, male petitioners in 1773 Boston, exclaiming, "We have no wives!" Carretta writes that Wheatley "had much to gain in terms of security by marrying," or at least hoped so. Shuffleton suggests that one of the conditions helping to sponsor her addressing new audiences was her economic instability as an unmarried woman in Boston, although Carretta adds, "She knew that marriage would mean losing the independence she had enjoyed during the previous five years." That was because she had already rejected a marriage proposal by powerful white males to a man she had never met, to return under his authority to the distant place remote from friends and the prospect of publishing, even if somehow she had been able to combine writing poetry with the demands of a missionary role subordinate to her husband and to Hopkins. Quaque's letters allow us to imagine the road she chose not to take.[26]

Robinson points out, "Every known piece of writing published by Phillis after marriage used her married name." This was the case in the advertisement for a second book of poems, which, in Carretta's view "probably indicated that her husband played a dominant role in that planning of the new book" and that "her identity was submerged beneath that of her husband." One can imagine other reasons for Wheatley using the name Phillis Peters, including the mark of self-assertion against the Hopkins/Thornton choice of her husband, echoing the general choice made by free black people to form their own families after slavery.[27]

More to the point, however, as we have seen, there were very significant developments in Wheatley's poetry, which she wrote until the end of her life in 1784. Carretta himself says the contents of Wheatley's formal book proposal of 1779 "indicates a writer of transatlantic stature," including poems on British public figures as well as those "prominent American military figures" Washington, Lee, and Wooster. Some had been written years before, one of them entitled and dated "Farewell to England 1773." There was a large advertisement for it in the *Boston Evening Post and General Advertiser* on October 30, 1779, soliciting subscriptions, repeated twice in November issues and three times in December. There were thirty-three poems, along with thirteen letters, including the one to Dartmouth, three to the Countess of Huntingdon, one to Susanna Wheatley, and one to "Dr. B. Rush, Phila," all under the name "Phillis Peters." They were to be dedicated to "Right Hon. Benjamin Franklin, Esq.," whom Wheatley had met in London, prior to the revolution. Now she added to his title, "One of the Ambassadors of the United States to the Court of France." Presumably she hoped for his patronage.[28]

Accompanying the "Proposals" was a letter addressed to "Messieurs Printers," stating that the collection "was put into my hands by the desire of the ingenious author," adding that she was "a female African, whose lot it was to fall into the hands of a generous master and great benefactor." Its phrasing suggests that it was written by Wheatley herself, expressing the values she placed on reading her poetry, and hoping to stimulate purchasers by referring to her youth, gender, and Africanness, but again without the invidiousness of "a negro girl." "The learned and ingenuous, as well as those who are pleased with novelty, are invited to encourage the publication by a generous subscription the former"—the learned—"that they may fan the sacred fire which is self-enkindled in the breast," which in "Liberty and Peace" Wheatley calls "Freedom," "The generous Spirit that Columbia fires," and elsewhere represented her poetic drive as fire. Here she continues, referring to the latter, the "ingenuous," "that they by reading this collection have a large play for their imagination," a "queen" she called it in her poem "On Imagination," singing of its force and power, here hoping that hers will be transmitted to inspire others, to "be excited to please and benefit mankind by some brilliant production of their own pens." She applied, too, to "Those who are always in search of some new thing, that they may obtain a sight of this *rara avis in terra*," referring again to "novelty," the Latin phrase evidence of this young African poet's progress in "the Latin Tongue" to which her *Poems* had said she had "a great Inclination." She wanted to be further "encouraged to improve her own mind, benefit and please mankind." She had hoped to sell the book for "Twelve Pounds, neatly Bound and Lettered, and Nine Pounds sew'd in blue paper, one Half to be paid on Subscribing, the other Half on Delivery of the Books." But the lack of subscribers prevented publication.[29]

She and her husband left Boston in 1780 (they "disappeared from public view until 1784"); she was unable to promote herself there. She published "Liberty and Peace" as a four page pamphlet "by Phillis Peters, Boston. Printed by WARDON and RUSSELL, At Their Office in Marlborough Street, MDCC, LXXXIV." Other poems and songs entered the market then, like hers, capitalizing on the celebration of peace. Her 1779 "Proposals" were reprinted along with "TO Mr. and Mrs.—on the Death of Their Infant Son," "as a Specimen of her Work."[30]

The newly married couple must have seen Wheatley's poetry and fame as their best economic resources. Peters "was almost certainly in jail for debt." His ability to earn money had been very uneven, although later, in 1784, he "successfully petitioned town officials . . . to allow him to sell liquor at the shop . . . in North Boston 'for the purpose of supporting himself & Family.'" The effects of wartime and postwar depression must have been compounded by racism. She was unable to get her second book published. In fact, Wheatley's *Poems* had been rejected in colonial Boston, despite the Wheatleys' network; she had been able to publish it in London with the very powerful support of the Huntingdon Connexion (Lady Huntingdon, Dartmouth, Thornton, and others), but also with the endorsement of those eighteen American political and religious leaders transcending their enmity at a moment of possible reconciliation between Britain and her American mainland colonies, validating this African phenomenon. After 1783, "for all its talk about universal liberty and rights," the United States "was a nation of white people," its leaders defining themselves against blacks, a view essentially challenged by Wheatley.[31]

The corollary of marriage was pregnancy. The June after her November marriage, Wheatley faced pregnancy for the first time, a condition then more fraught with risk and consequently apprehensions over the outcome for mother and child. She may have expressed hers in a prayer ascribed to her, entitled "Sabbath—June 13, 1779," transcribed "from a badly damaged manuscript" by the Schomburg Center, "said to have been found accidentally in her bible." Shields prints it in Wheatley's *Collected Works* as if it were a poem:

> Oh my Gracious Preserver!
> hiterhero thou hast brot [me,]
> be pleased when thou bringest
> to the birth to give [me] strength
> To bring forth living & perfect a
> being

Stillbirths and infant mortality among her white contemporaries, and presumably among black women, too were proportionate to their high birthrate (although both groups—free blacks even more than whites—were exercising birth control to limit births during and after the Revolutionary Period). Susanna Wheatley saw three of her children die before she acquired Phillis.[32]

Her prayer continues,

> Who shall be greatly instrumental in promoting thy [glory]
> Tho conceived in Sin & brot forth
> In iniquity yet thy infinite wisdom
> Can bring a clean thing out of an
> unclean, a vesse[l] of Honor filled for thy glory.

There was, perhaps, a parallel in Wheatley's mind between her own and her child's emergence here, and her salvation from Africa, indicated by the repeated "brot me," along with "bring," invoking "On being brought from AFRICA to AMERICA." Whether the first word of the second line, "hiterhero," she intended to be "hither" or "hitherto," its conflation intensifies this reference.[33]

And "Sabbath" may well have resonated with her recollections of the mothers on whom she had focused her talents to bring them comfort with scenes of happiness to be enjoyed by their children, once they had made the crossing to rebirth in immortal life:

> Th' unhappy mother sees the sanguine rill
> Forget to flow, and nature's wheels stand still,
> But see from earth his spirit far remov'd,
> And know no grief recals your best-belov'd:
> He upon pinions swifter than the wind,
> Has left mortality's sad scenes behind
> For joys to this terrestrial state unknown,
> And glories richer than the monarch's crown.
> Of virtues steady course the prize behold!
> What blissful wonders to his mind unfold!

Such a view, frequently expressed by women's poetry then and later, must have borne a relation to the general re-evaluation of the previous denigration of Eve among liberal Protestants (Abigail Adams, for example), although evidently evangelical women like Wheatley perpetuated at least some of it in her view of copulation.[34]

In "Sabbath," after writing that she hoped to see her child "a vessel of Honour for God's glory," Wheatley prayed,

> Grant me
> to live a life of gratitude to thee
> for the innumerable benefits—
> O Lord my God! Instruct my ignorance
> & enlighten my Darkness.

She adds sinfulness to ignorance, as the meaning of "my Darkness."

> Thou art my King take [thou]
> the entire possession of [all] my
> powers & faculties & let me be
> no longer under the dominion of sin–

These passages express, it seems, an even clearer parallel to her interpretation of "being brought from AFRICA TO AMERICA," conveying, too, Wheatley's ongoing sense of self in its religious mode.

> . . . Give me a sincere &
> hearty repentance for all my
> [grievous] offences & strengthen
> by thy grace my resolutions
> on amendment & circumspection
> for the time to come—

when she hopes to participate in the pleasures she forecasts for Mrs. Boylston's child, for little Charles Eliot, and the other dead children about whom she has written.

> Grant me
> [also] the spirit of Prayer & Suppli[cation]

according to thy own
most gracious Providence.

This pregnancy seems to have resulted in a live birth, and Wheatley may have had another two pregnancies at least. We saw that Peters referred to his "Family" in a surviving document.[35]

Wheatley died on December 5, 1784. John Peters was probably in jail for debt at the time. We do not know if her children were with her or any fellow Christian, like those who were with Sarah Wheatley, embarking on her last voyage, as Phillis recorded it. One hopes at the end she beheld the "blissful wonders" she imagined on behalf of her predecessors.[36]

Antislavery and Colonization

The enslavement of Africans and their descendants had become an immense political and social problem because of the American Revolution. Hopkin's proposal to send Quamine, Yamma, and Wheatley to Anomabu initiated the American linkage between the moral imperative of emancipation and the colonization of black people to Africa, with Christianizing purpose. In 1789, "inspired and counselled" by Hopkins, the "officers of the Free African Union Society of Newport Rhode Island," declared that "being strangers in a strange land," and appalled by the state of their enslaved brethrens, many of "whom are treated in the most inhumane and cruel manner, and . . . sunk down in ignorance, stupidity and vice," looked to Africa. There, African nations were in "heathenish darkness and barbarity," selling "one another into slavery." These black, Rhode Island followers of Hopkins asked God "to pour down his spirit upon us and cause us and them to become a wise, virtuous, and Christian people. And . . . open a safe and prosperous way for our returning to Africa."[37] Overwhelmingly, however, African Americans stayed in America, although a few did take the opportunity to sail to what became Liberia, akin to its predecessor, the British colony of Sierra Leone, which was established by British abolitionists in 1787. In sharp contrast, to return African Americans to Africa after they were manumitted became the central purpose of white American abolitionists, a goal in which they were joined by some slaveholders, who wished to dry up the sea in which escapees could swim, until this vision was challenged in the 1830s. Hopkins died in 1803.[38]

The chief advocate for the establishment of Sierra Leone, to be "the Province of Freedom" for emancipated black people was Granville Sharp. He had heard from Hopkins directly that some recently freed people in postwar New England "had already expressed a desire to re-establish themselves in liberty in their native Africa." (We can suggest a connection here between Hopkins's proposal to Wheatley, and Sharp's associate Thornton's endorsement of it, following both men's acquaintance and conversations with Wheatley in London.) Sharp committed himself to Sierra Leone because he thought it "the most effectual way of destroying the *slave trade*," but he was also concerned about the effect of growing numbers of free blacks on the British population: "Inter-racial sexual liaisons were becoming commonplace and noticed, a threat to the purity of white womanhood" and to "the future whiteness of the British nation." This seems to have been a growing apprehension from the Mansfield decision through the intensifying revolutionary conditions, to the end of the century and beyond. So racism was a factor in Britain as it was in America, although, as in the case of Hopkins, fervent supporters of the plan, headed by the Teston Circle, including Ramsay as well as Sharp, believed that the establishment of a colony of Christianized ex-slaves in Africa would contribute to the end of slavery.[39]

Sharp (an opponent of Britain's war with America) believed the establishment of a colony of ex-slaves would help redeem Britain and restore its ancient liberty. American revolutionaries also maintained that the eighteenth-century British government had deviated from that tradition, turning to arbitrary government, while Americans had upheld it. The Rev. Thompson had interpreted the outbreak of the Seven Years' War as God's punishment for Britain's sins, although he had not considered the slave trade and slavery to be among those sins. After Britain's victory over the French, Benezet (Sharp's inspiration and collaborator) had warned Britain and her colonies of God's "future reckoning." He asked the white inhabitants to "consider how you shall come off in the great and awful Day of account. You may heap up riches and live in pleasure," but in doing so by being "thieves and murderers," enslaving Africans, "you are treasuring up to yourselves wrath against the day of wrath, and vengeance shall come upon the workers of iniquity," unless they repent. Religious Britons explained Britain's stunning defeat by Americans as the result "of their own failings in the sight of God." They included slavery, "so productive of worldly profit and luxury." Not only was antislavery "seized on to redeem the nation as a patriotic act," but it "reaffirmed Britons' unique commitment to liberty, in contrast to the victorious Americans." First Britain ended the slave trade in 1807 and then, in the 1830s, slavery, which helped legitimize imperial Britain's "claims to be arbiters of the civilized and uncivilized world." This was to be largely the achievement of Britain's self-identification with evangelical Christianity: "Nineteenth-century Great Britain was still Israel."[40]

Competition between Britain and America as nations of virtue and freedom had another expression. Wheatley's "Liberty and Peace" repeated the American adaptation of the trope of "virtue in distress" to its oppression by Britain, which Wheatley had presented in her earlier poem "America" as a "senseless, cruel, parent," which "scourged the innocent weeping son," betraying the tie of kindred. "Liberty and Peace" recalled the same cruelty, although both sides fought with "fraternal arms" and "mother Earth . . . smoak'd with kindred Gore." Wheatley's poetry proved useful to the antislavery movement. The first American edition of her *Poems* was published in Philadelphia in 1786, although Silverman suggests that this was in part, at least, to satisfy a patriotic market for American poetry. That same year, the most influential antislavery figure outside Parliament in Britain, the Rev. Thomas Clarkson, quoted her in his *An Essay on the Slavery and Commerce of the Human Species, Particularly the African* (1786). Like Hopkins and other predecessors, including the Rev. Lawrence Sterne (Clarkson was to publish an extensive and detailed account of them in *The History of the Rise, Progress and Accomplishment of the Abolition of the African Slave Trade by the British Parliament* in 1808), Clarkson argued forcefully for the common humanity, the kinship of whites and blacks. He found it essential to explain that color, the barrier to white sympathy for enslaved blacks, was the result merely of environmental, climatological factors. (Of course, geneticists have now shown that the evolutionary deviance to be explained is whiteness.)[41]

Clarkson quoted extracts of Wheatley's poetry, including "On Imagination," and he praised Sancho's prose, both emblematic of African capacities, to refute the argument that because they were lower on the great chain of being, they were designed for slavery. In this Clarkson also took up precisely the opinion of Wheatley's *Poems* expressed by the *Critical Review* in 1773, which asserted that "the Negroes of Africa are . . . fit only to be slaves . . . incapable of any considerable attainments in the liberal arts and sciences," to declare that "a poet or poetess among them . . . would be a prodigy." This meant Wheatley. Clarkson wrote that she and Sancho were "above mediocrity in the literary way," but refuted the objection that they were "prodigies," and that Africans in general were "inferior . . . and are made for slavery." Freed Africans were as capable "of the highest intellectual attainment as any Europeans," and in general, "their abilities were equal."[42]

Clarkson's *Essay* immediately provoked Jefferson's contemptuous dismissal of Wheatley's poetry. He was only apparently less contemptuous of Sancho's prose in the most widely read English edition of his *Notes on the State of Virginia* (1787).[43] Having dismissed black people's achievements in all areas (with a sort of exception in music), Jefferson turned to poetry. "Misery is often the parent of the most affecting touches in poetry—Among the blacks is misery enough, God knows, but no poetry. Love is the oestrum of the poet." The only love he has in mind is heterosexual love, leaving aside other expressions, of parents for children, for example. Black people's "love is ardent but it kindles the senses only, not the imagination." Given his next sentence, Jefferson approaches a version of Samuel Foote's and the *London Advertizer's* representation of Wheatley as a lusty black wench, but he swerves to another kind of putdown. "Religion has indeed produced a Phyllis Wheatley, but it could not produce a poet. The compositions under her name are below the dignity of criticism." Bad as the poems are, Jefferson insinuates that a black person is incapable even of them, the same insinuation with which he concluded his criticism of Sancho's letters. Jefferson ended his criticism of Wheatley by comparing her blackness implicitly to Pope's spinal deformity, aware of her admiring emulation of the greatest Anglophone poet of the era. "The heroes of the *Dunciad* are to her, as Hercules to the author of that poem."[44]

Jefferson's denigration of Wheatley and Sancho was part of a chapter in which he proposed the emancipation of all slaves at a future date. The "females should be eighteen, and the males twenty one, when they should be colonized" to some proper place, declaring them "a free and independent people" and extending "to them our alliance and protection until they have acquired strength." His answer to the question, why not "incorporate the blacks into the State"—Virginia—appears to be the same as Hopkins's for the exclusion of blacks from America: "Deep-rooted prejudices entertained by the whites," but he adds, "ten thousand recollections by the blacks of the injuries they have sustained; new provocations," and then Jefferson's now famous, then influential, scientized racism, repudiating Clarkson, and almost absent from Hopkins, "the real distinctions which nature has made." To avoid "staining the blood" of whites, "he is to be removed beyond the reach of mixture." Jefferson's words on slavery remained ambiguous, but he kept his slaves, only silently freeing his children stained by Sally Hemings, his African American "substitute wife."[45]

After the Revolution, the slave trade was reopened and the U.S. Constitution sanctioned it for another twenty years, along with the perpetuation of slavery. "The word does not appear. And yet slavery is all over the document." The clauses sanctioning slavery debated by the delegates to the 1787 convention "are many more . . . with greater implications for slavery than those contained in the Articles of Confederation," which had ostensibly banned the slave trade in 1774, and to whose delegates Hopkins had appealed to end slavery.[46]

In his view, the economic and social distress accompanying and then following the war for independence and its aftermath were God's expression of displeasure with white Americans' refusal to end slavery. In 1793, Hopkins published a second antislavery pamphlet, the text of a speech he gave at the Baptist meeting house in Providence in 1793 before a group he had helped establish, the Providence Society for Abolishing the Slave-Trade. It was entitled *A Discourse upon the Slave-Trade, and the Slavery of the Africans.* He reiterated that there was a dynamic relationship in the inconsistency of white Americans' opposing their own enslavement by the British government as they enslaved Africans: the former was God's threat in retaliation for the latter.[47]

This second pamphlet further developed the colonization scheme rooted in those 1773 and 1776 circulars. Quamine had died at sea in 1779, five years before Wheatley died in Boston, and Yamma was "a free laborer in North Carolina." Hopkins's 1793 sermon's text was Mark 16:15, "GO YE INTO ALL THE WORLD, AND PREACH THE GOSPEL TO

EVERY CREATURE." The "offer of salvation," Christ said, should "be made to all mankind, of whatever nation or complexion, Jews or Gentiles, rich or poor, white or black." Hopkins lists the benefits of the gospel, that it "turns men from darkness to marvelous light." If it finds them "in a state of savage, ignorance and barbarity, it civilized them, and forms them to be intelligent and good members of society."[48]

Again he asks why the appeal of the enslaved has not stimulated white sensibility into action. "Why are not the cries of the millions of Africans in bondage heard by all? Why do they make no more impression on the public mind and raise all to feel for the wretchedness of so great a part of their fellow men, and to exertion for their relief?" In his earlier pamphlet, Hopkins's answer had been racism ("it is because they [slaves] are Negroes"). At this point in his second, post–Constitutional Convention pamphlet, he leaves that implicit, but invokes the same process he had hoped to see in members of the Continental Congress, arousal of feeling, followed by action: "May we not hope . . . that benevolence and compassion toward the miserable Africans will be so sensibly . . . exercised towards them, by people in general, that . . . proper measures will be taken up to make them a free and happy people." Then follows his acknowledgement of the limitations of such benevolence, only operable by the exclusion of emancipated "Africans" from "the people in general," whites. "And if it be necessary in order to this [making blacks a free and happy people], that they should return to Africa, the continent which seems to be best suited to their constitution, may we not wish and hope that such a desire to compensate them as far as we may, for the injuries we have done them," may be implemented. The resemblance to Jefferson's unimplemented plan in *Notes on the State of Virginia* is apparent. But Jefferson did not share the second paramount element of Hopkins's vision, the Christianization of Africans in Africa.[49]

To Hopkins, this would be a resounding vindication of the slave trade: its being concluded in this way was perhaps "design'ed by the Most High to be a means of introducing the gospel to the nation in Africa, while [those] among us who have been or may be in some good measure civilized and instructed, will by our assistance return to Africa and spread the light of the gospel." Hopkins paints a rosy picture of freed American slaves successfully following their missionary work by propagating arts and science among Africans, replacing ignorance and barbarity with civilization. "Thus all the past and present evil which the Africans have suffered by the Slave-trade and . . . slavery . . . may be the occasion of overbalancing good."[50] The difference from those like Whitefield, who said that slavery was good in the end because it Christianized Africans, was that Hopkins's scheme would reverse the direction of the Middle Passage and, at the same time, rid white Americans both of their fateful sin and of black people. In his earliest version, Wheatley, at that time the most famous, successfully Christianized African woman, properly subordinated to a properly Christianized African husband, was to return to Anomabu to assist him in Christianizing the pagan land. To her, however, the Rev. Quaque signified its dubiety, if not futility. In any case, she had found herself as a poet in revolutionary America.

ACKNOWLEDGMENTS

The person to whom I am most indebted for myriad insights is anthropologist Linda Layne. My dedication is a mere token of this and all the love she gives me, all the time.

I am extremely grateful to my dear friend John Callahan, novelist and distinguished scholar of African American culture, for his tough-minded advice, on reading an earlier version of this manuscript.

Lori Saba's endless diligence and generosity in turning my manuscripts into typescript have sustained my efforts for decades.

David Alexander, another distinguished scholar, but of eighteenth-century prints and books, was very helpful on specific matters and generally, along with his gracious spouse, Helena Moore.

It was while working with distinguished feminist historian and life-long friend Catherine Clinton that I first encountered Phillis Wheatley.

I have been so very lucky in the sustaining friendship of Lawrence Wittner ever since we arrived at SUNY Albany in 1975, a champion of civil rights and the nobler aspects of American history; and of his fellow champion, Dorothy Tristman.

My dear friend Lian Xi, historian of Christianity in China, has given me his unfailing support over the years.

Poet Marc Weber gave me valuable advice toward the end.

The three anonymous reports for NYU Press offered fruitful redirection and encouragement, and I am very grateful to Clara Platter and her assistant, Amy Klopfenstein, my editors, for eliciting them, and for their own, ongoing encouragement, all under their chief, Ilene Kalish, who has again been decisive in getting my work out, after her extraordinary feat in re-issuing my first book after a quarter of a century. Thank you, Ilene!

The thoughtful assistance of Timothy Jackson, Head of Interlibrary Loan at SUNY Albany, in speeding materials to me over thousands of miles for years, has been invaluable.

I have been sustained, too, by the generosity and good humor of Tony and Tere Axon since my youth; and of Gary Holden and his family for the last twenty years. My stepsons, Fletcher Layne Wilson and Jasper Layne Wilson, have been joys since their childhoods. My brother's family, Ingrid, Sigrid, Erika, and Karen, have been loving all the while—Erika and Lian Xi dropped everything to pull me through a very tough spot. I have been stimulated by conversations with two more brilliant scholars, Barbara Bodenhorn and Linda Jacobs. Other friends in Cambridge, Andrew Taylor, David Smith, Tim Cottage, Brian Lewsey, Michael Brown, and Brent Greenwood, have cheered me over many a lunch at Clare Hall.

This book, as the rest of my historical writing, is rooted in the mentoring and friendship of Donald Meyer, abetted by his dear spouse, Jean. Another root was Jack Gallagher of Trinity College, Cambridge, who first taught me American history, and paved my way to UCLA, where I met Don.

–2011—Cambridge; Averill Park, NY; Falls Church, VA; Evergreen, CO; and finally, Cambridge again—2017

NOTES

INTRODUCTION

1 Vincent Carretta, *Phillis Wheatley: Biography of a Genius in Bondage* (Athens, GA: University of Georgia Press, 2011), 4–6; G-Ugo Nwokeji, "African Conception of Gender and the Slave Traffic," *William and Mary Quarterly*, 3d Series, LVIII, 1 (January 2001), 47–68, *passim;* William H. Robinson, *Phillis Wheatley and Her Writings* (New York: Garland, 1984), 5–8.

2 Phillis Wheatley, "To the Right Honourable WILLIAM, Earl of DARTMOUTH, His Majesty's Principal Secretary of State for North America, &c.," in *The Collected Works of Phillis Wheatley*, ed. John C. Shields (New York: Oxford University Press, 1988), 73 (hereafter referred to as *Collected Works*). In this edition, Wheatley's *Poems on Various Subjects, Religions and Moral* (London: A Bell, 1773) is included as a facsimile of that edition, along with her other writings. William H. Robinson also included a facsimile in *Phillis Wheatley and Her Writings*, cited in the previous note. Recommended is *The Poems of Phillis Wheatley*, ed. Julian D. Mason (Chapel Hill, NC: University of North Carolina Press, rev. ed. 1989). In addition, Vincent Carretta edited *Complete Writings of Phillis Wheatley* (New York: Penguin, 2001).

3 *The Life and Letters of Philip Quaque: The First African Anglican Missionary*, ed. Vincent Carretta and Ty M. Reese (Athens, GA: University of Georgia Press, 2010). The frequency of my references to this work in my first two chapters, and to Carretta's biography of Phillis Wheatley cited in n. 1, above, indicate my indebtedness to his work. I am equally grateful for his edition of *The Letters of Ignatius Sancho, An African* (New York: Penguin, 1998).

4 Wheatley, *Collected Works*, 24.

5 Wheatley, *Collected Works*, 74.

6 Wheatley, *Collected Works*, 11.

7 Wheatley, *Collected Works*, 101–3.

8 Sondra O'Neale, "A Slave's Subtle War: Phillis Wheatley's Use of Biblical Myth and Symbol," *Early American Literature* 21, no. 2 (Fall 1986), 144–45; Cynthia J. Smith, "'To Maecenas': Phillis Wheatley's Invocation of an Idealized Reader," *Black American Literature Forum* 23, no. 3 (Autumn 1989): 579–92; Lucy K. Hayden, "Classical Tidings from the Africa Muse: Phillis Wheatley's Use of Greek and Roman Mythology," *CLA Journal* 35, no. 4 (June 1992): 432–47; James A. Levernier, "Phillis Wheatley and the New England Clergy," *Early American Literature*

26, no. 1 (1991): 21–38; Frank Shuffleton, "Phillis Wheatley, the Aesthetic, and the Form of Life," *Studies in Eighteenth Century Culture* 26, ed. Sydney M. Conger and Julie C. Hayes (Baltimore, MD: John Hopkins University Press, 1998): 73–85; 75; Shuffleton, "On Her Own Footing: Phillis Wheatley in Freedom," in *Genius in Bondage: Literature of the Early Black Atlantic*, ed. Vincent Carretta and Philip Gould (Lexington, KY: University Press of Kentucky, 2001): 175–89; Christine Levecq, *Slavery and Sentiment: The Politics of Feeling in Black Atlantic Antislavery Writing, 1770–1850* (Hanover, NH: University Press of New England, 2008), chaps. 1 and 4. While her writing is "clearly implicated in discourses of empire, of freedom, and of redemption, its mastery of feeling and estrangement finally matter more than the political messages ideological critics have decoded." Shuffleton, "Phillis Wheatley, the Aesthetic, and the Form of Life," 75. For an account of critical responses to Phillis Wheatley and her poetry, see John C. Shields, *Phillis Wheatley's Poetics of Liberation: Backgrounds and Contexts* (Knoxville, TN: University of Tennessee Press, 2008), chaps. 2 and 3. See, too, William H. Robinson, *Phillis Wheatley: A Bio-Bibliography* (Boston, MA: G. K. Hall, 1981), *passim.*

9 Levecq, *Slavery and Sentiment*, 6; Shuffleton, "On Her Own Footing," 188.

10 Winthrop D. Jordan, *White Over Black: American Attitudes Toward the Negro, 1550–1812* (Baltimore, MD: Penguin, 1969), 289.

CHAPTER 1. BRITAIN SENDS AN AFRICAN MISSIONARY TO AFRICA

1 William St. Clair, *The Grand Slave Emporium: Cape Coast Castle and the British Slave Trade* (London: Profile Books, 2007), 43–46; the English text of the treaty is printed in *The Life and Letters of Philip Quaque, The First African Anglican Missionary*, ed. Vincent Carretta and Ty M. Reese (Athens, GA: University of Georgia Press, 2010), 187–88 (hereafter referred to as *Letters of Quaque*).

2 For playoff diplomacy in British North America, see Gary B. Nash, *Red, White and Black: The Peoples of British North America* (Englewood Cliffs, NJ: Prentice Hall, 1974), chap. 10; for India, see Barbara D. Metcalf and Thomas R. Metcalf, *A Concise History of Modern India* (Cambridge, UK: Cambridge University Press, 2012), 45, 49–50.

3 Thomas Thompson to the Rev. Moore, February 10, 1762, in *Letters of Quaque*, 190–91; Thomas Thompson, *An Account of Two Missionary Voyages: By the Appointment of the Society of the Propagation of the Gospel in Foreign Parts, the one to New Jersey in North America, the other from America to the Coast of Guinea* (London: Benjamin Dod, 1778), 66–67 (hereafter referred to as *Voyages*); Travis Glasson, *Mastering Christianity: Missionary Anglicanism and Slavery in the Atlantic World* (Oxford: Oxford University Press, 2012), 135, 179.

4 Thompson, *Voyages*, 67; St. Clair, *Grand Slave Emporium*, 184; Rebecca Shumway, *The Fante and the Transatlantic Slave Trade* (Rochester, NY: University of Rochester Press, 2011), 112, 117 (hereafter referred to as *The Fante*).

5 Thompson, *Voyages*, 67; Carretta and Reese, "Introduction," in *Letters of Quaque*, 8–9.

6 Glasson, *Mastering Christianity*, 172–173; Thompson, *Voyages*, 1–2; G. J. Barker-Benfield, *The Culture of Sensibility: Sex and Society in Eighteenth-Century Britain* (Chicago: University of Chicago Press, 1992), 57; Jon Butler, *Awash in a Sea of Faith: Christianizing the American People* (Cambridge, MA: Harvard University Press, 1990), 102, 139 (hereafter referred to as *Awash*).

7 Thompson, *Voyages*, 42; Butler, *Awash*, chap. 6.

8 Thompson, *Voyages*, 11–12; Butler, *Awash*, 159; Edmund S. Morgan, *American Slavery, American Freedom* (New York: W.W. Norton, 1975).

9 John A. Schutz, "Christopher Codrington's Will: Launching the S.P.G. into the Barbadian Sugar Business," *Pacific Historical Review* 15, no. 2 (June 1946): 192–200; 192; Glasson, *Mastering Christianity*, 23; Fleetwood, quoted in Butler, *Awash*, 135–36; Butler, *Awash*, 136–38. For the SPG and its Codrington slaveholdings, see Glasson, *Mastering Christianity*, chap. 5.

10 Thompson, *Voyages*, 23; Frank L. Klingberg, "Philip Quaque, Pioneer Native Missionary on the Gold Coast, 1765–1816," *Journal of Negro Education* 8, no. 4 (October 1939): 666–72; 666; Glasson, *Mastering Christianity*, 175.

11 Thompson, *Voyages*, 24–25, 33–24; Melvil, quoted in *Letters of Quaque*, 189; Thompson, *Voyages*, 36.

12 Glasson, *Mastering Christianity*, 175–76; Thompson, *Voyages*, 35, 47.

13 "The Royal African: or memoirs of the young prince of Annamaboe," etc., (London: W. Reeve, G. Woodfall, and J. Barnes, 1749); Wylie Sypher, *Guinea's Captive Kings: British Anti-Slavery Literature of the XVIIIth Century* (Chapel Hill, NC: University of North Carolina Press, 1942); Thompson, *Voyages*, 58–59.

14 Glasson, *Mastering Christianity*, 173; Thompson, *Voyages*, 53–54, 68.

15 Thompson, *Voyages*, 69–75; Shumway, *The Fante*, 133.

16 Thompson, *Voyages*, 71, 72–73, 77, 78–80.

17 Klingberg, "Philip Quaque," 667–68; Carretta and Reese, "Introduction," 8; Glasson, *Mastering Christianity*, 176; Moore, quoted in *Letters of Quaque*, 194. Travis Glasson writes that the "Society's use of enslaved catechists was one of the many techniques experimented to convert black people around the British Atlantic world." *Mastering Christianity*, 171.

18 Moore, quoted in *Letters of Quaque*, 194; Quaque to the Reverend Doctor Daniel Burton March 14 and September 28, 1766, in *Letters of Quaque*, 39, 43.

19 Carretta and Reese, "Introduction," 9; Quaque to Burton, March 15, 1765, in *Letters of Quaque*, 31; Seymour Drescher, *Abolition: A History of Slavery and Antislavery* (Cambridge, UK: Cambridge University Press, 2009), 8. For Whitefield, see below, pp. 50–51; Phillis Wheatley, "On being brought from AFRICA to AMERICA," in *The Collected Works of Phillis Wheatley*, ed. John C. Shields (New York: Oxford University Press, 1988), 18.

20 Quaque to Burton, March 15, 1765, *Letters of Quaque*, 31–32.

21 Quaque to Burton, February 29, 1766, *Letters of Quaque*, 35.

22 Quaque to Burton, [between September and October] 1767, *Letters of Quaque*, 58; Glasson, *Mastering Christianity*, 181; Quaque to Burton, [between September

and October] 1767, *Letters of Quaque*, 54, 55. Another of Quaque's interpreters was John Acqua, who, with George Sackee, had been sent from Cape Coast Castle to London to learn English in the 1750s, both returning to work as "brokers" for the CMTA on the slave trade. *Letters of Quaque*, 65 n. 9.

23 Margaret Priestley, *West African Trade and Coast Society: A Family Study* (London: Oxford University Press, 1969), 207–9, 182; Quaque to Burton, March 7, 1767, *Letters of Quaque*, 46–47; St. Clair, *Grand Slave Emporium*, 185.

24 Quaque to Burton, [between September and October] 1767, *Letters of Quaque*, 54–56.

25 Quaque to Burton, [between September and October] 1767, *Letters of Quaque*, 55; Quaque to Burton, April 19, 1771, *Letters of Quaque*, 98.

26 Quaque to Burton, [between September and October] 1767, *Letters of Quaque*, 51.

27 John Hippisley to the African Committee, March 20, 1766, *Letters of Quaque*, 195; Quaque to Burton, March 7, 1767, *Letters of Quaque*, 46–47; Quaque to Burton, [between September and October] 1767, *Letters of Quaque*, 52.

28 Quaque to Burton, September 5, 1769, *Letters of Quaque*, 84–85. Thompson reported that he was at Cape Coast Castle, by "Favor of the Governor . . . often invited to his Table and he was in every Respect very kind and civil to me." Thompson, *Voyages*, 37, and see 74.

29 Quaque to Hind, April 11, 1777, *Letters of Quaque*, 130; Quaque to Morice, June 12, 1780, *Letters of Quaque*, 144, 149, and n. 1.

30 Carretta and Reese, "Introduction," 5; Quaque to Burton, February 1766, *Letters of Quaque*, 35.

31 Quaque to Burton, September 28, 1766, *Letters of Quaque*, 41; Quaque to Burton, March 7, 1767, *Letters of Quaque*, 45.

32 Quaque to Burton, September 5, 1769, *Letters of Quaque*, 86; Carretta and Reese, "Introduction," 13 (Glasson assumed she was African, too, *Mastering Christianity*, 181), in contrast to St. Clair, *Grand Slave Emporium*, 161.

33 Quaque to Burton, September 5, 1769, *Letters of Quaque*, 86.

34 Quaque to Burton, April 12, 1770, *Letters of Quaque*, 88.

35 Quaque to Burton, March 8, 1772, *Letters of Quaque*, 99–101.

36 Quaque to Morice, October 20, 1781, *Letters of Quaque*, 154; Quaque to Morice, August 6, 1782, *Letters of Quaque*, 158. He had buried one of his children, he reported to Morice, June 12, 1780, *Letters of Quaque*, 147.

37 Quaque to Morice, October 20, 1781, *Letters of Quaque*, 154. In his verse *Description of the West Indies* (1767–77), John Singleton presented "a Negro funeral" in which,

> some veteran pours,
> His mercenary panegyric forth
> In all the jargon of mysterious speech[.]

Quoted in Sypher, *Guinea's Captive Kings*, 145.

38 Quaque to Morice, June 30, 1783, *Letters of Quaque*, 163; Quaque to Morice, [August 23, 1787], *Letters of Quaque*, 165–66.

39 Quaque to Morice, January 28, 1789, *Letters of Quaque*, 174.

40 Quaque to Morice, June 9, 1795, *Letters of Quaque*, 185–6; Governor Archibald Dalziel reported Quaque's request, and the Committee's refusal, *Letters of Quaque*, 201.

41 Quaque to Hind, July 30, 1775, *Letters of Quaque*, 126.

42 Quaque to Morice, [October 13, 1811], *Letters of Quaque*, 185.

43 Quaque to Morice, [October 13, 1811], *Letters of Quaque*, 185–86; Quaque to Morice, June 12, 1780, *Letters to Quaque*, 146.

44 Quaque to Morice, [October 13, 1811], *Letters of Quaque*, 186; Dawson to the African Committee, October 4, 1816, *Letters of Quaque*, 201.

45 Quaque to Burton, February 1766, *Letters of Quaque*, 35; St. Clair, *Grand Slave Emporium*, 148–49, 156–57, and chap. 6 *passim*. There were comparable relationships in British-conquered India: "Nabobs and common soldiers alike customarily lived openly with Indian mistresses, called *bibis*." Metcalf and Metcalf, *Concise History of Modern India*, 66. For more wide-ranging parallels, see Ronald Hyam, *Understanding the British Empire* (Cambridge, UK: Cambridge University Press, 2010), chap. 13. But for a deeper, more recent account of the significance of "multi-ethnic" families where Europeans met native peoples, see Anne F. Hyde, *Empires, Nations, and Families: A New History of the North American West, 1800–1860* (New York: Harper Collins, 2012).

46 Thomas Thompson, *A Discourse Relating to the Present Times, Addressed to the Serious Consideration of the Public* (London: printed for the author by J. Oliver, [1757]), 8. Ecco Edition reproduced from the copy in the British Library.

47 Quaque to Rev. Samuel Johnson, November 25, 1767, *Letters of Quaque*, 67.

CHAPTER 2. PROSPECTS OF AN AMERICAN MISSION TO ANOMABU

1 Quaque to Burton, March 7, 1767, *The Life and Letters of Philip Quaque, the First African Anglican Missionary*, ed. Vincent Carretta and Ty M. Reese (Athens, GA: University of Georgia Press, 2010), 47 (hereafter referred to as *Letters of Quaque*); Quaque to Burton October 20, 1767, *Letters of Quaque*, 65.

2 Quaque to Johnson, November 26, 1767, *Letters of Quaque*, 68.

3 Quaque to Johnson, April 5, 1769, *Letters of Quaque*, 76, 77; Peter Fryer, *Staying Power: The History of Black People in Britain* (London: Philo Press, 2010 [1984]), 74; Seymour Drescher, *Abolition: A History of Slavery and Antislavery* (Cambridge, UK: Cambridge University Press, 2009), 98.

4 Quaque to Johnson, April 5, 1769, *Letters of Quaque*, 77.

5 Quaque to Burton, April 13, 1769, *Letters of Quaque*, 79; Quaque to Burton, February 6, 1771, *Letters of Quaque*, 94.

6 *Ibid.*, and 96 n. 1.

7 Quaque to Burton, August 19, 1771, *Letters of Quaque*, 97.

8 Thomas Thompson, *The African Trade for Negro Slaves Shown to be Consistent with the Principles of Humanity and the Laws of Revealed Religion* (Canterbury: Simons and Kirkby, also London: Robert Baldwin [1772]), Ecco reprint from the British Library. Hereafter referred to as *African Trade*.

9 Thompson, *African Trade*, 7–8. See my "Sensibility in Black and White," forthcoming, but the briefs are readily accessible.

10 Thompson, *African Trade*, 9.

11 Thompson, *African Trade*, 9–10; John Hippisley, *Essays On the Populousness of Africa*, etc. (London: T. Lownds, 1764), 4. This, too, is an Ecco edition, reprinted from the Goldsmith's Library of the University of London.

12 Thompson, *African Trade*, 10–11, 11–12; "Other critics" included West Indian Samuel Estwick, *Consideration on the Negro Cause Commonly So Called, Addressed to the Right Honourable Lord Mansfield* (London: J. Dodster, 1772), and Edward Long, *Candid reflections Upon a Judgement lately awarded by the Court of King's Bench in Westminster, on what is Commonly called the Negroe Cause* (London: T. Lowndes, 1772); Anthony Benezet, *A Caution and Warning to Great Britain* (Philadelphia: Henry Miller, 1766).

13 Thompson, *African Trade*, 12–17, 21, 23, 24, 25–26, 30–31.

14 Max Weber, *The Protestant Ethic and the Spirit of Capitalism*, trans. Talcott Parsons (New York: Charles Scribner's Sons, 1958), 79ff, and R.H. Tawney, *Religion and the Rise of Capitalism: An Historical Study* (Gloucester, MA: Peter Smith, 1962 [1920]); Richard Baxter, *The Practical Works of Richard Baxter* (Morgan, PA: Soli Deo Publications, 2000 [1846]), 461 (for Baxter's context, see Eamon Duffy, *Reformation Divided: Catholics, Protestants, and the Conversion of England* [London: Bloomsbury, 2017]); Benezet, *A Caution and Warning to Great Britain*, 37–38; Thompson, *African Trade*, 26, 29.

15 Quaque to Burton, August 19, 1771, *Letters of Quaque*, 98; Quaque to Hind, January 17, 1778, *Letters of Quaque*, 136.

16 *Letters of Quaque*, 101 n. 1; Quaque to Burton, March 8, 1772, *Letters of Quaque*, 99.

17 Quaque to Hind, May 12, 1773, *Letters of Quaque*, 109–10.

18 James A. Levernier, "Phillis Wheatley and the New England Clergy," *Early American Literature* 26, no. 1 (1991), 21–38; 26; Stanley K. Schultz, "The Making of a Reformer: The Reverend Samuel Hopkins as an Eighteenth-Century Abolitionist," *Proceedings of the American Philosophical Society* 115, no. 5 (October 15, 1971), 350–65; 350; Allan Yarema, *The American Colonization Society: An Avenue to Freedom?* (Lanham, MD: University Press of America, 2006), 4; Paul Gilroy, *The Black Atlantic: Modernity and Double Consciousness* (Cambridge, MA: Harvard University Press, 1993), 199ff; Adam Hochschild, *King Leopold's Ghost: A Story of Greed, Terror and Heroism in Colonial Africa* (New York: Mariner Books, 1999), 79–80, 182. For Hopkins and antislavery, see David Brion Davis, *The Problem of Slavery in the Age of Revolution, 1770–1823* (New York: Oxford University Press, 1999 [1975]), 217–18 n. 6.

19 Schultz, "The Making of a Reformer," 350, 354.

20 Mary Beth Norton, *Liberty's Daughters: The Revolutionary Experience of American Women, 1750–1800* (Boston: Little Brown, 1980), 129–33; David Grimsted, "Anglo-American Racism and Phillis Wheatley's 'Sable Veil,' 'Lengthen'd Chains,' and 'Knotted Heart,'" in *Women in the Age of the American Revolution*, ed. Ronald

Hoffman and Peter J. Albert (Charlottesville, VA: University Press of Virginia, 1989); Christopher Leslie Brown, *Moral Capital: Foundation of British Abolitionists* (Chapel Hill: University of North Carolina Press, 2006), 350.

21 Samuel Hopkins and Ezra Stiles, "To the Public" (Newport, 1776). The 1776 version simply added five pages to the original three (dated August 31, 1773), largely reporting on and quoting from Quaque's reply.

22 Quaque to Hind, March 19th, 1774 *Letters of Quaque*, 119–20; Randy L. Sparks, *The Two Princes of Calabar: An Eighteenth-Century Atlantic Odyssey* (Cambridge, MA: Harvard University Press, 2004), 149.

23 Hopkins and Stiles, "To the Public," 2.

24 Hopkins and Stiles, "To the Public," 2–3.

25 Hopkins and Stiles, "To the Public," 3; John Wesley, "Thoughts Upon Slavery," (London: R. Hawes, 1774).

26 Quaque to Hind, May 12, 1773, *Letters of Quaque*, 110.

27 Quaque to Hopkins, May 19, 1773, *Letters of Quaque*, 111; G. J. Barker-Benfield, *The Culture of Sensibility: Sex and Society in Eighteenth-Century Britain* (Chicago: University of Chicago Press, 1992), 66–71; R. S. Crane, "Suggestions toward a Genealogy of the 'Man of Feeling,'" *English Literary History* 1, no. 3 (December 1934), 205–30.

28 Quaque to Hopkins, May 19, 1773, *Letters of Quaque*, 111–12; Phillis Wheatley, "On being brought from AFRICA to AMERICA," in *The Collected Works of Phillis Wheatley*, ed. John C. Shields (New York: Oxford University Press, 1988), 18 (hereafter referred to as *Collected Works*); Winthrop D. Jordan, *White Over Black: American Attitudes toward the Negro, 1550–1812* (Baltimore, MD: Penguin, 1969), 17–20.

29 Quaque to Hopkins, May 19, 1773, *Letters of Quaque*, 112; Quaque to Morice, June 12, 1780, *Letters of Quaque*, 148.

30 Quaque to Hopkins, May 19, 1773, *Letters of Quaque*, 111–14. Quotations in the preceding five paragraphs are all from this letter.

31 Hopkins to Quaque, December 10, 1773, *Letters of Quaque*, 114–15.

32 Hopkins and Stiles, "To the Public," 4–5.

33 This is the subject of chapter 5, below.

34 Hopkins and Stiles, "To the Public," 5.

35 Vincent Carretta, *Phillis Wheatley: Biography of a Genius in Bondage* (Athens, GA: University of Georgia Press, 2012), 5.

36 Hopkins and Stiles, "To the Public," 5; Phillis Wheatley to Samuel Hopkins, February 9, 1774, *Collected Works*, 176.

37 Hopkins and Quaque [n.c.], *Letters of Quaque*, 115; Wheatley, "Proposals for Printing by Subscription," *Collected Works*, 188–89.

38 Hopkins and Stiles, "To the Public," 5–6. Grant writes "Job's joy was inexpressible," then quotes him: "I must have you to guess . . . the Raptures and pleasure I enjoy'd . . . Floods of Tears burst their way and some little time afterward we recover'd." But Grant includes a contrasting account of the reception of Job:

"All his relatives and friends poured out to welcome him, dancing and singing, and Job himself galloped his horse wildly up and down firing off guns and
pistol." He rode so furiously that his horse "drop'd down under him." Douglas
Grant, *The Fortunate Slave: An Illustration of African Slavery in the Early Eighteenth Century* (London: Oxford University Press, 1968), 170. This is a uniquely
detailed and first-rate book on the subject. A contemporary account of Job's
stay in London, *en route* home after being "redeemed" from enslavement in
Maryland, notably combined British political interest in the slave trade with
an appeal to sensibility. Thomas Bluett, *Some Memoirs of the Life of Job, the Son
of Solomon, the High Priest of Boonda in Africa* (London: Richard Ford, 1734).
An electronic edition is available from Academic Affairs Library, University of
North Carolina at Chapel Hill, 1999.

39 Hopkins and Stiles, "To the Public," 6.

40 Hopkins and Stiles, "To the Public," 6–7.

41 Hopkins and Stiles, "To the Public," 7.

42 *Ibid.*

43 Hopkins and Stiles, "To the Public," 7–8.

44 Hopkins and Stiles, "To the Public," 8; Levernier, "Phillis Wheatley and the New
England Clergy," 27.

45 To this is added, *with an Address to the Owners of such Slaves, Dedicated to the
Honorable the Continental Congress* (Norwich, [CT]: Judah P. Spooner, 1776).
Ecco Edition, reproduced from the Library of Congress. Hereafter referred to
as *Dialogue.*

46 Hopkins, *Dialogue,* 30; David Waldstreicher, *Slavery's Constitution: From Revolution to Ratification* (New York: Hill and Wang, 2009), 45, 53.

47 Hopkins, *Dialogue,* 7; for Christianity and brotherhood, see Michael Banner, *The Ethics of Everyday Life: Moral Thought, Social Anthropology, and the
Imagination of the Human* (Oxford: Oxford University Press, 2014), 42–43; for
the ideal of brotherhood in the Enlightenment, see Steven J. Bullock, *Revolutionary Brotherhood; Freemasonry and the Transformation of the American Social
Order, 1730–1840* (Chapel Hill, NC: University of North Carolina Press, 1996),
passim.

48 Hopkins, *Dialogue,* 9, 10, 28, 35. Whole families could be enslaved in Africa, and
so could be shipped together, albeit separated by gender, finally to be torn apart
upon being sold on the docks in America. Marcus Rediker, *The Slave Ship: A Human History* (New York: Penguin, 2008), 304–5.

49 Hopkins, *Dialogue,* 42; Adam Smith, *The Theory of Moral Sentiments,* ed. D. D.
Raphael and A. L. Macfie (Indianapolis: Liberty Classics, 1982 [1759]), 9.

50 Hopkins, *Dialogue,* 34, 31.

51 Hopkins, *Dialogue,* 34, 31, 50, 56; David Brion Davis, *The Problem of Slavery in
Western Culture* (New York: Oxford University Press, 1966), 371; Schultz, "The
Making of a Reformer," 355 n. 24; Hopkins, *Dialogue,* 53–54. Davis writes of Hop-
kins's rhetoric in his *Dialogue*: it "was an imaginative conflation of freedom from

sin with freedom from secular bondage—both the bondage of Negroes and the bondage with which the colonists were threatened." Here and in his subsequent remarks on Hopkins, Davis is extremely suggestive. Davis, *Problem of Slavery in the Age of Revolution*, 293–95.

52 Hopkins, *Dialogue*, 7, 8, 9; Schultz, "The Making of a Reformer," 355.

53 Hopkins, *Dialogue*, 7, 12.

54 Hopkins, *Dialogue*, 13.

55 Hopkins, *Dialogue*, 15, 43, 44

56 Hopkins, *Dialogue*, 46, 47. Best known of the expression of such fears is Jefferson's, who conjectured that the emancipation of slaves would "produce convulsions, which will probably never end but in the extermination of the one or other race." He proposed, therefore, that "they should be colonized" outside the United States. Jefferson, *Notes on the State of Virginia* (New York: Harper and Row, 1962 [1st English ed. 1787]), 132. For the big picture, see Robert G. Parkinson, *The Common Cause: Creating Race and Nation in the American Revolution* (Chapel Hill, NC: University of North Carolina Press, 2016), *passim*.

57 Hopkins, *Dialogue*, 48.

58 Frank Shuffleton, "On Her Own Footing: Phillis Wheatley in Freedom," in *Genius in Bondage: Literature of the Early Black Atlantic* (Lexington, KY: University Press of Kentucky, 2001), 175–89; 178.

59 Felix, [Petition], *A Documentary History on the Negro People in the United States*, ed. Herbert Aptheker (New York: Citadel Press, 1968), 1:6–7. For context, see Bernard Bailyn, *The Ordeal of Thomas Hutchinson* (Cambridge, MA: Harvard University Press, 1974), chap. VI.

60 Peter Bestes et al., [Petition: Printed Leaflet], in *Documentary History of the Negro People*, 1:7–8; Phillis Wheatley to Samson Occom, February 11, 1774, *Collected Works*, 177.

61 Describing this and other such proposals, Christine Levecq writes, "Black emigration (to Nova Scotia, to Sierra Leone) occurred for various reasons and in various circumstances, and so its political significance varies and each case needs to be evaluated individually." Levecq, *Slavery and Sentiment: The Politics of Feeling in Black Atlantic Antislavery Writing, 1770–1850* (Hanover, NH: University Press of New England, 2008), 46.

62 Leon Litwack, *North of Slavery: The Negro in the Free States* (Chicago: University of Chicago Press, 1961); Ira Berlin, *Slaves Without Masters: The Free Negro in the Antebellum South* (Oxford: Oxford University Press, 1974). For those who were interested, in addition to Levecq's book cited in the previous note, see Simon Schama, *Rough Crossings: The Slaves, the British, and the American Revolution* (New York: Harper Collins, 2006), and Stephen Braidwood, *Black Poor and White Philanthropists: London's Blacks and the Foundation of the Sierra Leone Settlement, 1786–91* (Liverpool: Liverpool University Press, 1994). See Jordan, *White Over Black*, and Sondra O'Neale, "Phillis Wheatley's Use of Biblical Myth and Symbol," *Early American Literature* 21, no. 2 (Fall 1986): 144–65; 145–6; Parkinson, *Common Cause*.

CHAPTER 3. FROM AFRICA TO AMERICA

1 Edwin Welch, *Spiritual Pilgrim: A Reassessment of the Life of the Countess of Huntingdon* (Cardiff: University of Wales Press, 2013), 112, 195, 197. See also Boyd Stanley Schleuther, "Hastings [nee Shirley], Selina, countess of Huntingdon (1707–1791), founder of the Countess of Huntingdon's Connexion," *Oxford Dictionary of National Biography* (Oxford: Oxford University Press 2004–12), www.oxforddnb.com, and F. Cook, *Selina, Countess of Huntingdon: Her Pivotal Role in the 18th Century Evangelical Awakening* (Edinburgh: Banner of Truth, 2001).

2 Quoted in Welch, *Spiritual Pilgrim*, 177.

3 Welch, *Spiritual Pilgrim*, 33, 44, 18; G. J. Barker-Benfield, *The Culture of Sensibility: Sex and Society in Eighteenth-Century Britain* (Chicago: University of Chicago Press, 1992), 193–98, 352. For a definition of Bluestocking feminism, see Gary Kelly, "Introduction: Sarah Scott, Bluestocking Feminism, and Millenium Hall," in Sarah Scott, *Millenium Hall*, ed. Gary Kelly (Peterborough, Ontario: Broadview Press 1995 [1762]), 11–43. See also Benjamin Dabby, *Women as Public Moralists in Britain: From the Bluestockings to Virginia Woolf* (Woodbridge, Suffolk: Boydell Press, 2017).

4 Elaine Chalus, "Elite Women, Social Politics, and the Political World of Late Eighteenth-Century England," *Historical Journal* XLIII (2000), 669–97; Amanda Foreman, *Georgiana, Duchess of Devonshire* (New York: Modern Library, 2001), *passim*; Regina Knowles, "The general election of 1784," RegencyHistory.net.

5 *Complete Letters of Lady Mary Wortley Montague*, ed. Robert Halsband (Oxford: Oxford University Press), 2:136; Welch, *Spiritual Pilgrim*, 27.

6 Welch, *Spiritual Pilgrim*, 52, 59; Harry S. Stout, *The Divine Dramatist: George Whitefield and the Rise of American Evangelicalism* (Grand Rapids, MI: William B. Eerdmans Publishing Company, 1998), 172, 213–16.

7 N.E. Now, *Memorial of Selina, Countess of Huntingdon*, rev. ed. (New York: 1858), 353; W. E. Painter, *The Life and Times of Selina Countess of Huntingdon*, (London: 1740), 2:266; Welch, *Spiritual Pilgrim*, 205, 47, 209; Maurice Jackson, *Let This Voice Be Heard: Anthony Benezet, Father of American Abolitionism* (Philadelphia, PA: University of Pennsylvania Press, 2000), 216.

8 Anthony Benezet, *A Caution to Great Britain and Her Colonies in a Short Representation of the Calamitous State of the Enslaved Negroes in the British Dominions* (London: James Phillips, 1785 [1766]), 12; Wylie Sypher, *Guinea's Captive Kings: British Anti-Slavery Literature of the XVIIIth Century* (Chapel Hill, NC: University of North Carolina Press, 1942), 91; Daniel Boorstin, *The Americans*, vol. 1, *The Colonial Experience* (New York: Penguin, 1965), chaps. 13–16. See also Christine Levecq, *Slavery and Sentiment: The Politics of Feeling in Black Atlantic Writing, 1770–1850* (Hanover, NH: University Press of New England, 2006), 420.

9 Quoted in Vincent Carretta, *Phillis Wheatley: Biography of a Genius in Bondage* (Athens, GA: University of Georgia Press, 2011), 75.

10 Whitefield to Mr. B, March, 22, 1751, *Works of George Whitefield on* CD-ROM
    (Weston Rhyn, UK: Quinta Press, 2001), 2:DCCCLXXXVII; *The Collected Works of
    Phillis Wheatley*, ed. John C. Shields (New York: Oxford University Press, 1988),
    24 (hereafter referred to as *Collected Works*); Welch, *Spiritual Pilgrim*, 145; Travis
    Glasson, *Missionary Anglicanism and Slavery in the Atlantic World* (Oxford: Ox-
    ford University Press, 2012), 141 and chap. 5 *passim*.

11 Jackson, *Let This Voice Be Heard*, 216–17; Welch, *Spiritual Pilgrim*, 145. "Writ-
    ing to those who were administering her estate in Georgia in 1771, the
    Countess asked them to buy a black female slave for her: 'I must request that
    a woman slave be purchased . . . and that she might be named Selina after
    me.'" Helen M. Burke, "The Rhetoric and Politics of Marginality: The Subject
    of Phillis Wheatley," *Tulsa Studies in Women's Literature* 10, no. 1 (Spring 1991),
    21–45; 39.

12 Phillis Wheatley to the Countess of Huntingdon, July 17, 1773, *Collected Works*, 168.

13 For the Rev. Shirley, see Welch, *Spiritual Pilgrim*, 101–2. John Albert Ukawsaw
    Gronniosaw and Walter Shirley, *A Narrative of the Most Remarkable Particulars of
    the Life of James Albert Gronniosaw, an African Prince, as Related by Himself* (Bath:
    W. Gye, 1770; Electronic Edition, University of North Carolina Press, 2001), 23, 25,
    iii–iv. Hereafter referred to as *Narrative*.

14 [Shirley], "The Preface: To the Reader," in Gronniosaw, *Narrative*, iii–iv.

15 Christopher Leslie Brown, *Moral Capital: Foundation of British Abolitionism*
    (Chapel Hill, NC: University of North Carolina Press, 2006), 284. Relevant to
    historical questions raised by the white, English lady taking down Gronniosaw's
    narrative is John West Davidson and Mark H. Lytle, "The View from the Bottom
    Rail," in *After the Fact: The Art of Historical Detection*, ed. Davidson and Lytle
    (New York: Knopf, 1982), 177–206.

16 Shirley, "The Preface." Compare Randy J. Sparks, *The Two Princes of Calabar: An
    Eighteenth-Century Atlantic Odyssey* (Cambridge, MA: Harvard University Press,
    2004), 119 and ch. 5 *passim*.

17 Shirley, "The Preface"; David Brion Davis, *The Problem of Slavery in Western Cul-
    ture* (New York: Oxford University Press, 1967), 84. Peter Fryer notes that "John
    Marrant, a black man from Nova Scotia, was ordained a minister of the Countess
    of Huntingdon's Connection." Peter Fryer, *Staying Power: The History of Black
    People in Britain* (London: Pluto Press, 2010 [1984], 75. Like Marrant, Gronnio-
    saw had been a seaman.

18 Phillis Wheatley to the Countess of Huntingdon, October 25, 1770, *Collected Works*,
    162; Charles Scruggs, "Phillis Wheatley (1753–1784)," in *Portraits of American
    Women: From European Settlement to the Present*, ed. G. J. Barker-Benfield and
    Catherine Clinton (New York: Oxford University Press, 1998 [1991]), 106.

19 Vincent Carretta, *Phillis Wheatley*, 8–9.

20 Marcus Rediker, *The Slave Ship: A Human History* (New York: Penguin, 2008),
    268; Edward E. Baptist, *The Half Has Never Been Told: Slavery and the Making of
    American Capitalism* (New York: Basic Books, 2014), 3.

21 William H. Robinson, *Phillis Wheatley and Her Writings* (New York: Garland, 1984), 1–8; Carretta, *Phillis Wheatley*, 6–4.

22 Carretta, *Phillis Wheatley*, 4, 7, 8. "The proportion of African women and children carried across the Atlantic . . . varied strongly by region [of origin] and over time." G. Ugo Nwokeji, "African Conception of Gender and the Slave Traffic," *William and Mary Quarterly*, 3d Series, Vol. LVIII, no. 1 (January 2001), 48–68; 48.

23 Rediker, *Slave Ship*, 277; see also James Walvin, *Crossings: Africa the Americans and the Atlantic Slave Trade* (London: Reaction Books, 2013).

24 Rediker, *Slave Ship*, 277–79; 274–75.

25 Wheatley, "To the Right Honourable WILLIAM, Earl of DARTMOUTH, His Majesty's Principal Secretary of State for North America, &c.," in *Collected Works*, 73–75, 29; for her mother's bereavement, see chap. 5, below.

26 Rediker, *Slave Ship*, 304, 104, 69, 311.

27 Rediker, *Slave Ship*, 7, 146–47, 152.

28 Rediker, *Slave Ship*, 270–71; Walvin, *Crossings*, 98.

29 Walvin, *Crossings*, 82, 13; Robinson, *Phillis Wheatley*, 23.

30 David Grimsted, "Anglo-American Racism and Phillis Wheatley's 'Sable Veil,' 'Lengthen'd Chains,' and 'Knitted Heart,'" in *Women in the Age of the American Revolution*, ed. Ronald Hoffman and Peter J. Albert (Charlottesville, VA: University Press of Virginia, 1989), 338–44 (hereafter referred to as "Anglo-American Racism"); Rediker, *Slave Ship*, 124, 2; Carretta, *Phillis Wheatley*, 13–14.

31 Rediker, *Slave Ship*, 124; Jerome Handler, "Survivors of the Middle Passage: Life Histories of Enslaved Africans in British America," *Slavery and Abolition: A Journal of Slave and Post Slave Studies* 23 (2002): 25–56; 41.

32 Wheatley, *Collected Works*, 18. For a helpful reading of this poem see Sondra O'Neale, "A Slave's Subtle War: Phillis Wheatley's Use of Biblical Myth and Symbol," *Early American Literature* 21 (1986), 144–65; 147–48; 150–52.

33 Jerome McGann, *The Poetics of Sensibility: A Revolution in Literary Style* (Oxford: Clarendon Press, 1996), 7; "The occasion for which she was most frequently called upon to verify was . . . death." Robinson, *Phillis Wheatley and Her Writings*, 100.

34 Wheatley, *Collected Works*, 83, 85, 94.

35 Wheatley, *Collected Works*, 80–81.

36 Wheatley to Obour Tanner, March 21, 1774, *Collected Works*, 177–78. Obour Tanner outlived Wheatley by half a century, into the 1830s, as her "sister's" poetry was reprinted and disseminated with antislavery literature, notably in Garrison's *Liberator*, as ammunition for abolitionism on both sides of the Atlantic (see Robinson, *Phillis Wheatley: A Bio-Bibliography* [Boston: G.K. Hall, 1981], 34–67). Tanner gave the letters she had preserved to Mrs. William Beecher, who wrote:

> They were given to me ages since by the person to whom they were addressed. She was then a very little, very old, very infirm, very, very black woman, with a great shock of the whitest of wool all over her head,—a picture well photographed on my mind's eye. She died in the odor of sanctity, sometime in 1833 or '4, an uncommonly pious, sensible, and intel-

ligent woman, respected and visited by every person in Newport who could appreciate excellence.

The letter was printed as a footnote to the first year's meeting of the Massachusetts Historical Society in 1863. The body of the text was comprised of Wheatley's *Letters*, introduced by the chairman, Mr. Dean, who recalled on reading an earlier letter, "It seemed to me at the time to indicate much maturity of mind, and refinement of delicacy and character." Mr. William Beecher to Rev. E. Hale, October 28, 1868, *Proceedings of the Massachusetts Historical Society (1863)*, 267.

37 Scruggs, "Phillis Wheatley," 106; Leslie Stephen, "Thornton, Henry," *Dictionary of National Biography, 1885–1900*, 56, en.wikisource.org (DNB00).

38 Wheatley to John Thornton, March 29, 1774, *Collected Works*, 178–80; Wheatley to John Thornton, October 30, 1774, *Collected Works*, 182–84.

39 Carretta, *Phillis Wheatley*, 43; observer quoted in Rediker, *Slave Ship*, 301; Wheatley to Abour [sic] Tanner, May 19, 1772, *Collected Works*, 165.

40 Robert Hayden, "A Letter from Phillis Wheatley, London, 1773" in Hayden, *Collected Poems*, ed. Frederick Glaysher (New York: Liveright/Norton, 2013), 147–48. I am grateful to John F. Callahan for this reference.

41 Grimsted, "Anglo-American Racism," 373, 376; Carretta, *Phillis Wheatley*, 65.

42 Carretta, *Phillis Wheatley*, 66; Stanley K. Schultz, "The Making of a Reformer: The Reverend Samuel Hopkins as an Eighteenth-Century Abolitionist," *Proceedings of the American Philosophical Society* 115, no. 5 (October 15, 1971): 350–65; 353.

43 Wheatley, *Collected Works*, 25, 29. Compare Grimsted, "Anglo-American Racism," 356.

44 Wheatley to Thornton, March 29, 1774, *Collected Works*, 179–80.

45 Wheatley to Abour Tanner, May 19, 1772, *Collected Works*, 165; Grimsted, "Anglo-American Racism," 379; Wheatley, *Collected Works*, 133; William, Lord Bishop of Glocester, "Sermon Preached before the Incorporated Society for the Propagation of the Gospel in Foreign Parts etc.," February 21, 1766 (London: E. Owen and T. Harrison, 1766); Charles W. Akers, "Our Modern Egyptians; Phillis Wheatley and the Whig Campaign Against Slavery in Revolutionary Boston," *Journal of Negro History* 60 (July 1975): 397–410; 397; Carretta, *Phillis Wheatley*, 66.

46 Carretta, *Phillis Wheatley*, 42; Robinson, *Phillis Wheatley: A Bio-Bibliography*, 12.

47 Quoted in Robinson, *Phillis Wheatley: A Bio-Bibliography*, 12–13, 16.

48 Wheatley, *Collected Works*, 69–71; Andrews, quoted in Robinson, *Phillis Wheatley*, 13. Frank Shuffleton remarks of this poem's publication, "It migrated from the edges of the public sphere, where it was bound by intimate relationships, to a clarified public subjectivity; it moved from a private scene defined by kinship and shared grief to a communal vision of conversation and power in which the slave becomes masterful." Shuffleton, "Phillis Wheatley, the Aesthetic, and the Form of Life," in *Studies in Eighteenth-Century Culture* 26, ed. Sydney M. Conger and Julie C. Hayes (Baltimore, MD: Johns Hopkins University Press, 1998), 73–85; 81.

CHAPTER 4. WHEATLEY GAINS HUNTINGDON'S PATRONAGE

1 William H. Robinson, *Phillis Wheatley: A Bio-Bibliography* (Boston: G.K. Hall, 1981), 7; *The Collected Works of Phillis Wheatley*, ed. John C. Shields (New York: Oxford University Press, 1988), 282 (hereafter referred to as *Collected Works*).

2 Wheatley, *Collected Works*, 22–24.

3 Charles Scruggs, "Phillis Wheatley (1753?–1784)," in *Portraits of American Women: From European Settlement to the Present*, ed. G. J. Barker-Benfield and Catherine Clinton (New York: Oxford University Press, 1998 [1991]), 106; Wheatley, *Collected Works*, 287.

4 Whitefield had expressed his sympathy for Americans in resisting the Stamp Act and other British imperial measures. Carretta observes, "Poets depicted the late Whitefield as America's friend and defender." Vincent Carretta, *Phillis Wheatley: Biography of a Genius in Bondage* (Athens, Georgia: University of Georgia Press, 2011), 74. Another scholar writes that Wheatley was "likely to have encountered *Three Letters from the Reverend George Whitefield*, including the one addressed to the inhabitants of Maryland, Virginia, North and South Carolina," calling them "monsters of barbarity." He suggests it was "Whitefield's deep concern for the welfare of Boston's slaves that prompted Wheatley to write the elegy that made her famous, for in this elegy she specifically refers to Whitefield's preaching among the *Africans* of Boston." James A. Levernier, "Phillis Wheatley and the New England Clergy," *Early American Literature* 26, no. 1 (1991), 21–28, 31.

5 Robinson, *Phillis Wheatley*, 6–7; David Grimsted, "Anglo-American Racism and Phillis Wheatley's 'Sable Veil,' 'Lengthen'd Chain,' and 'Knitted Heart,'" in *Women in the Era of the American Revolution*, ed. Ronald Hoffman and Peter J. Albert (Charlottesville, VA: University Press of Virginia, 1989), 338–444 (hereafter referred to as "Anglo-American Racism"); Robinson, *Phillis Wheatley*, 6–7.

6 Ignatius Sancho to Lawrence Sterne, July 1766, *Letters of the Late Ignatius Sancho, An African*, ed. Vincent Carretta (New York: Penguin, 1998 [1782]), 73–74. Sterne's daughter, Lydia Sterne Medalle, published this and the subsequent brief surviving correspondence in *Letters of the Late Rev. Mr. Lawrence Sterne to His Most Intimate Friend* in 3 volumes in 1775, making Sancho's appeal well-known.

7 Wheatley, *Collected Works*, 162, 16–17.

8 G. J. Barker-Benfield, *The Culture of Sensibility: Sex and Society in Eighteenth-Century Britain* (Chicago: University of Chicago Press, 1992), 46–47; David S. Shields, *Civil Tongues and Polite Letters in British America* (Chapel Hill, NC: University of North Carolina Press, 1997), 214–15.

9 G. J. Barker-Benfield, *Abigail and John Adams: The Americanization of Sensibility* (Chicago: University of Chicago Press, 2010), 310–11, 321.

10 Wheatley, *Collected Works*, 131–32; Scruggs, "Phillis Wheatley," 112–13; Jay Fliegelman, *Prodigals and Pilgrims: The American Revolution against Patriarchal Authority* (Cambridge, UK: Cambridge University Press, 1982), pt. I. For an exegesis of Wheatley's use of "the Christian historicity vested in the term 'Ethiopian'" and

other Biblical references, see Sondra O'Neale, "A Slave's Subtle War: Phillis Wheatley's Use of Biblical Myth and Symbol," *Early American Literature* 21, no. 2 (Fall 1980): 144–65.

11 See n. 9, and Barker-Benfield, *Culture of Sensibility*, chaps. 2 and 5; see also Barker-Benfield, *Abigail and John Adams*, 127–28 and chaps. 7 and 9.

12 Wheatley, *Collected Works*, 134.

13 Maurice Jackson, *Let This Voice Be Heard: Anthony Benezet, Father of Atlantic Abolitionism* (Philadelphia: University of Pennsylvania Press, 2009), 118, 121; Rush's pamphlet in its 1775 edition, published by Judah P. Spooner in Norwich, has been reprinted from the Cornell University Digital Collection. For Rush's context, including the relation between sensibility, reform, revolution, and antislavery in Philadelphia, see Michael Meranze, *Laboratories of Virtue: Punishment, Revolution, and Authority in Philadelphia, 1760–1835* (Chapel Hill, NC: University of North Carolina Press, 1996), 120–21, 296–301, and Sarah Knott, *Sensibility and the American Revolution* (Chapel Hill, NC: University of North Carolina Press, 2009), 65, and *passim*.

14 Rush, "Address to the Inhabitants of the British Settlements in America upon Slave Keeping," (New York: Arno Press and the New York Times, 1969[1773]), 3 (hereafter referred to as "Address to the Inhabitants"). Rush was an advocate for giving "the sex"—women—an improved education. He helped found the Philadelphia Young Ladies Academy, to make women better qualified to be wives and mothers of male republicans. May Beth Norton, *Daughters of the Republic: The Revolutionary Experience of American Women* (Boston: Little Brown, 1980), 267–69.

15 *Compact Edition of the Oxford English Dictionary*; Samuel Johnson, *Lives of the English Poets* (London: J.M. Dent, 1946), 1:1–2. For Jefferson, see my conclusion.

16 Rush, "Address to the Inhabitants," 16, 22; Christian Levecq, *The Politics of Feeling in Black Atlantic Antislavery Writing, 1770–1850* (Hanover, NH: University Press of New England, 2006), 44–45.

17 Richard Nisbet, *Slavery Not Forbidden By Scripture, Or, A Defence of the West-India Planters, From The Aspersions Thrown Out Against Them, By the Author of A Pamphlet Entitled, "An Address to the Inhabitants Of the British Settlements In America, Upon Slave-Keeping,"* (Philadelphia: 1773), also reprinted from Cornell University Library's Digital Collection, 20–21, 22–23, 63 n.

18 James Axtell, "Dr. Wheelock's Little Red Schoolhouse," in Axtell, *The European and the Indian: Essays in the Ethnohistory of Colonial North America* (New York: Oxford University Press, 1982), 87–109; 92, 95, 96. Hereafter referred to as "Dr. Wheelock's Schoolhouse."

19 Neal Salisbury, *Manitou and Providence: Indians, Europeans, and the Making of New England, 1500–1643* (New York: Oxford University Press, 1982).

20 Axtell, "Dr. Wheelock's Schoolhouse," 97; Ramsay's book was published in London by the Quaker printer James Phillips, who published Benezet's and other antislavery works. Christopher Leslie Brown, *Moral Capital: Foundation of British Abolitionists* (Chapel Hill: University of North Carolina Press, 2006), 377, 417–18.

21 Axtell, "Dr. Wheelock's Schoolhouse," 101, 102, 103, 105.

22 Carretta, *Phillis Wheatley*, 45–46; Grimsted, "Anglo-American Racism," 381.

23 Axtell, "Dr. Wheelock's Schoolhouse," 103, 108.

24 Robinson, *Phillis Wheatley and Her Writings* (New York: Garland, 1984), 113.

25 Wheatley to John Thornton, April 21, 1772, *Collected Works*, 163–64.

26 Rev. Richard Carey to the Countess of Huntingdon, May 15, 1772, in Robinson, *Phillis Wheatley: A Bio-Bibliography*, 12; and see Carretta, *Phillis Wheatley*, 91–92. The following year, Carey would help distribute Wheatley's *Poems* (published under Huntingdon's *aegis*) to a number of Boston lady readers. Grimsted, "Anglo-American Racism," 389.

27 Susanna Wheatley to the Countess of Huntingdon, February 20, 1773, in Sara Dunlap Jackson, "Letters of Phillis Wheatley and Susanna Wheatley, *Journal of Negro History* 57, no. 2 (April 1972), 211–15; 212–13 (hereafter referred to as "Letters").

28 Susanna Wheatley to the Countess of Huntingdon, April 30, 1773, in Dunlap Jackson, "Letters," 213–14.

29 *Op cit.*; Grimsted suggests that Susanna Wheatley became "the countess's principal cooperator in the colonies." Grimsted, "Anglo-American Racism," 384.

30 Quoted in Carretta, *Phillis Wheatley*, 92; Wheatley, "To the Publick," *Collected Works* (unpaginated).

31 Compare James D. Hartman, "Providence Tales and the Indian Captivity Narratives: Some Transatlantic Influences on Colonial Puritan Discourse," *Early American Literature* 32, (1997): 66–81; and Kenneth Silverman, *A Cultural History of the American Revolution: Painting, Music, Literature, and the Theatre in the Colonies and the United States from the Treaty of Paris to the Inauguration of George Washington* (New York: Crowell, 1976), 215.

32 Richard L. Bushman, *The Refinement of America: Persons, Houses, Cities* (New York: Knopf, 1992), xiv, 55–58, 132–33, 446. Very suggestive on interpersonal performance is Rhys Isaac, *The Transformation of Virginia, 1740–1790* (Chapel Hill, NC: University of North Carolina Press, 1982), *passim*.

33 Wheatley, *Collected Works*, 43–50, 283; Scruggs, "Phillis Wheatley," 111.

34 Thomas Wooldridge to the Earl of Dartmouth, November 24, 1772, in Robinson, *Phillis Wheatley and Her Writings*, 454; Peter Marshall, "Legge, William, second earl of Dartmouth," *Dictionary of National Biography* (Oxford: Oxford University Press, 2004–12), www.oxforddub.com (10/5/2012), 1–6; 2, 3 (hereafter referred to as "Dartmouth"). For illustrations of the countess's relations with Dartmouth, one seeking his help when he was president of the Privy Council, another, sending him music of hymns collected for her Connexion, see Edwin Welch, *Spiritual Pilgrim: A Reassessment of the Life of the Countess of Huntingdon* (Cardiff: University of Wales Press, 1995), 134, 201. The "too much religion" quotation is in Bernard Bailyn, *The Ordeal of Thomas Hutchinson* (Cambridge, MA: Harvard University Press, 1974), 326.

35 Vincent T. Harlow, *The Founding of the Second British Empire, 1763–1793*, 2 vols. (London: Longmans, Green, 1962–64); James Otis, "The Rights of the British Colonies Asserted and Proved," in *The American Republic: Primary Sources*, ed. Bruce Frohnen (Indianapolis, IN: Liberty Fund, 2007).

36 Wheatley, *Collected Works*, 137; see John C. Shields, "Phillis Wheatley's Struggle for Freedom, in Her Poetry and Prose," in Wheatley, *Collected Works*, 229–20; 233, for the specifics of Snider's murder. For "revolutionary events that took place near her home," see Robinson, *Phillis Wheatley and Her Writings*, 17.

37 Marshall, "Dartmouth," 3; Brown, *Moral Capital*, 176.

38 Wooldridge to Dartmouth, November 24, 1772, in Robinson, *Phillis Wheatley and Her Writings*, 453.

39 Grimsted, "Anglo-American Racism," 389; John Russell, *The Life of Mozart* (Cambridge, UK: Cambridge University Press, 1998), 18; Shields, *Civil Tongues*, chap. 2; Wheatley, *Collected Works*, 124.

40 William H. Robinson, "Phillis Wheatley in London," *College Language Association Journal* 21 (1977): 187–201; 193.

41 Wheatley to the Earl of Dartmouth, October 10, 1772, *Collected Works*, 166–67.

42 *Collected Works*, 73–75; Sondra O'Neale, "A Slave's Subtle War," 156; Helen M. Burke, "The Rhetoric and Politics of Marginality: The Subject of Phillis Wheatley," *Tulsa Studies in Women's Literature* 10, no. 1 (Spring 1991): 31–45; 36. We saw that in "An Address to the Deist" and "America" Wheatley suggests an Ethiop has a particular love of liberty. These were not included in her *Poems*. See, too, Peter Coviello, "Agonizing Affection," *Early American Literature* 37, no. 3 (2002): 439–68; 445–46, and Christine Levecq's discussion of Coviello in Levecq, *Slavery and Sentiment: The Politics of Feeling in Black Atlantic Antislavery Writing, 1770–1850* (Hanover, NH: University Press of New England, 2008), 53–54.

43 Wheatley, *Collected Works*, 323–24.

44 For significant qualifications to the meaning of Lady Huntingdon's patronage, see Cynthia J. Smith, "'To Maecenas': Phillis Wheatley's Invocation of an Idealized Reader," *Black American Literature Forum* 23, no. 3 (Autumn 1989): 579–92; 580, 582; Susanna Wheatley to the Countess of Huntingdon, April 30, 1773, in Dunlap Jackson, "Letters," 213–14. William Piercy led the group Lady Huntingdon sent to sort out affairs in Bethesda after Whitefield's death; for his activities there, see Welch, *Spiritual Pilgrim*, 136–47 and chap. 10. Carretta provides a more accurate transcription of most of this letter in *Phillis Wheatley*, 95.

45 Grimsted, "Anglo-American Racism," 342.

46 Quoted in Carretta, *Phillis Wheatley*, 93.

47 The relevant extract from Calef's letter to Susanna Wheatley, June 5, 1773, was published in "Notes and Queries," *Historical Magazine* 2 (June 1858), 179. On Wheatley to Occom, see Carretta, *Phillis Wheatley*, 92.

48 Walt Nott, "From 'uncultivated Barbarian' to 'Poetical Genius,' The Public Presence of Phillis Wheatley," *MELUS* 18, no. 3 (Fall 1993): 23–32; 24.

CHAPTER 5. THE PUBLICATION OF WHEATLEY'S *POEMS ON VARIOUS SUBJECTS, RELIGIOUS AND MORAL*

1 Vincent Carretta, *Phillis Wheatley: Biography of a Genius in Bondage* (Athens, GA: University of Georgia Press, 2011), 95–97; *The Collected Works of Phillis Wheatley*, ed. John C. Shields (New York: Oxford University Press, 1988), i–vii (hereafter referred to as *Collected Works*).

2 Wheatley, *Collected Works*, iv–v; in a letter, written after her *Poems'* publication, Wheatley told John Thornton that Susanna Wheatley had "applied unwearied diligence to instruct in the principles of the Religion." Wheatley to Thornton, October 30, 1774, *Collected Works*, 183. According to a descendant, Susanna Wheatley's daughter, Mary, eighteen when her parents brought the African child home, "tutored her to read and write." David Grimsted, "Anglo-American Racism and Phillis Wheatley's 'Sable Veil,' 'Lengthen'd Chains,' and Knitted Heart,'" in *Women in the Age of the American Revolution*, ed. Ronald Hoffman and Peter J. Albert (Charlottesville, VA: University Press of Virginia, 1989), 341 (hereafter referred to as "Anglo-American Racism"). In her 1784 "An Elegy to the Memory of that Great Divine, the Reverend and Learned D. Samuel Cooper," Wheatley called him "A Friend sincere, who mild indulgent grace/Encourag'd oft, and oft approv'd her lays." Wheatley, *Collected Works*, 153. Cooper had baptized the fifteen-year old Wheatley in 1771, and was one of the ministers who publicly attested to Wheatley's ability and authenticity in another prefatory document to her *Poems*. The second on that list, the Rev. Matthew Byles, seems to have "served as a tutor" to Wheatley. Grimsted, "Anglo-American Racism," 341. See, too, John C. Shields, "Phillis Wheatley and Mather Byles: A Study in Literary Relationship," *College Language Association Journal* 23, no. 4 (June 1980), 377–90 (hereafter referred to as "Wheatley and Byles").

3 Wheatley, *Collected Works*, vi; Wheatley to John Thornton, October 30, 1774, *Collected Works*, 184. For Wheatley's demonstration of her literary abilities in person, see my previous chapter.

4 Alan Taylor, *American Colonies: The Settling of North America* (New York: Penguin, 2002), 359–60, 338.

5 Wheatley, *Collected Works*, vii; Advertisement, *Boston Censor*, February 29, 1772, in William H. Robinson, *Phillis Wheatley: A Bio-Bibliography* (Boston, MA: G.K. Hall, 1981), 11.

6 Henry Louis Gates, Jr., *The Trials of Phillis Wheatley: America's First Black Poet and her Encounters with the Founding Fathers* (New York: Basic Books, 2003), 5, 7, 16.

7 Ignatius Sancho to Mr. [Jabez] F[isher], January 27, 1778, *Letters of the Late Ignatius Sancho, An African*, ed. Vincent Carretta (New York: Penguin, 1998 [1782]), 288, 111–12. For a later but still Rousseau-istic contrast celebrating nature, see Elizabeth Inchbald, *Nature and Art* (Peterborough, Ontario: Broadview Press, 2005 [1796]).

8 Markman Ellis has a more qualified view of the effect of Sancho's letter on Sterne. Ellis, *The Politics of Sensibility: Race, Gender and Commerce in the Sentimental Novel* (Cambridge, UK: Cambridge University Press, 1996), chap. 2.

9 Laurence Sterne, "The Sermons of Laurence Sterne," in *The Florida Edition of the Works of Laurence Sterne*, ed. Melvyn New (Gainesville, FL: University Press of Florida, 1996), IV:27.

10 William H. Robinson, *Phillis Wheatley and Her Writings* (New York: Garland, 1984), 39; Helen M. Burke, "The Rhetoric and Politics of Marginality: The Subject of Phillis Wheatley," *Tulsa Studies in Women's Literature* 10, no. 1 (Spring 1991): 31–45, 39. Among "other scholars" are Sondra O'Neale, "Phillis Wheatley's Use of Biblical Myth and Symbol," *Early American Literature* 21, no. 2 (Fall 1986): 144–45; Betsy Erkkila, "Revolutionary Women," *Tulsa Studies in Woman's Literature* 6, no. 2 (1987): 189–220; James A. Levernier, "Style as Protest in the Poetry of Phillis Wheatley," *Style* 27, no. 2 (1993): 172–93.

11 James A. Levernier, "Phillis Wheatley and the New England Clergy," *Early American Literature* 26, no. 1 (1991): 21–38.

12 Wheatley, *Collected Works*, 116–18.

13 Charles W. Akers, "'Our Modern Egyptians': Phillis Wheatley and the Whig Campaign against Slavery in Revolutionary Boston," *Journal of Negro History* 60 (July 1975): 397–410; 403; Shields, "Wheatley and Byles," 377–90; Grimsted, "Anglo-American Racism," 388; Wheatley to Rev. Samuel Hopkins, May 6, 1774, *Collected Works*, 181, 137; Levernier, "Phillis Wheatley and the New England Clergy," 23, 25; Robinson, *Phillis Wheatley and Her Writings*, 19.

14 Robinson, "Phillis Wheatley in London," *College Language Association Journal* 21 (1977): 187–201; 189–90; Wheatley, *Collected Works*, 13.

15 Robinson, *Phillis Wheatley: A Bio-Bibliography*, 18–20; for a detailed account of these announcements, the variants in them, and their titles, see Mukhtar Ali Isani, "Wheatley's Departure for London and her 'Farewell to America,'" *South Atlantic Bulletin* 42, no. 4 (November 1977): 123–29.

16 Robinson, *Phillis Wheatley: A Bio-Bibliography*, 19–20; *The Poems of Phillis Wheatley*, ed. Julian D. Mason (Chapel Hill, NC: University of North Carolina Press, 1989), 154; Isani, "Wheatley's Departure for London," 125.

17 Wheatley, *Collected Works*, 119–22; G. J. Barker-Benfield, *Abigail and John Adams: The Americanization of Sensibility* (Chicago: University of Chicago Press, 2010), 87, 212–13; Wheatley to John Thornton, March 29, 1774, *Collected Works*, 178–80; 179; Jerome McGann, *The Poetics of Sensibility: A Revolution in Literary Style* (Oxford: Oxford University Press, 1996), 7.

18 These lines are all from "Farewell to America." To Mrs. S. W. Wheatley, *Collected Works*, 119–22; for London's attractions to young women, see G. J. Barker-Benfield, *The Culture of Sensibility: Sex and Society in Eighteenth-Century Britain* (Chicago: University of Chicago Press, 1992), 182–90, and moralistic concerns over them, 190–205. Compare Mrs. Trevelyan's apprehensions of her ward, Kitty, going to London: "the hot house of vice where virtue had long been banished . . . and

Wickedness of every description was gaining ground—that Kitty . . . was the last girl in the world to be trusted in London, as she would be totally unable to withstand temptation." Jane Austen, "Catherine or the Bower," in *Love and Freindship and Other Juvenile Writing*, (New York: Penguin), 258.

19 Wheatley, *Collected Works*, 221. Isani sees "a gain in clarity, view and directness." Isani, "Wheatley's Departure for London," 125.

20 Carretta, *Phillis Wheatley*, 128–31, 135–37; Carretta refers to Orlando Patterson, *Slavery and Social Death: A Comparative Study* (Cambridge, MA: Harvard University Press, 1985). Isani suggests Nathaniel Wheatley, who accompanied Phillis Wheatley across the Atlantic, was worried about this possibility. Isani, "Phillis Wheatley in London: An Unpublished Letter to David Wooster," *American Literature* 51, no. 2 (May 1979): 253–60; 258 n. 6.

21 Carretta, *Phillis Wheatley*, 121.

22 Wheatley to the Countess of Huntingdon, June 27, 1773, *Collected Works*, 167–68; Edwin Welch, *Spiritual Pilgrim: A Reassessment of the Life of the Countess of Huntingdon* (Cardiff: University of Wales Press, 1995), 80.

23 This letter in Wheatley's *Collected Works* has the phrase "uppity Criticism," evidently a misprint.

24 Carretta, *Phillis Wheatley*, 126; Wheatley to David Wooster, October 18, 1773, in Isani, "Phillis Wheatley in London," 255–60; 256 n. 3, 259. It is also printed in Wheatley, *Collected Works*, 169–71.

25 Carretta, *Phillis Wheatley*, 106; Robinson, *Phillis Wheatley and Her Writings*, 41.

26 Wheatley to David Wooster, October 18, 1773, *Collected Works*, 169–71; for Alderman Kirkman, see www.tonykirkman.pwp.blueyonder.co.uk. Wheatley's editorial decisions for her London audience are described by Grimsted, "Anglo-American Racism," 349ff, and see John C. Shields, *Phillis Wheatley and the Poetics of Liberation* (Knoxville, TN: University of Tennessee Press, 2008), 95–96; Wheatley, "On the Death of Mr. Snider, Murder'd by Richardson," *Collected Works*, 136. For the lost poem, see Wheatley, *Collected Works*, 338.

27 Wheatley, *Collected Works*, 17, 73–75.

28 See note 26; "Sir Brook Watson," *Virtual American Biographies*, taken from *Appleton's Encyclopedia 2001*, www.famousamericans.net.

29 Peter Marshall, "Legge, William, second earl of Dartmouth," *Dictionary of National Biography* (Oxford: Oxford University Press, 2004–12), 1–6; see www.oxforddub.com; David Waldstreicher, *Slavery's Constitution: From Revolution to Ratification* (New York: Hill and Wang, 2009), 53; Dartmouth, quoted in Wylie Sypher, *Guinea's Captive Kings: British Anti-Slavery Literature of the Eighteenth Century* (Chapel Hill, NC: University of North Carolina Press, 1942), 65.

30 Isani, "Phillis Wheatley in London," 256. These are more quotations from Wheatley's letter to Wooster.

31 "Daniel Solander, 1733–1782," *Wikipedia*, en.wikipedia.org; "Joseph Banks, 1743–1820," *Wikipedia*, en.wikipedia.org; Robert J. Taylor, "Israel Mauduit," *New*

England Quarterly 24, no. 2 (June 1951), 208–30; Franklin, quoted in Isani, "Phillis Wheatley in London," n. 6.

32 Wheatley to Wooster, October 18, 1773, *Collected Works*, 169; Grimsted, "Anglo-American Racism," 386–87; Christopher Leslie Brown, *Moral Capital: Foundations of British Abolitionism* (Chapel Hill, NC: University of North Carolina Press, 2006), 175.

33 Grimsted, "Anglo-American Racism," 385; Carretta, "Phillis Wheatley, the Mansfield Decision of 1772, and the Choice of Identity," in *Early America Re-Explored: New Readings in Colonial, Early National, and Antebellum Culture*, ed. Klaus H. Schmidt and Fritz Fleischman (New York: Peter Lang, 2000): 208; Carretta, *Phillis Wheatley*, 118, 132.

34 Wheatley to Huntingdon, July 17, 1773, *Collected Works*, 168–69. Carretta suggests that "her return voyage had been planned rather than in response to 'a message that Mrs. Wheatley was seriously ill,'" as Julian Mason writes in the introduction to his edition of *The Poems of Phillis Wheatley* (Chapel Hill, NC: University of North Carolina Press, 1989), 8. Wheatley did find Susanna near to death on her return.

35 Robinson, *Phillis Wheatley: A Bio-Bibliography*, 21.

36 Charles Scruggs, "Phillis Wheatley (1753–1784)," in *Portraits of American Women: From European Settlement to the Present*, ed. G. J. Barker-Benfield and Catherine Clinton (New York: Oxford University Press, 1998 [1992]), 107; Lathrop, quoted in Robinson, *Phillis Wheatley and Her Writings*, 17, 124–50.

37 Scruggs, "Phillis Wheatley," 108; for Yearsley, see Elizabeth Eger and Lucy Peitz, *Brilliant Woman: 18th Century Bluestockings* (London: National Portrait Gallery, 2008), 45–48.

38 Carretta, *Phillis Wheatley*, 106; Wheatley, *Collected Works*, 276; Cynthia J. Smith, "'To Maecenas': Phillis Wheatley's Invocation of an Idealized Reader," *Black American Literature Forum* 23, no. 3 (Autumn 1989), 579–92; 579; Scruggs, "Phillis Wheatley," 111. Paula Bennett writes that "To Maecenas" was one of a group of poems asserting Wheatley's "legitimation of her right to practice her vocation." Bennett, "Phillis Wheatley's Vocation and the Paradox of the Afric Muse," *PMLA* 113, no. 1 (1998): 64–76; 64.

39 Wheatley, *Collected Poems*, 9–12; Alexander Pope, "An Essay on Man," *The Poems of Alexander Pope*, ed. John Butt (New Haven, CT: Yale University Press, 1963 [1733–34]), Epistle II: ll, 108–110; Smith, "To Maecenas," 586; Helen M. Burke notes that "the young writer's self-deprecation here is as conventional as that young Pope's in his 'Essay on Criticism' where the latter similarly defines himself as an unworthy inheritor of the classical tradition." Burke, "The Rhetoric and Politics of Marginality," 34. See also Phillip M. Richards's observation that "similar rhetorical gestures" can be found "in American colonial poets beginning with Anne Bradstreet and continuing through Matthew Byles," that correspondent of Pope's who is believed to have had an influence on Wheatley. Richards, "Phillis

Wheatley and Literary Americanization," *American Quarterly* 44, no. 2 (June 1992): 163–91; 173.

40 Gordon Willis Williams, "Terence," in *Oxford Classical Dictionary*, ed. N. G. L. Hammond and H. H. Scullard (Oxford: Clarendon Press, 1970), 1043–44; David McCullough, *John Adams* (New York: Simon and Schuster, 2001), 259; John Adams to John Quincy Adams, December 25, 1780, *Adams Family Correspondence*, ed. L. H. Butterfield et al. (Cambridge, MA; Belknap Press of Harvard University Press, 1963—), IV:80; Thomas Jefferson, *Notes on the State of Virginia* (New York: Penguin, 1999 [1785]), 149, 147.

41 While Wheatley "sometimes mirrored usual linguistic assumptions by using 'dark' and 'black' to denote evil or a state of damnation, she was careful to differentiate these associations from human skin color." Sondra O'Neale, "A Slave's Subtle War: Phillis Wheatley: Use of Biblical Myth and Symbol," *Early American Literature* 21, no. 2 (Fall 1986): 144–65; 146.

42 Wheatley, *Collected Works*, 9–12.

43 Wheatley, *Collected Works*, 95–97. For the meaning of "humanity," see Barker-Benfield, *Abigail and John Adams*, 115–26, 396, 402.

44 Wheatley, *Collected Works*, 291–92.

45 Lucy K. Hayden, "Classical Tidings from the Afric Muse: Phillis Wheatley's Use of Greek and Roman Mythology," CLA *Journal* 35, no. 4 (June 1992): 432–47; 437; Jennifer Thorn, "'All Beautiful in Woe': Gender, Nation and Phillis Wheatley's 'Niobe,'" *Studies in Eighteenth-Century Culture* 37 (2008): 233–58; 240; David Alexander, personal communication, May 29, 2017.

46 Wheatley, *Collected Works*, 101–13.

47 Wheatley, *Collected Works*, 98–100; Robinson, *Phillis Wheatley and Her Writings*, 20; Wheatley, *Collected Works*, 29–30.

48 Hayden, "Classical Tidings," 435–36.

49 Ovid, *Metamorphosis*, trans. A.D. Melville (Oxford: Oxford University Press, 1986), Book VI, 125–30.

50 Wheatley, *Collected Works*, 113.

51 Wheatley, *Collected Works*, 113. For more context of the presentation of Niobe in "the age of sensibility," see Barker-Benfield, *Culture of Sensibility*, 64–65.

52 Hayden, "Classical Tidings," 443; Christine Levecq, *Slavery and Sentiment: The Politics of Feeling in Black Atlantic Antislavery Writing, 1770–1850* (Hanover, NH: University Press of New England, 2008), 66; Jennifer Thorn, "'All Beautiful in Woe': Gender, Nation, and Phillis Wheatley's 'Niobe,'" *Studies in Eighteenth-Century Culture* 37 (2008): 233–58; 245. For other differences between Ovid and Wheatley, see Robinson, *Phillis Wheatley and Her Writings*, 99.

53 Grimsted, "Anglo-American Racism," 369.

54 Wheatley, *Collected Works*, 114–15; Robinson, *Phillis Wheatley and Her Writings*, 274. Robinson writes that the ad "may or may not refer to Scipio"; R.W.B. Lewis and Nancy Lewis, *American Characters: Selection from the National Portrait Gallery, Accompanied by Literary Portraits* (New Haven, Yale University Press, 1999), 380.

55 "The Life of Terence," *Works of C. Suetonius Tranquilus*, trans. J. C. Rolfe (Cambridge, MA: Harvard University Press, 1997), II:431.

56 Eg. Austen, *Love and Freindship*, 8 and 367 n. 11.

57 Wheatley, *Collected Works*, 9.

58 Hayden, "Classical Tidings," 435–36; Wheatley, *Collected Works*, 31–42.

59 Wheatley to Samson Occom, February 11, 1774, *Collected Works*, 176–77; Barker-Benfield, *Culture of Sensibility*, 355–57, 351–52. Compare Shields, *Phillis Wheatley and the Poetics of Liberation*, 32–34.

60 Robinson, *Phillis Wheatley: A Bio-Bibliography*, 18–27; Mukhtar Ali Isani, "The Contemporaneous Reception of Phillis Wheatley: Newspaper and Magazine Notices during the Years of Fame, 1765–1774," *Journal of Negro History* 85, no. 4 (Autumn 2000), 260–73.

61 Frank Shuffleton, "On Her Own Footing: Phillis Wheatley in Freedom," in *Genius in Bondage: Literature of the Early Black Atlantic*, ed. Vincent Carretta and Philip Gould (Lexington, KY: University Press of Kentucky, 2001): 175–89; 175; Sondra O'Neale, "Phillis Wheatley's Use of Biblical Myth and Symbol," 158; Voltaire, quoted in Kenneth Silverman, *A Cultural History of the American Revolution: Painting, Music, Literature, and the Theatre in the Colonies and the United States from the Treaty of Paris to the Inauguration of George Washington, 1763–1789* (New York: Thomas Y. Crowell, 1976), 217; Phillip M. Richards, "Phillis Wheatley and Literary Americanization," *American Quarterly* 44, no. 2 (June 1992): 163–91; 188 n. 4.

62 *London Chronicle*, September 18, 1773, 277; *Critical Review* 36 (September 1773), 456.

63 *Gentleman's Magazine* 43 (September 1773), 456; *Scots Magazine* 35 (September 1773), 484–85; Ignatius Sancho to Jabez Fisher, January 27, 1778, *Letters of the Late Ignatius Sancho, An African*, 112.

64 *Monthly Review* 49 (December 1773): 458–59.

65 Quoted in Robinson, *Phillis Wheatley and Her Writings*, 39.

66 *Pennsylvania Chronicle*, September 13, 1773, quoted in Isani, "Reception of Phillis Wheatley," 263.

67 *Sentimental Magazine* 2 (September 1774): 416.

68 Robinson, *Phillis Wheatley and Her Writings*, 39–40.

69 See n. 62.

70 See n. 62.

71 Lawrence Sterne to Ignatius Sancho, July 27, 1766, *The Florida Edition of the Works of Lawrence Sterne*, vol. VIII, *The Letters, Part 2: 1765–1768*, ed. Melvyn New and Peter de Voogd (Gainesville, FL: University Press of Florida 2009), 504–5; Ignatius Sancho to Lawrence Sterne, July 17[6]6, *Letters of the Late Ignatius Sancho, An African*, 73–74; Lawrence Sterne, *The Life and Opinion of Tristram Shandy, Gentleman*, ed. James Aiken Workman (New York: Odyssey Press, 1940 [1759–1767]), 606–7.

72 Quoted in Carretta, *Phillis Wheatley*, 35–37; Robinson, *Phillis Wheatley: A Bio-Bibliography*, 20, 25.

73 Lawrence Sterne, *The Beauties of Sterne* (London: T. Davies, 1782), Preface, 75–78; Alan B. Howes, *Yorick and the Critics: Sterne's Reputation in England, 1760–1868* (Hamden, CT: Archon Books, 1971), 62–63, 65; Thomas Clarkson, *The History of the Rise, Progress, and Accomplishment of the Abolition of the African Slave Trade*, (Lexington, KY: Filiquarian Publishing, 2013 [transcribed from first ed., 2 vols. Pub. London: Richard Taylor, 1808]) 1:22.

74 Samuel Foote, *The Cozeners; A Comedy in Three Acts* (London: T. Cadell, 1778 [1774]), in *The Dramatic Works of Samuel Foote, Esq.: The Commissary. The Lame Lover, The Bankrupt, The Cozeners* (n.p.: Nabu Public Domain Reprints; see www.jcgtesting.com), 67–68, 78–81; see, too, Sypher, *Guinea's Captive Kings*, 238–39; Susan Lamb, "The Popular Theater of Samuel Foote and British National Identity," *Comparative Drama* 30, no. 2 (Summer 1996): 245–61; 245–46, 248–9.

75 Peter Fryer gives further evidence that black women and men were stereotyped as lustful. Fryer, *Staying Power: The History of Black People in Britain* (London: Pluto Press, 2010 [1984]), 139–40, 159, 164, 170–71, 317–19.

76 Mary Scott, *The Female Advocate: A Poem Occasioned by Reading Mr. Duncombe's Feminead* (1774), reprinted as William Andrews Clark Memorial Library Publication, Number 24 (Los Angeles, CA: UCLA, 1984), with a valuable introduction by Gae Holladay, iii–xiv, which includes an identifying list of all fifty-one women described by Scott.

77 Barker-Benfield, *Culture of Sensibility*, xix, ff, chaps. 4, 5, 6; Scott, *Female Advocate*, iv; ll 21–24; vi.

78 Wheatley, *Collected Works*, 96; Scott, *Female Advocate*, II, 247–52. See, too, Holladay's introduction to Scott, *Female Advocate*, v–vi.

79 Wheatley, *Collected Works*, 13–14.

80 Elizabeth Eger and Lucy Petz, *Brilliant Women: 18th Century Bluestockings* (London: National Portrait Gallery, 2008), 95; Scott, *Female Advocate*, II, 313–20; Barker-Benfield, "Mary Wollstonecraft: Eighteenth-Century Commonwealthwoman," *Journal of the History of Ideas* 50, no. 1 (January–March 1989), 95–115. Wollstonecraft and Macaulay's ideas on democracy, equality, and women's rights were "remarkably close." Bridget Hill, "The Links between Mary Wollstonecraft and Catherine Macaulay," *Women's History Review* 4, no. 2 (1995): 177–92; 177.

81 Robinson, *Phillis Wheatley and Her Writings*, 16, 17, 92; Levecq, *Slavery and Sentiment*, 59, 61.

CHAPTER 6. MARRIED IN AFRICA OR FREE IN AMERICA

1 William H. Robinson, *Phillis Wheatley: A Bio-Bibliography* (Boston, MA: GK Hall, 1981), 23; Wheatley to David Wooster, October 18, 1773, *The Collected Works of Phillis Wheatley*, ed. John C. Shields (New York: Oxford University Press, 1988), 170 (hereafter referred to as *Collected Works*).

2 For Mauduit, see chap. 5, n. 31.

3 William H. Robinson, *Phillis Wheatley and Her Writings* (New York: Garland, 1984), 52.

4 "Proceedings of the Massachusetts Historical Society" 7 (1863–64): 168–279; 276 n. 1.

5 John Andrews to William Barrell, January 28, 1774, Robinson, *Phillis Wheatley: A Bio-Bibliography*, 25.

6 Wheatley to Obour Tanner, October 10, 1773, *Collected Works*, 171–72. It was this letter that inspired Robert Hayden's "A Letter from Phillis Wheatley, London, 1773," quoted p. 60, above.

7 Wheatley to Tanner, October 10, 1773, *Collected Works*, 171–72.

8 Wheatley to John Thornton, December 1, 1773, *Collected Works*, 172–75.

9 Quoted in Robinson, *Phillis Wheatley and Her Writings*, 311.

10 Quoted in Vincent Carretta, *Phillis Wheatley: Biography of a Genius in Bondage* (Athens, GA: University of Georgia Press, 2011), 116. It was dated June 2, 1774, but its references suggest it was written closer in time to when "Phillis the African Girl . . . staid with me." Thornton's warning to Wheatley brings to mind Toni Morrison's words: "Female freedom always means sexual freedom, even when—especially when—it is seen through the prism of economic freedom." Morrison, "Foreword," *Sula* (New York: Vintage International, 2004), xiii.

11 Wheatley to Hopkins, February 9, 1774, *Collected Works*, 175–76; Carretta, *Phillis Wheatley*, 43.

12 See chap. 2.

13 Wheatley to Hopkins, February 9, 1774, *Collected Works*, 175–76; Robinson, *Phillis Wheatley and Her Writings*, 43–44.

14 Wheatley, "On the Death of the Rev. Mr. GEORGE WHITEFIELD, 1770," *Collected Works*, 23; Wheatley to Hopkins, February 9, 1774, *Collected Works*, 176. The Rev. Shirley is quoted earlier.

15 Quoted in Robinson, *Phillis Wheatley and Her Writings*, 44.

16 Wheatley to Occom, February 11, 1774, *Collected Works*, 176–77; Wheatley, "An HYMN to HUMANITY, To S.P.G. Esq.," *Collected Works*, 95–97.

17 Wheatley to Occom, February 11, 1774, *Collected Works*, 177.

18 *Collected Works*, 15–16; Lawrence W. Levine, *Black Culture and Black Consciousness: Afro-American Folk Thought from Slavery to Freedom* (New York: Oxford University Press, 1977). See also Sondra O'Neale, "A Slave's Subtle War: Phillis Wheatley's Use of Biblical Myth and Symbol," *Early American Literature* 21 (1986): 144–65.

19 Carretta, *Phillis Wheatley*, 31, 32. See also Tim Lockley, "David Margrett: A Black Missionary in the Revolutionary Atlantic," *Journal of American Studies*, doi: 10.1017/s0021875811001277.

20 Wheatley to Occom, February 11, 1774, *Collected Works*, 177; Robinson, *Phillis Wheatley and Her Writings*, 120–21.

21 Wheatley to Thornton, March 29, 1774, *Collected Works*: 178–180; 180; Robinson, *Phillis Wheatley: A Bio-Bibliography*, 26–27; Robinson, "Phillis Wheatley in London," *College English Association Journal* 21 (1977): 187–201; 200.

22 Wheatley to Obour Tanner, March 21, 1774, *Collected Works*, 177–78.

23 Robinson, *Phillis Wheatley and Her Writings*, 124.

24 Wheatley to Thornton, March 29, 1774, *Collected Works*, 178–81.

25 Wheatley to Obour Tanner, May 6, 1774, *Collected Works*, 181.

26 Wheatley to Hopkins, May 6, 1774, *Collected Works*, 181–82.

27 Wheatley to Thornton, October 30, 1774, *Collected Works*, 182–84.

28 The expectation in New England Protestant tradition that wives' tongues be silent is indicated in M.J. Lewis, "Anne Hutchinson," in *Portraits of American Women: From European Settlement to the Civil War*, ed. G. J. Barker-Benfield and Catherine Clinton (New York: Oxford University Press, 1998 [1992]), 35–53; see also Mary Beth Norton, *Liberty's Daughters: The Revolutionary Experience of American Women, 1750–1800* (Boston: Little Brown, 1980), 14–15, 61–70, 230–31; Nancy F. Cott, *The Bonds of Womanhood: Women's Sphere in New England, 1780–1835* (New Haven, CT: Yale University Press, 1977), chap. 1. One can add another perspective to Wheatley's expected purpose in the Thornton-Hopkins proposal. Of the eighty-six freed black people who agreed to sail as the American Colonization Society's first emigrants to what became Liberia, fifty-eight were "women and children, hired as seamstresses, nurses, and laundry workers." Allan Yarema, *The American Colonization Society: An Avenue to Freedom?* (Lanham, MD: University Press of America, 2006), 38.

29 G.J. Barker-Benfield, "Marriage as Slavery," forthcoming.

30 Wheatley, *Collected Works*, 140–44. For approaches and interpretations different from the one I offer, see Mukhtar Ali Isani, "Gambia on My Soul: Africa and the African in the Writings of Phillis Wheatley," *MELUS: Journal of the Society for the Study of Multi-Ethnic Literature of the Limited States* 6 (1979): 364–72; 364–5; David Grimsted, "Anglo-American Racism and Phillis Wheatley's 'Sable Veil,' 'Lengthen'd Chains,' and Knitted Heart,'" in *Women in the Age of the American Revolution*, ed. Ronald Hoffman and Peter J. Albert (Charlottesville, VA: University Press of Virginia, 1989), 338–444; 341 (hereafter referred to as "Anglo-American Racism"), 361; Charles Scruggs, "Phillis Wheatley (1753-1784)," in *Portraits of American Women*: 109–11. Robinson addresses the episode very briefly, concluding, "Phillis seemed resolved . . . to live out the rest of her life as a black American." Robinson, *Phillis Wheatley and Her Writings*, 113. Carretta quotes some of the letters and notes that "in a February 14, 1776 [Letter] to Obour Tanner [Wheatley] mentions that she had 'passed the evening very agreeably' with 'Mr. Quamine' in Providence." Carretta, *Phillis Wheatley*, 161–64. We saw in her October 30, 1774, letter to Thornton that she told him she was "unacquainted" with Quamine and Yamma "in person." One could infer she knew of them at a distance, perhaps through Obour Tanner.

31 "Poetical Essays," *Royal American Magazine* (December 1774), 473.

32 Carretta, *Phillis Wheatley*, 148–52.

33 For example:
Though *Winter* frowns to Fancy's captur'd eyes.
The fields may flourish, and gay scenes arise;

The frozen deeps may break their iron bands;
And bid the waters murmur o'er the sands,
Fair *Flora* may resume her fragrant reign,
And with her flow'ry riches deck the plain;
Wheatley, "Imagination," *Collected Works*, 66.

34 And Edward Long wrote in 1774 in his influential *History of Jamaica* that the minds of "the negroes" of "Guinea are . . . incapable of strong exertions. The climate seems to relax their mental powers still more than those of the body; they are, therefore, in general found to be stupid, indolent, and mischievous." Quoted in Wylie Sypher, *Guinea's Captive Kings: British Anti-Slavery Literature of the Eighteenth Century* (Chapel Hill, NC: University of North Carolina Press, 1942), 55.

35 Sypher, *Guinea's Captive Kings*, 33–36; Maurice Jackson, *Let This Voice Be Heard: Anthony Benezet, Father of American Abolitionism* (Philadelphia, PA: University of Pennsylvania Press, 2009), 92–94; Francis Hargrave, "An Argument in the Case of James Somerset," in *Slavery, Race, and the American Legal System*, ed. Paul Finkelman (New York: Garland Publishing 1988), 1–82. Carretta suggests Wheatley here was indebted to Benezet's quotation of Adanson. Carretta, *Phillis Wheatley*, 152.

36 Wheatley, "THE ANSWER [BY THE GENTLEMAN OF THE ROYAL NAVY]," *Collected Works*, 142. Her vision here might be compared to Olaudah Equiano's construction of Africa "as a pastoral and idyllic land" before being "corrupted by European contact," a "convention frequently promoted by white abolitionists." Carretta, "Questioning the Identity of Olaudah Equiano, or Gustavus Vassa, the African," in *The Global Eighteenth Century*, ed. E. Felicity Nussbaum (Baltimore: Johns Hopkins University Press, 2003), 228. Wheatley's lines, though, Shuffleton writes, "were the first by a black American writer to offer such a romantic, longed-for vision of Africa as a lost homeland of pleasure, love and song." Frank Shuffleton, "On Her Own Footing: Phillis Wheatley in Freedom," in *Genius in Bondage: Literature of the Black Atlantic*, ed. Vincent Carretta and Philip Gould (Lexington, KY: University Press of Kentucky 2001), 175. Levecq writes of this poem's vision of Africa: it is "a world that needs to be discovered and communicated with . . . Wheatley's ideological ground was shifting very quickly." Christine Levecq, *Slavery and Sentiment: The Politics of Feeling in Black Atlantic Antislavery Writing, 1770–1850* (Hanover, NH: University Press of New England, 2008), 68–69.

37 Wheatley, "THE ANSWER [BY THE GENTLEMAN OF THE ROYAL NAVY]," *Collected Works*, 141–43.

38 *Collected Works*, 143–45.

39 Jerome McGann, *The Poetics of Sensibility: A Revolution in Literary Style* (Oxford: Clarendon Press, 1996), 1, chap. 1, 15; Alexander Pope, "An Essay on Man," Epistle II: Sec. III, *The Poems of Alexander Pope*, ed. John Butt (New Haven, CT: Yale University Press, 1963), 519–22.

40 McGann, *Poetics of Sensibility*, 15–16.

CHAPTER 7. FREEDOM AND DEATH

1 Frank Shuffleton, "On Her Own Footing: Phillis Wheatley in Freedom," in *Genius in Bondage: Literature of the Early Black Atlantic* ed. Vincent Carretta and Philip Gould (Lexington, KY: University Press of Kentucky, 2001), 176.

2 Phillis Wheatley, "To HIS EXCELLENCY GENERAL WASHINGTON," *The Collected Works of Phillis Wheatley,* ed. John C. Shields (New York: Oxford University Press, 1988), 145–46. Hereafter referred to as *Collected Works.*

3 Ron Chernow, *Washington: A Life* (New York: Penguin, 2010), 200; Vincent Carretta, *Phillis Wheatley: Biography of a Genius in Bondage* (Athens, GA: University of Georgia Press, 2011), 156, 157.

4 Thomas J. Steele, "The Figure of Columbia: Phillis Wheatley plus George Washington," *New England Quarterly* 54, no. 2 (June 1961): 264–66; 264.

5 Shuffleton, "On Her Own Footing," 186–87.

6 Shuffleton, "On Her Own Footing," 186.

7 Phillis Wheatley to George Washington, October 26, 1775, *Collected Works,* 185.

8 George Washington to Phillis Wheatley, February 28, 1776, *Collected Works,* 305; Carretta, *Phillis Wheatley,* 156.

9 Richard Bushman, *The Refinement of America: Persons, Houses, Cities* (New York: Knopf, 1992); Alexis de Tocqueville, *Democracy in America,* trans. Henry Reeve, rev. Francis Bowen, ed. Phillips Bradley (New York: Vintage, 1945 [1835, 1840]), Bk II, Chap. II; David Hume, "My Own Life," in Hume, *The History of England from the Invasion of Julius Caesar to the Revolution of 1688,* (London: 1778), 1:2.

10 Kenneth Silverman, *A Cultural History of the American Revolution: Painting, Music, Literature, and the Theatre in the Colonies and the United States from the Treaty of Paris to the Inauguration of George Washington* (New York: Thomas Crowell, 1976), 286–95. Carretta suggests that the meeting was "very unlikely." Carretta, *Phillis Wheatley,* 157.

11 Washington to Joseph Reed, February 10, 1776, *Collected Works,* 305–6; Chernow, *Washington,* 217, 214, 219; Silverman, *Cultural History of the American Revolution,* 285.

12 Silverman, *Cultural History of the American Revolution,* 296, 317.

13 Chernow, *Washington,* 173.

14 Carretta, *Phillis Wheatley,* 87; Wheatley to Mary Wooster, July 15, 1778, *Collected Works,* 186.

15 Wheatley, "Ode in the Death of General Wooster," *Collected Works,* 149–50; Jan Lewis, *The Pursuit of Happiness: Family and Values in Jefferson's Virginia* (Cambridge, UK: Cambridge University Press, 1983), 11; see also Gordon Wood, *The Radicalism of the American Revolution* (New York: Vintage, 1991), 215–20.

16 C. S. Lewis, *The Allegory of Love: A Story in Medieval Tradition* (London: Oxford University Press, 1938); E. McClung Fleming, "From Indian Princess to Greek Goddess: The American Image, 1783–1815," *Winterthur Portfolio: A Journal of Material Culture* 3, no. 1 (1967), 37–66; Alexander Pope, "An Essay on Man," *The*

Poems of Alexander Pope, ed. John Butt (New Haven, CT: Yale University Press, 1963), 515–25.

17 Christopher Leslie Brown, *Moral Capital: Foundations of British Abolitionism* (Chapel Hill, NC: University of North Carolina Press, 2006), 107 and see chap. 2, above.

18 Shuffleton, "On Her Own Footing," 182; Wheatley to Mary Wooster, July 15, 1778, *Collected Works*, 186.

19 Wheatley, *Collected Works*, 146–48.

20 Mary Beth Norton, *Liberty's Daughters: The Revolutionary Experience of American Women, 1750–1800* (Boston, MA: Little Brown, 1980), 128, 178–80; [Esther DeBerdt Reed], "The Sentiments of an American Woman," in *American Women Writers to 1800*, ed. Sharon M. Harris (New York: Oxford University Press), 256–59.

21 [Reed], "Sentiments of an American Woman"; Mercy Otis Warren, *History of the Rise, Progress and Termination of the American Revolution*, 2 vols. (Indianapolis: Liberty Classics, 1988 [1805]); McClung Fleming, "From Indian Princess to Greek Goddess," *passim*; G. J. Barker-Benfield, *Abigail and John Adams: The Americanization of Sensibility* (Chicago: University of Chicago Press, 2010), chap. 7; Norton, *Liberty's Daughters*, chap. 2.

22 Wheatley, *Collected Works*, 154–56.

23 Shuffleton, "On Her Own Footing," 176; Carretta, *Phillis Wheatley*, 189; Wheatley, *Collected Works*, 150–52.

24 Carretta, *Phillis Wheatley*, 173; Wheatley to Obour Tanner, May 29, 1778, *Collected Works*, 185; Carretta, *Phillis Wheatley*, 153–54, 172.

25 Phillip M. Richards, "Phillis Wheatley and Literary Americanization," *American Quarterly* 44, no. 2 (June 1992): 163–91; 164; Jennifer Thorn, "'All Beautiful in Woe': Gender, Nation, and Phillis Wheatley's 'Niobe,'" *Studies in Eighteenth Century Culture* 37 (2008): 233–58; 249; Barker-Benfield, *Abigail and John Adams*, 20–21.

26 Carretta, *Phillis Wheatley*, 174; Shuffleton, "On Her Own Footing," 176.

27 William H. Robinson, *Phillis Wheatley and Her Writings* (New York: Garland, 1984), 58; Carretta, *Phillis Wheatley*, 175, 181.

28 Carretta, Phillis Wheatley, 178–79; Robinson, *Phillis Wheatley and Her Writings*, 123; "Advertisement," *Boston Evening Post and General Advertizer*, October 30, 1779; Robinson, *Phillis Wheatley: A Bio-Bibliography* (Boston: G. K. Hall, 1981), 31 and see Wheatley, *Collected Works*, 190–202; Carretta, *Phillis Wheatley*, 179–80.

29 Quoted in Carretta, *Phillis Wheatley*, 180–81; Wheatley, "On IMAGINATION," *Collected Works*, 65–66.

30 Carretta, *Phillis Wheatley*, 189; Wheatley, *Collected Works*, 309; Silverman, *Cultural History of the American Revolution*, 426–27.

31 Carretta, *Phillis Wheatley*, 190, 184, 177; Robinson, *Phillis Wheatley and Her Writings*, 56–57; Shuffleton, "On Her Own Footing," 176. John Wesley published Wheatley's penultimate "An ELEGY on leaving—" in 1784 (pastoral apolitical, and therefore inoffensive), and several others of hers in his *Arminian Maga-*

zine during the 1780s, all in the interests of the antislavery movement. Carretta, *Phillis Wheatley*, 177, 188–89, 195. Carretta contends that had she chosen to "self-emancipate" in 1773 in London, knowing as she must have done of the Mansfield decision, "she probably would have found a publisher for her second volume." Carretta, "Phillis Wheatley, the Mansfield Decision of 1772, and the Choice of Identity," in *Early America Re-explored: New Readings in Colonial, Early National and Antebellum Culture*, ed. Klaus H. Schmidt and Fritz Fleischman (New York: Peter Lang, 2000), 220.

32 Barker-Benfield, "Sensibility and Stillbirth: The Case of Abigail and John Adams," *Early American Studies* 10, no. 1 (January 2012): 2–29; 5–6, n. 8; Susan E. Klapp, *Revolutionary Conceptions: Women, Fertility, and Family Limitations in America, 1760–1820* (Chapel Hill, NC: University of North Carolina Press, 2009), chap. 1; Wheatley, *Collected Works*, 194, 318; Robinson, *Phillis Wheatley: A Bio-Bibliography*, 31; Carretta, *Phillis Wheatley*, 14.

33 "Sabbath–June 13, 1779," Wheatley, *Collected Works*, 194.

34 Wheatley, "To a LADY and her Children, on the Death of her Son and their Brother," *Collected Works*, 82–83; Barker-Benfield, "Sensibility and Stillbirth," 25–26. Robinson comments that lines in "Sabbath" intimate "something of a puritanical revulsion at the awareness of her personal involvement in conjugal realities." Robinson, *Phillis Wheatley and Her Writings*, 56.

35 Carretta has found "no birth, baptismal, or burial records . . . for any children of Phillis and John Peters." Carretta, *Phillis Wheatley*, 177.

36 Carretta, *Phillis Wheatley*, 190.

37 Quoted in Robinson, *Phillis Wheatley and Her Writings*, 116.

38 Allan Yarema, *The American Colonization Society: An Avenue to Freedom?* (Lanham, MD: University Press of America, 2006); Denis Brennan, *The Making of an Abolitionist: William Lloyd Garrison's Path to Publishing* The Liberator (Jefferson, NC: McFarland, 2014). See also Craig Steven Wilder, *Ebony and Ivory: Race, Slavery, and the Troubled History of American Universities* (New York: Bloomsbury, 2013), chap. 8.

39 Simon Schama, *Rough Crossings: The Slaves, The British, and the American Revolution* (New York: Harper Collins, 2006), 189, 188; Peter Fryer, *Staying Power: The History of Black People in Britain* (London: Pluto Press, 2010 [1984]), 164 (Fryer's book includes an excellent account of the eighteenth-century origins and planning of the Sierre Leone colony, 196–203); Christopher Leslie Brown, *Moral Capital: Foundations of British Abolitionism* (Chapel Hill, NC: University of North Carolina Press, 2006), 316; Beilby Porteus, Bishop of Chester, "Sermon before the Society of the Propagation of the Gospel," February 21, 1783 (London: Rivington, 1784), 22–24. See also Stephen Braidwood, *Black Poor and White Philanthropists: London's Blacks and the Founding of the Sierra Leon Settlement, 1786–91* (Liverpool, UK: Liverpool University Press, 1994).

40 Bernard Bailyn, *The Ideological Origins of the American Revolution* (Cambridge, MA: Belknap Press of Harvard University Press, 1967) chaps. II and III; Rev. Thomas

Thompson, *A Discourse Relating to the Present Times, Addressed to the Serious Consideration of the Public* (London: J. Oliver, 1757); Anthony Benezet, *A Caution and Warning to Great Britain and Her Colonies in a Short Representation of the Clamitous State of the Enslaved Negroes* (London: James Phillips, 1785 [Philadelphia, 1766]), 44–45; Linda Colley, *Britons: Forging a Nation, 1707–1837* (New Haven, CT: Yale University Press, 1993), 353, 354, 359–60.

41 Robinson, *Phillis Wheatley: A Bio-Bibliography*, 33–66; Carretta, *Phillis Wheatley*, 196–202; Silverman, *Cultural History of the American Revolution*, 493; Thomas Clarkson, *An Essay on the Slavery and Commerce of the Human Species, Particularly the African* (Charleston, SC: Bibliobazaar, 2014) (hereafter referred to as *Essay on Slavery*).

42 Clarkson, *Essay on Slavery*, 122–24.

43 Thomas Jefferson, *Notes on the State of Virginia*, ed. Frank Shuffleton (New York: Penguin, 1999), see "A Note on the Text," xxxiii–xxxiv. Hereafter referred to as *Notes on Virginia*.

44 Jefferson, *Notes on Virginia*, 147; Barker-Benfield, *Abigail and John Adams*, 406–7, 408–10. See also John C. Shields, *Phillis Wheatley's Poetics of Liberation: Backgrounds and Contexts* (Knoxville, TN: University of Tennessee Press, 2008), 1–3.

45 Jefferson, *Notes on Virginia*, 144–45, 151; Annette Gorden-Reed, *The Hemingses of Monticello* (New York: Norton, 2008).

46 David Waldstreicher, *Slavery's Constitution: From Revolution to Ratification* (New York: Hill and Wang, 2009), 3; see also Edward E. Baptist, *The Half Has Never Been Told: Slavery and the Making of American Capitalism* (New York: Basic Books, 2014), 7–21.

47 Samuel Hopkins, *A Discourse upon the Slave-Trade, and the Slavery of the Africans* (Providence, RI: J. Carter, 1793).

48 Yarema, *American Colonization Society*, 4; Hopkins, *Discourse upon the Slave Trade*, 11, 5.

49 Hopkins, *Discourse upon the Slave Trade*, 16, 18.

50 Hopkins, *Discourse upon the Slave Trade*, 18, 19.

INDEX

Scruggs, Charles, 79, 104; sensibility of, 26, 40, 69, 90, 96, 122, 125, 156, 178; poetics of, 152

"The Sentiments of an American Woman" (Reed), 163, 164

Sharpe, Granville, 31, 70, 139; and establishment of Sierra Leone, 174; shows Wheatley around London, 102–103

Shields, John C., 54, 170

Shirley, Rev. Walter, 51–52, 53, 76, 88, 89, 151

Shuffleton, Frank, 119, 155, 162, 168

Shumway, Rebecca, 9

Sierra Leone, 173, 174

Silverman, Kenneth, 158

slavery, 6, 173, 177; as metaphor for Britain's treatment of white American colonists, 40, 70, 79, 117, 159; U.S. Constitution on, 177

slave trade, 13, 26–27, 40–45, 49, 61; Christianizing Africa and, 31; perpetuated by U.S. Constitution, 177

Smith, Adam, 42

Smith, Cynthia J., 105, 106

Society for Propagation of Christian Knowledge (SPCK), 6, 48

Society for the Propagation of the Gospel in Foreign Parts (SPG), 1, 5, 6, 33, 48

Society for the Reformation of Manners, 6

Solander, David, 102

Somerset, James, 147. See also Mansfield decision

Stamp Act, 99, 100, 101, 126

Stanfield, James Field, 56

St. Clair, William, 19, 20

Sterne, Lawrence, 67, 90, 122–123

Stiles, Rev. Ezra, 29, 40

Stout, Harry, 49

Sugar Act, 126

Sypher, Wylie, 147

Tarleton, Banastre, 162

Taylor, Alan, 88

Terence, 107, 114, 152

Teston Circle, 59, 174

Thompson, Rev. Thomas, 5, 73, 132; criticism of Mansfield decision, 25–27; mission to Guinea, 7, 9; views of whites' sexual relations with Africans, 20

Thomson, James, 147, 149

Thorn, Jennifer, 113

Thornton, John, 2, 4, 98, 102, 121, 128, 153; design to send Wheatley to Africa, 130, 139, 144; instructs Wheatley, 75; role in Wheatley's manumission, 126; sponsors Occom, 2, 72, 130, 136, 138; Wheatley stays with in London, 59, 84

Thoughts on Slavery (Wesley), 51

"Thoughts on the Works of Providence" (Wheatley), 78

"To a GENTLEMAN and a LADY on the Death of the Lady's Brother and Sister, . . . (Wheatley), 58

"TO A GENTLEMAN OF THE NAVY" (Wheatley), 143

"To a LADY and her Children on the Death of her Son and their Brother" (Wheatley), 58

"To a LADY on her remarkable Preservation in a Hurricane in North Carolina" (Wheatley), 58–59

"To a Lady on the Death of her Husband" (Wheatley), 61, 109–110

"TO HIS EXCELLENCY GENERAL WASHINGTON" (Wheatley), 154–157, 158

"To His Honour the Lieutenant-Governor, on the Death of his Lady . . ." (Wheatley), 90–92

"To Maecenas" (Wheatley), 3, 105–107, 149

"To Mr. and Mrs.—, On the Death of Their Infant Son," (Wheatley), 166–167, 169

"To S.M. a young African Painter, on seeing his Works" (Wheatley), 114–117

ABOUT THE AUTHOR

G. J. Barker-Benfield was born in London. After taking a BA (hons) from Trinity College, Cambridge, he went to the University of California, Los Angeles, for a PhD. Specializing in American History, he spent most of his career as a professor at the State University of New York, Albany. He has published books on the history of gender in the eighteenth and nineteenth centuries in America and Britain.